A Struggle for Heritage

Cultural Heritage Studies

UNIVERSITY PRESS OF FLORIDA

Florida A&M University, Tallahassee
Florida Atlantic University, Boca Raton
Florida Gulf Coast University, Ft. Myers
Florida International University, Miami
Florida State University, Tallahassee
New College of Florida, Sarasota
University of Central Florida, Orlando
University of Florida, Gainesville
University of North Florida, Jacksonville
University of South Florida, Tampa
University of West Florida, Pensacola

A STRUGGLE FOR HERITAGE

Archaeology and Civil Rights in a Long Island Community

Christopher N. Matthews

UNIVERSITY PRESS OF FLORIDA
Gainesville · Tallahassee · Tampa · Boca Raton
Pensacola · Orlando · Miami · Jacksonville · Ft. Myers · Sarasota

Published in the United States of America

25 24 23 22 21 20 6 5 4 3 2 1

Library of Congress Cataloging-in-Publication Data
Names: Matthews, Christopher N., 1965– author.
Title: A struggle for heritage : archaeology and civil rights in a Long Island community / Christopher N. Matthews.
Other titles: Cultural heritage studies.
Description: Gainesville : University Press of Florida, [2020] | Series: Cultural heritage studies | Includes bibliographical references.
Identifiers: LCCN 2020017096 (print) | LCCN 2020017097 (ebook) | ISBN 9780813066684 (hardback) | ISBN 9780813057682 (pdf)
Subjects: LCSH: Excavations (Archaeology)—New York (State)—Setauket. | Civil rights—New York (State)—Setauket—History. | Setauket (N.Y.)—History. | Long Island (N.Y.)—History.
Classification: LCC F129.S65 M38 2020 (print) | LCC F129.S65 (ebook) | DDC 974.7/21—dc23
LC record available at https://lccn.loc.gov/2020017096
LC ebook record available at https://lccn.loc.gov/2020017097

The University Press of Florida is the scholarly publishing agency for the State University System of Florida, comprising Florida A&M University, Florida Atlantic University, Florida Gulf Coast University, Florida International University, Florida State University, New College of Florida, University of Central Florida, University of Florida, University of North Florida, University of South Florida, and University of West Florida.

University Press of Florida
2046 NE Waldo Road
Suite 2100
Gainesville, FL 32609
http://upress.ufl.edu

DEDICATED TO ROBERT E. LEWIS

CONTENTS

FIGURES

TABLES

FOREWORD

Time passes. I wonder, in all the history of my life, is what I have learned something finite, or is there more to it that my lifespan will never be allowed to see? Is all that I have learned and will learn just a certain, fixed quantity of learning and understanding, and you're done? If this is the case, I am therefore just a machine. Realizing that the human lifespan is so very short, I wonder if I have learned anything at all. I think about all the incalculable ways through which I assumed, and felt comfortable with the thoughts that went through my head, that my mind would lead me, I had a companion of sorts, and I had to trust something. However, nothing attended my growth, my being, more significantly than the thoughts that told me I had to believe in something, or someone, other than myself, for an increase in my capacity to reason. We are all faced with this juncture at some point in life. At the moment of this realization, I felt that I had finally, truly learned something useful, a dimension that stretches far beyond the thinking capacity of the mind. There is a part of me, and every other person in the world, that is not restricted to the finiteness of earth or death or what is considered to be relegated to the past.

When a venture is begun with the intent of probing an aspect of the history of human life on earth, and should that venture be led with prescribed procedures of academic or scientific evaluation, we must engage in this venture always knowing beforehand that people encountered in the past are worlds unto themselves and that whether it is manifestly evident or not, the genius of creativity is a quality within every person and a portion of what is connected to people is not restricted to the finiteness of this world. We who probe into history, especially a specific history, must inspect and respect everything connected to that inquiry, with special attention to the beliefs of individuals. Beliefs arrange thinking and actions, particularly in adults. To ignore this seemingly insurmountable complexity and refuse to bend to the humility and empathy it demands renders all inquiry to misinterpretation, misunderstanding, and a perpetuation of falsehoods, and a crippling ignorance.

R. E. Lewis
Higher Ground Intercultural and Heritage Association

SERIES FOREWORD

Beneath the Façade of Suburbia

Driving through Long Island on one of its many highways it is easy to conclude that the suburban boom of the 1950s continues. These highways are dominated by shopping strip malls and housing developments. One can quickly come to the conclusion that any deep, complicated, long-term history is non-existent. However, Christopher Matthews's *A Struggle for Heritage: Archaeology and Civil Rights in a Long Island Community* counters this narrative. He provides an in-depth look into one community on the north shore of Long Island. The Town of Setauket is near Stony Brook University, Brookhaven Laboratories, as well as major medical facilities and shopping opportunities. While many people work locally, some residents also commute to New York City for employment. It is a community that is relatively well-off and is thriving in a suburban-like atmosphere. Yet, beneath this façade of suburbia is a history and heritage that has been whitewashed over time. Much of the heritage narrative in this community boasts of the achievements of the former estate holders and community entrepreneurs. The town's residents are also proud of the community's role in the Revolutionary War. However, after digging through the archives and performing archaeological excavations Matthews skillfully uncovers a forgotten history of the African American and Native American presence on the landscape.

A Struggle for Heritage is about the historical archaeology of social justice. Matthews remarks: "Archaeology, especially the historical archaeology of common people and marginal communities, provides a counter-narrative to most of what we know about the past. At Lloyd Manor, for example, there is rich documentary record that gives us insight on the homeowners and their families, business interests. There is much less, and at times nothing at all, written about those who did the everyday work at the estate. At Lloyd Manor, this included enslaved African-descended laborers whose worldview was quite different, yet whose presence and labor were essential to the whole of the site's history."

Using historical archaeology and grounding it in concepts of social justice is an important part of Matthews's scholarship. He shows that people lost to history can be found with archaeology. His archaeology in Setauket focuses on two families of color, and he shows through the archaeological record the different strategies these families used to survive in an increasingly racist society.

An important part of this work is that the author goes beyond artifact description. Matthews does an extraordinary job placing the history of these forgotten families and the archaeological collections in a larger context and he uses these assemblages to discuss race and labor and industrialization from the early nineteenth century to the mid-twentieth century and how it plays out in the material culture record. Equally important is that this project sets a standard for working collaboratively with a descendant community left out of the dominant narrative. His research is tied to the politics of inclusion and he brings attention to the continuous and gradual and effective economic assault on people of color living in a traditional neighborhood in Setauket as the area has rapidly suburbanized.

Matthews expertly shows how and why specific heritage stories are selected and by whom. He points out that the civil rights struggle in Setauket can probably date to the mid-seventeenth century when Setauket was first settled by English colonists. They brought with them enslaved Africans and indentured local Native Americans. However, Setauket today is an affluent village and its official history is tied to the American Revolution and its well-preserved historic housing.

While sites, events, and people from the Native and African American community are quite visible they do not conveniently contribute to the history that controls the past. They become part of the landscape with the development of counter maps and challenge the dominant narrative. Matthews develops a counter narrative through the material culture remains, telling the story of work, race, and racism from the early nineteenth century through the middle of the twentieth century. For instance, census data from 1790 to 1900 present a clear trend of increasing residential segregation in the Town of Brookhaven over the course of the nineteenth century.

Matthews writes, "Setauket's population has always been diverse including colonial English settlers, Native Americans, Africans and African Americans, Quakers, Catholics, Jews, and immigrants and migrants from many states and nations. Together these groups built a successful coastal village and left cultural legacies including churches, cemeteries, and gathering places. Nevertheless, the historical narrative in Setauket is dominated by stories of the protestant white property-owners and patriots." He notes that while everyone may have a past, not all pasts are treated nor understood equally. Heritage professionals must realize that our responsibility is not to the resource, but to those the resource belongs to. And, I would like to add, it is imperative that we work toward developing a more inclusive past, because this work can help us develop a more inclusive present and future.

Paul A. Shackel
Series Editor

ACKNOWLEDGMENTS

This book is the culmination of work by many people who contributed their time, effort, thought, and challenging critiques over the last ten years. First and foremost is Robert Lewis, founder and president of Higher Ground Intercultural and Heritage Association. Robert has been my host and collaborator in Setauket, and his invaluable input since the day we met has opened up vistas onto history, archaeology, heritage, culture, and community that have influenced both my research and the way I live. It has been a great honor to know Robert and to be able count him as a collaborator and a friend.

Through Robert, I was introduced to the many wonderful members of the descendant community who claim Setauket as their ancestral home. At the top of this list are Pearl Lewis Hart and Carlton "Hubble" Edwards. Pearl and Hub freely shared their deep historical knowledge of the community and their memories of growing up as people of color in Setauket. Sadly, Pearl passed way in 2016, though her legacy lives on in her children and grandchildren and the stories she left behind. I also offer my gratitude to Helen "Hart of the Morning Star" Sells, president of the Setalcott Native American Council. Helen supported my research in Setauket since it began and has provided a perspective on this place that reflects her commitment to community's indigenous roots, while also reminding me that this is a story of her family. Vivian Nicholson and Simira Tobias, who found each other researching their Tobias family genealogies, shared their findings and knowledge of history freely and guided my understanding of the complex stories that were lives of their ancestors. I am also deeply indebted to Judith Burgess, who, along with Robert Lewis, has been a principle collaborator in the A Long Time Coming project. Many other Native and African Americans in Setauket contributed to the research presented here. These include Rev. Gregory Leonard, Violet Thompson, Michelle de Castillo,

Angel de Castillo, Kiara Settles, Jordan Brown, Marsha Calvin-Settles, Warren Stevens, Idamae Glass, Nellie Edwards, Rick "Long Tree" Sells, Michael Calvin, Renee Calvin, Ronald Keyes, Diana Keyes, Barbara Lewis, Julius Stith, Tori Green, Wayne Hart, and Kevin Sells.

This book also reflects the influence of many Long Island–based researchers and advocates for local history. I am especially grateful to Charla Bolton for speaking with me about Long Island's African diaspora history and for introducing me to Robert Lewis. Charla is among the most important preservationists that Long Island has known. Along with many others, I also gained much from the input of Bob Mackay, former director of the Society for the Preservation of Long Island Antiquities (now Preservation Long Island). Archivists Karen Martin and Barbara Russell helped me locate many resources that essential to this project. Beverly Tyler is the guiding force of Setauket history, and his interest and support of my work has been generous. Many others helped me through the tireless and underappreciated work they do to tell the story of Long Island especially Gaynell Stone, Judith Wellman, Georgette Grier-Key, Grania Marcus, Lynda Day, Floris Cash, Thelma Jackson-Abidally, Jenny Anderson, Mark Chambers, Bruce Robertson, Jim Moore, and Jim "Zak" Czakmary.

I reserve a special sort of appreciation for those who joined me in the field. These people know the joys of archaeological excavation and the sorrows of Long Island's vicious poison ivy. I am enormously indebted to Brad Phillippi, who worked with me at the Hart site and the Thompson house, his dissertation site. Brad remains a close friend and colleague, sharing his research and helping me sort through the complicated parts involved in making sense of Long Island's past. I am also so happy to have had the chance to work with and learn from Allison Manfra McGovern, who has made significant strides toward revising the historical narrative of Long Island's East End. For contributing directly to research reported here, I am extremely grateful to Judith Burgess, Judith Wellman, Mark Tweedie, Pam Crabtree, Justine McKnight, and Meta Janowitz. I also want to thank and recognize the contributions and support of Ross Rava, Meg Gorsline, and Jenna Coplin, who have left their mark on the archaeological history of Long Island as well as my own research. Finally, I am eternally grateful to Dave Bernstein, who not only provided mentorship about doing archaeology on Long Island but gave me a place to stay along with excellent meals and fantastic company.

This project also benefited from the contributions of many students and volunteers in both the field and the lab. The field crew in 2011 included Tami Longjohn, Ariel Flajnik, Rachel Iancangelo, Brandon Ungar, Desiree Palma, Bill

Keating, Dwayne Lindsey, and Brienne Giordano. The lab team in 2011–2012 included Emma Lagan, Joe Tonelli, Gabe Abinante, and Tess Jay. The 2013 field crew at the Thompson house consisted of Eve Dewan, Matthew Joseph, Cara Frissel, Brienne Giordano, Irene Satchwell, Caitlin Poore, Paul Moyer, Angela Moyer, Ben Hornstra, Joanne Liff, Annika Durham, Tiffany Carcamo, Ann Glickman, Josephine Virgintino, Siu Ying Ng, Alexandra Hourahan, Samantha Wade, and Stefanie D'Erasmo. The field and lab crew in 2015–2016 included Alexis Alemy, Jess Twal, Amber Johnson, Sophia Hudzik, Warren Bristol, Ryan Brophy, Nikolas Petrovsky, Sasha Romih, Karina Gomez, Scott Zukowski, Mark Tweedie, Jamie Ancheta, and Jim "Zak" Czakmary.

Research for this book was support by a grant from the Wenner-Gren Foundation (GR#9347) as well as funding and in-kind support from the New York Council for the Humanities, Hofstra University, Montclair State University, the National Center for Suburban Studies, and Preservation New York.

Finally, I thank those who took time to work me on the concepts, theories, and data contained in this book. These include my good friends and colleagues Zoë Burkholder, Brad Phillippi, Paul Mullins, Allison McGovern, Kurt Jordan, Dave Bernstein, Mark Tweedie, Susan Hussein, Sharryn Kasmir, Meredith Babb, Steve Mrozowksi, Paul Shackel, Chris Barton, and most of all Robert Lewis.

INTRODUCTION

A Long Time Coming

On a lovely summer day in 2008, I had the pleasure of hosting Robert and Barbara Lewis at the Joseph Lloyd Manor site in Lloyd Harbor, New York, where I was leading an archaeological excavation. Lloyd Manor is the home of the well-known African American poet and author Jupiter Hammon, as well as a number of other enslaved men and women who were owned and overseen by the prominent Lloyd family in the eighteenth and nineteenth centuries. Our excavations focused on exposing the architectural remains and cultural layers associated with an outbuilding depicted on an early hand-drawn illustration of the property. We were looking to see if any of the evidence from the excavation would show the building was a residence for enslaved persons, perhaps even the home of Jupiter Hammon. An educated and literate person of African descent, Hammon must have stood out to the owners who had known him since birth. It would have made sense for him to have a separate home on the site, where space was not in short supply. That said, the manor house was large enough and conspicuously segregated internally to suggest that at least some enslaved people lived there. Unfortunately, while the archaeological deposits clearly indicate that the small outbuilding was used for domestic purposes, since it contained mostly kitchen-related artifacts, there was not enough evidence to confirm it was occupied by people of color. Therefore, this question remains unanswered.

Nevertheless, the site proved to be a fascinating object for people across Long Island and beyond. Too few people know about the important works of Jupiter Hammon, whose writings were a major contribution to the first generation of African American authors (alongside those of Phyllis Wheatley and Lucy Terry Prince). The fact that an archaeological project researching the possible site of Hammon's home was open to view inspired hundreds of first-time visitors to Lloyd Manor, the bulk of them people of color. Though we offered site tours and coordinated special events with speakers on African American history and archaeology, we heard most often that the main attraction was the chance to visit an ancestral African heritage site and to commune with this history.

This heritage was one reason the Lewises came to the site, and they were among the many that told us how impressed they were with the memories that seem to come from the ground. Yet they came that day also because they were interested in learning more about the possibilities of archaeology. I had first met Robert Lewis a couple weeks before at a historic preservation award ceremony for a mutual friend, Charla Bolton. Charla and Robert worked together in 2005 to establish the Bethel–Christian Avenue–Laurel Hill Historic District (BCALH) in Robert's hometown of Setauket. This was one of the earliest and still one of the very few historic districts representing Long Island's many historic communities of color. At the reception that followed, Charla eagerly introduced Robert and me, since she saw in each of us a shared interest in not only history but also social justice. She was right, and Robert and I became friends and have worked together since.

Robert rightly asked that day how archaeology and civil rights fit together. It seemed to him an odd combination of a scholarly study of the past and activist focus on the present and future. I figured the best thing to do was to show rather than tell him my answer, so I invited him to come see the excavations at Lloyd Manor. During his visit he saw the field school crew exposing house foundations and collecting small household artifacts from the sifters. He and Barbara also pitched in and helped wash artifacts, giving them a direct experience with both the archaeology and the materiality of history artifacts provide. We discussed more fully how this work could support a social justice agenda. This book provides the full version of the answer to this question, but in short my answer focused on two things.

The first is that archaeology, especially the historical archaeology of common people and marginal communities, provides a counter-narrative to most of what we know about the past. At places like Lloyd Manor, for example, there is a rich documentary record that gives us insight on the home owners and their families, business interests, and additional worldly and otherworldly concerns. The Lloyds' home faces a waterway that connected the estate to a vast and developing colonial and commercial network. There is much less written about those who did the everyday work that sustained the position, wealth, and authority of the heads of these households. At Lloyd Manor, these everyday workers included enslaved African-descended laborers whose worldview was quite different yet whose presence and labor were essential to the site's history. Focused on collecting the material remains of everyday spaces and activities, archaeology is positioned to recover information that can address these missing pieces of the past, pieces which of course connect us to actual people who, despite the lack of other records, lived, worked, loved, and sometimes died where we dig. The idea that people lost to history can be found with archaeology was compelling to the Lewises.

The second aspect of archaeology that impressed them was that it was something they could do themselves. Helping us out by washing artifacts was a big deal, since it allowed common folks like them to handle artifacts and make a real contribution to the recovery of lost places and people. Unlike historical documents, which tend to be housed in carefully managed and guarded archives (though much more is now available online!), archaeological artifacts seemed more accessible. While excavations need to be supervised by professionals and require proper permits, they remain a hands-on, participatory means to make history that do not require advanced degrees, years of experience, and the right connections to be able to contribute. It only takes interest, time, and some ability, and, with typically limited funding, research archaeologists are usually quite happy for the help! This is even more the case when those helping out come from the very communities being studied.

For Robert and Barbara, finding a direct and different route to the past and relatively open access to the tools to discover it was powerful. Later, Robert used these attributes to describe archaeology as an "unconventional" way to do history. Conventional history for him came in the form of stories whose content and meaning were already fixed and whose sources were out of reach. Histories like this seemed a lot like many other forms of exclusion and oppression he was familiar with from both his personal experience and his political activism as a person of color.[1] As an elder, he was also aware of the impact of conventional thinking among the members of his community who were too often forced to accommodate the shortcomings of their poverty and the need to work instead of learning about and fighting the persistent racism that underlay their struggles. For Robert, people of color require unconventional methods of living and understanding if they are not only to pay their bills but also understand and develop an authentic and successful culture of their own. This unconventional spirit was alive during the civil rights era, but the passion for civil rights has since tempered as other pressing issues emerged. This decline is in part due to a backlash against civil rights that came with the rise of conservativism in the 1980s and after but also because, at the local level, the realities of the changing economy began to undercut the ability of many people of color to earn enough and thereby maintain their capacity to sustain autonomous and unconventional lives. In an unexpected way, the unconventionality of archaeology seemed to offer the chance to reignite that spark. This book tells the story of what we have done to bring this perspective to light.

A Long Time Coming

In a conversation with Judith Burgess, a cultural anthropologist and oral historian who rounded out our research team in 2010, Robert Lewis told us that Sam Cooke's 1964 civil rights–era anthem "A Change Is Gonna Come" was a beloved song among members of Setauket's mixed-heritage Native and African American community. Cooke wrote this moving tribute to the African American freedom struggle after being turned away from a hotel in Shreveport, Louisiana, because he and his wife were black. Cooke's song has sustained civil rights resistance ever since. We all knew this song and realized that the lyric "a long time coming" captured the essence of the work we were trying to do together, and we adopted "A Long Time Coming" as the title for our collaboration (figure I.1).

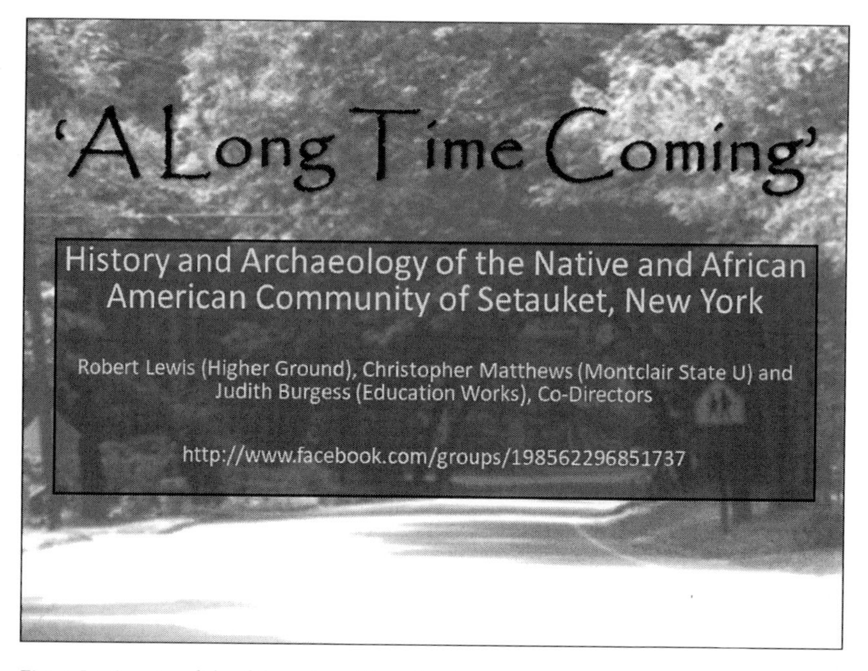

Figure I.1. Opening slide of the A Long Time Coming PowerPoint presentation. The background shows Christian Avenue in Setauket as it leads into the Bethel–Christian Avenue–Laurel Hill Historic District.

Why does "A Long Time Coming" work so well as a title? I mentioned that Robert and I found common ground in a social justice agenda, and Judith Burgess shares this interest as well. Therefore, the title is effective in the way it embodies the agenda of the civil rights–era struggle for social and racial justice that we see as a unifying force in our work. Second is the idea that what we would be doing is the result of a struggle that has lasted a "long time." Arguably, the civil rights struggle in Setauket dates to the mid-seventeenth century when English colonists settled there, indentured local Native Americans, and brought enslaved Africans to do the base labor required to build their homes, prepare and tend their fields, and care for their families. As I discuss in later chapters, historical documents though limited and biased are clear about the fact that people of color have always lived in Setauket and that they have always served as a lower-status group than whites.

Finally, the fact that "A Change Is Gonna Come" is still a beloved song in the community spoke to us about the importance of the articulation of past and present in our project. The memory of the song was tied to the part it played at the annual Hart-Sells family reunion. These reunions highlight the two principle families within Setauket's Native and African American community. While there are other family lines in the community, including the Scotts, Calvins, Bristols, Brewsters, Woodhulls, Lewises, and Tobiases, the Harts and Sells are connected to most of these through marriage so the reunions include everybody. The annual Hart-Sells reunions are held at the Irving Hart Legion Hall in the heart of the recently created historic district, where they have been taking place since the 1950s. Hundreds of people have attended these reunions, creating, among other community-building memories, a powerful chorus when the time comes to sing along to their favorite songs. In the 1990s these reunions helped people to compile two extensive genealogies documenting the presence of Harts and Sells in Setauket for the last 200 years (Hart-SellsFamily.com 2019).

Establishing the early origins of these two lineages makes a clear claim to the historical significance of the community of color in and around Setauket. Doing so in last decades of the twentieth century was also a response to other historical claims made in the village during those years. As I describe in chapter 1, this was the same time the conventional narratives that dominate the historical discourse in Setauket were laid out and institutionalized in local historical societies and schools and across the village landscape. That these narratives largely ignore the Native and African American community was certainly not lost on its members at the time. Recording their family genealogies provided a symbolic counterpoint to their absence from the historical discourse in their home town. We envisioned A Long Time Coming as an extension of this critical view of local history from the standpoint of Native and African American people. Chapter 2 presents one part of our contribution to this critique in the form of a "Counter-Map of Setauket." Other of our efforts and contributions are discussed in the following chapters, which detail the historical and archaeological research completed since 2010 to recover and understand the experience of Setauket's community of color over the last 200 years.

Higher Ground Intercultural and Heritage Association

All of this work rests on the foundational historical efforts of community members going back generations. The earliest of these efforts was the founding of the Bethel AME Church in 1848, its reestablishment in 1871 in a new location and again in 1909 after a fire. This was also when the AME church took over the independent management of Laurel Hill Cemetery, which had been in use since at least 1815, when it was formally set aside by the Town of Brookhaven as an African burial ground. Our work also builds on the community that settled around the AME church on Christian Avenue in the early twentieth century, a community led by strong and prominent women, including Rachel Midgett, Lucy Keyes, Sarah Ann Sells, and Ethel Lewis, as well as men like William Smith Sells, Harry Hart, Isaiah Hart, and Edward G. Calvin. This group became the core of the last enclave of Native and African Americans in Setauket. They built the Irving Hart Legion Hall in 1949, across the street from Bethel AME Church. The legion hall has been a gathering place and watering hole for the community ever since. In the next generation, people such as Ted Green, Carlton "Hubble" Edwards, Pearl L. Hart, Violet Thompson, Idamae Glass, Helen Sells, Billie Sells, Richard Sells, Marva Scott, Wilfred Scott, Richard Scott, James Thomas, and Eugene Hart continued investing time and effort in maintaining and improving the Hall. Under Ted Green and Hubble Edwards's leadership, the hall came to house a community museum with dozens of military portraits of community members and other photographs detailing the community's history lining its walls (figure I.2). Ted Green compiled a lengthy set of genealogies in the 1990s, and, along with Robert Lewis, started to collect and write historical narratives about the community. Green also led a revival of interest in the community's Native American heritage at that time. The local Native American community was later reconstituted by Helen "Hart of the Morning Star" Sells as the Setalcott Native American Tribal Council, a nonprofit 501c(3) organization. The Setalc-

Figure I.2. Judith Burgess and Carlton "Hubble" Edwards in the Irving Hart Legion Hall with Hofstra University students Ariel Flanjik and Tami Longjohn.

ott Nation Corn Festival has been held next to Setauket's historic village green every other year since 1992.

The most recent historical building block in the community was the founding of the Higher Ground Intercultural and Heritage Association, a community-based initiative that aims to support the neighborhood's well-being through historic preservation. In particular, Higher Ground formed to create the Bethel–Christian Avenue–Laurel Hill Historic District which was officially recognized by the Town of Brookhaven in 2005. The historic district is a roughly half-mile stretch of Christian Avenue that includes the community's landmarks as well as 30 residential lots. Until recently, these properties were all owned or occupied by members of the historic minority community. Starting in the 1970s, however, increasing economic hardships led some families to sell their lots to outsiders. In 2004 the sale of a lot across the street from Bethel AME Church led to the demolition of the historic R. W. Hawkins house. When a new house was built that was completely out of scale and character with the neighborhood, Robert Lewis organized the community to form Higher Ground and establish the historic district. Since 2005 Higher Ground has raised funds and worked to improve and monitor subsequent changes to the fabric of the community including compiling a massive cultural resources survey (Wellman 2016) that was the basis of the successful nomination of the BCALH to the National Register of Historic Places in 2017.

Establishing the historic district was a major accomplishment, and as in the case of Bethel AME Church, the legion hall, and the Setalcott Tribal Council, it was done for the benefit of the immediate community largely because they were excluded from other peer organizations in the area. The work of A Long Time Coming has sustained this self-driven, community-based agenda. Unlike traditional archaeologies, our work has not been done to bring to light ancient and forgotten sites and stories but to meet a much more pressing contemporary need. Despite Higher Ground's tireless efforts to preserve the fabric of the community, the number of families of Native and African American descent in the district is in decline. It has become increasingly hard to afford the cost of living in Setauket, especially given the loss of low-skill manual jobs that community members used to rely on. Since many young adults have left the area to get an education or to find work elsewhere, when elders pass away there is often no one nearby to keep the house in the family. One at a time homes have been sold to new people, most of whom are white, a process that is undermining the viability of this historic community.

This was the problematic context that Higher Ground faced after forming in 2005 and why, once Robert Lewis learned of the social justice possibilities of archaeology, he wanted to develop a project that included archaeology and oral history. Like all preservationists he saw the great value that historical resources can give beleaguered communities. Yet the resources on Christian Avenue are neither very ancient nor high style. They are the vernacular material culture of a small community of color that has lived in the village for a few hundred years and along Christian Avenue for the last century. On their own these houses and sites were not "significant" enough to be included in the Old Setauket Historic District when it was established in the 1970s. Still, for Higher Ground and the contemporary and historic community it represents, these vernacular sites are vital historical resources that need to be preserved. If any more homes are lost or families leave, it could easily lead to a total erasure of the community from the landscape and to their stories being forgotten.

This is where a connection to archaeology comes in. Archaeology is not limited by what already exists, is known, or is in view. In fact, the premise of the archaeological process is the idea that what we know and see now is necessarily built over the ruins of what came before. Often the break between past and present is stark, such that the world we live in today is unconnected to the remains of what came before. However, in many cases, especially for the descendants and survivors of the purges that created our contemporary world, what came before may very well contain the core of who they are. Despite being at times in ruins, these sources may still provide powerful and authentic sources of identity and power. Applying this idea in Setauket, A Long Time Coming has worked to broaden and deepen the critical historical resources Higher Ground can use to tell the story of their community. With the findings of archaeology and oral history, members of the mixed-heritage Native American and African American community can now be shown to have lived in every part of the village, ending up isolated on Christian Avenue only after being removed from other places. (See chapter 3 for more on this displacement.) Our excavations have also located a rich underground resource of remains and artifacts from some of these formerly occupied sections of the village that articulate the alternative and unconventional ways of life people of color practiced. These include ways of living that reflect both a distinct and authentic cultural heritage as well as a history of negotiation with the racist majority community around them. In other words, this is a community defined by both survival and resistance.

This book presents essential material and lays a groundwork for building these unconventional narratives. The book is also an application of a series of ideas and theories that have been developed in archaeology regarding its role in working with communities as well as ideas and theories that reflect on race and the production of counter-narratives. I offer a brief overview these source literatures in the following sections.

Historical Archaeology

First and foremost this book is a study in historical archaeology. Historical archaeology is an interdisciplinary practice focused the material and social record from the last 500 or so years (Deetz 1996; Little 2007; Little and Shackel 2014). This record is assembled from a wide range of sources, the primary, of course, being archaeological sites, or places where past people lived, worked, exchanged, worshiped, recreated, and took care of the other routine activities of their lives. These sites are often abandoned and buried, though sometimes they are still occupied and used, which means part of the material record exists aboveground in the form of standing structures and landscape features such as fences, pathways, roads, or grave markers. Most archaeology, however, is based on the recovery, recording, and analysis of excavated remains such as ceramic or glass vessel fragments, animal bones, and building materials as well as larger features such as house foundations or wells. Historical archaeologists also pair what they discover in the field with what they find in archives about the past people associated with the sites they study. Some of the sources consulted for this research include historic maps and photographs, census records, tax and property records, probates and wills, merchant account books, newspapers, institutional records, and personal and family papers. Historical archaeologists also collect oral histories when they can, and the research presented here draws from interviews conducted by A Long Time Coming since 2010 and in a previous project led by Glenda Dickerson in the 1980s. Interviews provide compelling personal narratives about Setauket's community of color since the 1930s that connect with the archaeology and documentary archival sources to construct a narrative of Native and African American people since the colonial era.

Historical archaeology benefits from this access to a broad range of source material. The theory is that by working with a combination of artifacts, archaeological sites, documentary sources, and oral histories, we are better equipped to develop unique insights on the everyday lives of historic people not available from any one source alone (Deetz 1996). Moreover, in the recovery of material culture associated with common and marginal people and communities, historical archaeology sometimes produces the only records directly associated with these people and groups. This process inherently creates new narratives and sometimes these are counternarratives that can change how we think about people and place. For example, the excavation of a plantation slave quarters such as by Charles Fairbanks (1972) or James Davidson (2015) at Kingsley Plantation in Florida provides direct access to the material culture of occupants who are otherwise entirely absent from the documentary record, at least through their own writings or actions. Research in historical archaeology makes it possible for marginal people who may or may not have been acknowledged by their contemporaries to be known through their own objects and actions, a process that provides a way around the biases embedded in most documentary sources.

An interest in recognition and counter-narratives is not only an attribute of research in historical archaeology but an artifact of the era we study: the modern age. Among the most powerful cultural transformations associated with modernity is the common acceptance of totalizing histories. Sweeping narratives about overcoming dark ages, religious dogma, and irrational devotion and the triumphs of a human-centered, scientific worldview have taken hold of the popular imagination. Yet envisioning our world as the result of a series of stages progressing toward the future constrains the development of historical consciousness, understanding, and critique. Yet many of those ignored, excluded, and displaced in modernity have survived and, because of their marginalized experiences, developed critical perspectives and alternative ways of life. When these community-based frameworks are included with other critical methods of inquiry, we may write a history of modernity that shows its claims to totality are partial and its progressive agenda more destructive than we realize. Historical archaeology is well positioned to contribute to this critical discourse.

Archaeologist Charles Orser (1996) provides a useful framework that captures many of the ways historical archaeology contributes to the study of the modern age. Orser identified four "haunts"—capitalism, colonialism, Eurocentrism, and modernity—that help define the contexts for most historical archaeological research. Specifically, the development and the rise to domination of a market-based capitalist political economic system lies within reach of historical archaeologists excavating homes and work sites, which Orser sees tied to an emergent global capitalist network. A component of global capitalism is the expansion of European people and cultures around the world, a process that involved the construction of colonial outposts and settlements used to organize the extraction of labor and raw materials. Beyond economic exploitation, colonialism also established a sharp cultural distinction between colonizers and colonized that produced powerful essentialist legacies tied to race and ethnicity still in place today. Tied up with colonialism, of course, is Eurocentrism, or the belief that European-descended people and cultures are superior and further that they possess a beneficial, rational, and objective "modern" worldview absent elsewhere. Finally, Orser sees modernity as a haunt influencing the worlds historical archaeologist study. Modernity is the sense that European-descended people see themselves as modern, progressive, and global in scope as compared to others who are taken to be primitive, static, and local. A desire for the modern is certainly embedded in capitalism and colonialism, though being modern is a somewhat distinct perspective that reflects more on politics, ideology, and being than economic and social relations.

Orser's global perspective and discussion of the four haunts has been widely embraced, though not without critique (e.g., Schmidt and Walz 2007), in historical archaeology. The key is to recognize how to draw these far-reaching and ethereal concepts and ideas down to the ground-level focus of archaeology. Works that succeed follow Orser's suggestion to "think globally, dig locally." This approach works for archaeology since our research is often placed-based and local and tied to specific sites and the people associated with them. With historical archaeology, that is, we are capable of engaging people and places in close detail and also connect these local experiences to larger global forces that impacted a wide range of people, if not the whole world.

Community Archaeology

Orser's framework is limited in that it does not examine connectivity at the local scale. Orser selected case studies of sites in nineteenth-century Ireland and Brazil to show that these far-flung locations were part of the same emerging global network built through the displacement of communities and the exploitation of labor. To this end, his book is quite successful. Less prominent is the role of the communities associated with these sites and histories today. Investigating local and descendant communities connected to the sites under study, however, opens a different set of concerns and opportunities that deserve the same level of attention as the structural and historical forces that created the modern world.

The field of community archaeology provides useful concepts and tools for grounding research on the haunts of the modern age in the contemporary contexts in which archaeologists work. In short, community archaeology is the practice of archaeology done in collaboration with communities invested in the research. These are typically but not exclusively descendant communities whose ancestors are the focus of the archaeological study or local communities whose neighborhood spaces and nearby histories are being examined. In many cases local and descendant communities are one and the same or have significant overlap, which is the case in this study. For clear reasons these groups have a stake in archaeological research, since the work—from design to results—has the potential to impact their community and heritage resources. Until recently communities like these had little to no role to play in the archaeology connected to them. It was only after a difficult fight and the climbing of a steep learning curve by archaeologists and their professional peers that communities came to be seen as legitimate stakeholders (e.g., Atalay 2012; Colwell-Chanthaphonh and Ferguson 2008; McDavid 1997; McDavid and Matthews 2016).

The most important and impactful community debate in historical archaeology took place in New York City at the site of the New York African Burial Ground. The African Burial Ground was a cemetery used by enslaved African-descended people in New York in the eighteenth century. By the early nineteenth century, the site was buried and built over as the city expanded northward. For the most part, it was also forgotten. This changed in 1991 when the physical remains of the site were rediscovered during the construction of a federal office building. The site was known to historians because it was clearly identified on historic maps and noted in other records, but it was widely assumed the burials would have been significantly disturbed by later construction. The new construction was thus permitted to proceed despite acknowledgment that it was a historic cemetery. This assumption was quite wrong, since the site had been buried by as much as 25 feet of fill, which protected the burials. Archaeologists were called in to rapidly remove the unexpected remains, and once word of this rush job got out archaeology was changed forever (LaRoche and Blakey 1997; Perry and Blakey 1997).

African Americans in New York and elsewhere immediately protested that they should have been consulted before the excavation work began. It was also discovered that the human remains were not being well cared for and equally that the research design was focused on the racial identification of the remains. The African American descendant community demanded a new team with a new research design be put in place. At the urging of the city's African American mayor and members of the Congressional Black Caucus, work at the site stopped. The project was put under the direction of Michael Blakey, then a professor of anthropology at Howard University. Blakey, along with Warren Perry, Cheryl LaRoche, and others (e.g., LaRoche and Blakey 1997; Perry and Blakey 1997; Perry et al. 2009) developed new research questions sensitive to the demands of the descendant community that focused on understanding the African and American origins of the burial population and evidence of their experience of and resistance to slavery. The point was to focus on the humanity of the deceased and the role that the study of their remains could play in vitalizing new narratives about African American origins and history.

The power of the descendant community to redirect the African Burial Ground project shattered any illusions historical archaeologists had about the objective basis of their research. As long as we study sites, events, and people connected to the rise and elaboration of capitalism, colonialism, Eurocentrism, and modernity, we have to be mindful of the way our research is implicated in the reproduction and critique of these haunts. Community archaeologists take this to heart and work to build spaces for collaboration and consultation where discussion about the framing and execution of archaeological research can be thought through (Atalay 2012). Ideally, these spaces of discussion remain open as projects develop because, as community archaeologists know well, local and descendant communities are apt to change and develop their membership, interests, and positions. More to the point, since descendants are not usually archaeologists, they are not going to be fully prepared to recognize what archaeology is and can do.

The struggle to preserve, memorialize, and address the racialized stories attached to the past and present at the African Burial Ground site were something

I witnessed firsthand as a graduate student. The impact of community meetings where the emotional and spiritual as well as political and material interests of the descendant community emerged remains with me. Thus, when Robert Lewis and I met to discuss doing archaeology in Setauket, we spoke about what happened at the African Burial Ground and its meaning to Native and African Americans in Setauket today as well as how this descendant community would be a partner in the project we wanted to create. While I feel that this goal has been mostly met and I have certainly gained so much from the stories and encounters that underlie this work, the struggle of this community remains. My hope is that this book and some of the other resources that have come out of the A Long Time Coming project will contribute to the new narrative we hoped to produce.

Decolonization

Stepping back, I see two intersecting themes in community archaeology we need to consider further. The first is decolonization. Decolonization refers to the process of examining, updating, and rethinking how and what we know about the world in light of colonialism and its enduring legacies. Following the theoretical premise that colonialism relies on presumptions about what constitutes knowledge and whose knowledge should take preference and be applied, decolonization offers useful methods of critical analysis (Atalay 2006; Smith 1999; Tallbear 2013). Decolonizing knowledge means first and foremost that there are multiple perspectives on any event and, equally, multiple knowledges and epistemologies that sustain these perspectives. With decolonization, nothing about archaeology is a simple as it seems, since our vision of even the most basic aspects of the world are informed by how we have been trained to see and respond to what we see. None of us experience the world exactly the same way; rather, through our own standpoint, culture, and heritage, we come to agreements about what the world is and what events within it mean. This does not mean we are unable to understand each other across cultures, but it does mean that understanding only begins after we recognize and appreciate difference.

Creating decolonized knowledge requires a democratic process in knowledge production (Little and Shackel 2007, 2014). Democracy emerges from an effort to build a level playing field that multiple voices and standpoints can share. Building this playing field collaboratively is the most important part of decolonization since it is the ground those working across cultures will share. In the practice of community historical archaeology, the playing field we build needs to address the impact and legacies of the haunts of the modern age. It must provide open spaces where colonialism, capitalism, Eurocentrism, and modernity can be discussed in reference both to the way past people were situated in distinct and unequal positions as well as the way our desire to know about their lives plays a role in overcoming the persistence of these inequalities now. Community engagement in archaeology is a busy thoroughfare where the discourses of past events and present relationships are put into conversation.

I did not engage members of the Setauket community in academic discussions on decolonization. These vital ideas were rather embedded in the routine practice of the work we did together. Part of this involved interrogating what my place as a white university professor and researcher was to be in this community of color. The result was a standpoint defined, for me, by consistent reflection on how my actions reflected specific goals and to ensure that those goals were shared with the community. It was welcoming when Reverend Gregory Leonard at Setauket's Bethel AME Church said that he saw me as part of his congregation and community. It was also heartwarming to be embraced by Helen Sells when I attended a Setalcott Pow Wow. At the same time, I was reminded in many ways that I was not part of the community and that I needed to work harder to understand the limits of what I knew. Fortunately, opportunities to do this extra work and reflection were available, confirming for me at least that the community held out some hope that I could be a useful collaborator.

Collaboration

A second key theme of community archaeology is collaboration. While collaboration is essential to decolonization, one aspect in particular stands out. This is simply the acknowledgment that when we collaborate we produce something qualitatively different than if we work separately. In the last decade archaeologists have published a number of important works on collaborative research (e.g., Atalay 2006, 2012; Colwell-Chanthaphonh and Ferguson 2008; Little and Shackel 2014). Accordingly, the value of collaboration is explained as the possibility for sustainability such that the knowledge produced is "relevant to, accessible by, and done for the benefit of local communities" (Atalay 2012:7). Under these conditions new knowledge is created in an inclusive and dialogic setting and can be integrated into communities with more impact. Collaborations can take many forms ranging from service learning and civic engagement practices to participatory action research to community-based participatory research and long-term collaboration. Colwell-Chanthaphonh and Ferguson (2008:10) and Atalay (2012:48) situate these practices along a continuum, reflecting the level of community engagement from sharing knowledge to co-creation. Advocates for collaboration show that engagement promotes not just decolonized knowledge. They also argue that by "grounding it in the experiences of the community members instead of abstract frameworks" (Colwell-Chanthaphonh and Ferguson 2008:13) collaboration humanizes research in ways that promote positive virtues, trust, and a clearer view on the moral implications of a project.

A Long Time Coming is a collaborative project that has brought together researchers based in anthropology and public history with members of Setauket's Native and African American descendant communities, represented by Higher Ground. For the last decade our collaboration has conducted research and excavations, run workshops, organized symposia, and prepared nominations, reports, and scholarly publications. I think the project meets the high expectations set by Atalay (2012) and others for community-based collaboration. I think we have also complimented these expectations for collaborative research in archaeology in an important way through a commitment not only to ethical practice and cultivated trust but also politics, specifically the politics of civil rights. Collaborative research is arguably an example civil rights activism, though few of those who write about collaborative archaeology identify civil rights and political action as goals. As it is usually presented, collaborative archaeology ignores one of the basic tenets of the civil rights agenda, which is that those who have been historically marginalized need to be not only recognized and included but also endorsed as citizens of the larger collective. Collaboration, in other words, should be tied to the politics of recognition and inclusion and be framed by an awareness that inclusion requires access to the resources of the majority that have been historically denied to minority communities. This claim draws directly from work that explains the way archaeology is political action.

Archaeology as Political Action

The leading voice on the intersection of archaeology and politics is Randall McGuire. An author of several works on the topic, McGuire (1992, 2008; Wurst et al. 2005) urges scholars to consider that it is not enough to know world, we also need to use knowledge to change it. McGuire (2008:3) advocates specifically for developing an emancipatory praxis in archaeology:

> Praxis refers to the distinctively human capacity to consciously and creatively construct and change both the world and ourselves. . . . Praxis becomes emancipatory when it advances the interests of the marginalized

and the oppressed against the interests of the dominant. Praxis implies a process of gaining knowledge of the world, critiquing the world, and taking action to change the world.

Collaboration is embedded in a praxis-based archaeology, since the interests of marginal groups can only be known and addressed through sustained interactions. The distinction between praxis-based and other collaborative approaches in archaeology is the underlying purpose of the work. One sort of collaboration is focused on the interactions between researchers and communities and seeks to develop awareness and understanding across social and cultural divides. This work is driven by a desire to produce archaeological interpretations meaningful to collaborators and reflecting on their cultural knowledge. A praxis-based collaboration follows this same path but also engages the issues and relationships—"the historical products of cooperation and struggle" (McGuire 2008:93)—that caused people to be marginalized and oppressed. This is the point where collaborative and political archaeologies divide, since praxis-based research is explicit about the political role of archaeological and related knowledges in both understanding the past and acting in the present.

McGuire (2008:91) suggests archaeologists answer three questions about their research: "Whose interests are served? How do those interests and their consequences relate to other communities and to the internal relations of the communities we serve? How do those interests correspond to our knowledge of the world?" This recognition of the political agency and efficacy of archaeology shifts the discourse from recognition to action, or in Hamilakis's (2007) terms, from "ethics to politics." This shift is mandatory since there is often more at stake in archaeological research than producing successful and meaningful archaeological knowledge.

There are many illustrations of archaeological praxis by McGuire and others. The protest and reinterpretation of the New York African Burial Ground site in New York is an excellent example. Others examples include the excavation of mass graves from the Spanish Civil War that allowed descendants to address the atrocities of fascism (Ballbè 2007); the archaeology of the Ludlow Massacre in Colorado (Larkin and McGuire 2009; McGuire et al. 1998; also see Nida 2013; Roller 2013) that put archaeological research in the service of the labor movement and working-class memory; the Undocumented Migration Project (De León 2015), which documents the life and death struggle of immigrants crossing US-Mexico border; and the Bakken Oil Field Man Camp project (Caraher and Weber 2017) that examines contingent labor in late capitalism. Similarly, Kostis

Kourelis (2017) has documented contemporary refugee camps in Greece (also see Hamilakis 2017); Reinhard Bernbeck and Susan Pollack (2007) undertook an "Archaeology of Perpetrators" to show how the one-sided story of World War II memorials hides the human capacity for evil; Larry Zimmerman and others (2010) and Rachel Kiddey (2017) have used archaeology to challenge the dehumanization and isolation of homeless people; black feminist archaeologists (Battle-Baptiste 2011; Franklin 2001) foreground the lives and perspectives of women of color and thus reintroduce missing voices and action to our knowledge of the past. Maggie Ronayne's (2007) study "The Culture of Caring and Its Destruction in the Middle East" shows that archaeological skills and community relationships with rural communities in Turkey helped to resist the construction of hydroelectric dams that would have displaced them. The key to success in Ronayne's case was making a pathway for women's traditional knowledge and social roles to be acknowledged in political discussions.[2]

This book shows the way A Long Time Coming employs a praxis-based approach to archaeology. Our research is framed as a counter-narrative to Setauket history. Chapter 1 shows that the authorized heritage discourse (Smith 2006) in Setauket is populated with a string of stories that connect the village to other normative aspects of American history, especially the American Revolution. Mainstream local histories like those in Setauket work most of all to control the past by bringing order to the multiple and messy human experiences all communities contain. In Setauket, furthermore, this controlled past is not an original invention but a mass-produced history borrowed from other prominent historical locations to make Setauket seem more important to history than it is. This narrative both ignores the history of people of color and undermines the legitimacy of their ancestral claims. Chapter 1 explains that their absence from the narrative is not an oversight but a telltale sign of the way local histories serve the interests of those writing and replaying them.

The unfortunate choice to focus on a very narrow historical discourse means that most people are unaware of a wide range of powerful and compelling source materials connected to communities like the Native and African Americans in Setauket. The story of this Setauket community gives us the chance to consider a long-term history of a people of color who survived slavery, cultural and material appropriation, and a violent legacy of racism that has devalued their history. Their persistence is a story from which we can all gain.

Chapters 1–3 review a range of sources that tell the story of this community, though it is important to note at the outset two of the most prominent records. The first is a set of early nineteenth-century paintings by locally born artist

William Sidney Mount. Mount was a highly regarded American genre painter, and many of his works depict everyday scenes in and around Setauket. Several paintings are studies of people of color who, unlike in the narratives we encounter in Setauket today, are not invisible but are in fact often the main subjects of his work. These individuals are painted realistically and with care, indicating a historical context when people of color in Setauket were less marginal to the local community than they had been or would become. This may reflect that Mount worked at the time slavery ended in New York, when the population of free people of color was on the rise. Moreover, being local, Mount knew the people he was painting, though he did not indicate their names in the painting titles or other records. One of the key questions explored in this book is whether Mount's work is a reflection of a period of racial amiability or ambiguity in which people negotiated the meanings of emancipation, citizenship, and freedom in the United States. Borrowing an idea from historian and musicologist Christopher Smith (2013), I describe moment as a time of "creole synthesis."

The other resource neglected by the authorized heritage discourse is the descendant community itself. Setauket's population has always been diverse, including English settlers, Native Americans, Africans and African Americans, Quakers, Catholics, and Jews, as well as migrants and immigrants from many states and nations. These people built a successful coastal village and left cultural legacies of various sorts including multiple churches, cemeteries, and gathering places. Nevertheless, the historical narrative in Setauket is dominated by stories of the protestant white property owners and Revolutionary-era patriots. Some recent efforts have been made to broaden the local narrative, including a dramatic performance about the Underground Railroad and an exhibit about the former racially mixed working-class Chicken Hill community. Yet the leading roles in the Underground Railroad performance are white Quakers, and in the Chicken Hill exhibit the racial diversity of the community is noted but unexamined. In both productions, the voices of people of color are included to serve as witnesses to the heroic deeds of others. This is quite the opposite of the sense we get from Mount's paintings and suggests that the potential creole synthesis of the emancipation era gave way to a "racial modernity" (Stewart 1998, 1999) that cast whites and people of color as inherently distinct and unequal.

Of course, being witnesses to the history of their hometown does not sit well with Native and African Americans. They are aware they have not only been present throughout the history of Setauket but also played an active role in the development of the village. On the one hand, they built a successful independent community that materialized and is visible in their own institutions in the village such as Bethel AME Church, Laurel Hill Cemetery, and the Irving Hart Legion Hall. Second, they have until recent years been a major component of the working population in the village in both domestic and commercial settings. Their basic labor was a key part of the foundation the village is built on, and notably the vast majority of those whose stories constitute the authorized heritage discourse, including William Sidney Mount, came from families that were either slaveholders or employers of free nonwhite labor (Phillippi and Matthews 2017).

Structural Racism

The absence of the mixed-heritage Native and African American community from Setauket's local narratives is evidence of structural racism. Structural racism is the normalization of implied and active understandings of racial difference and inequality. In contrast to overt forms of discrimination such as segregation, biased hiring, and racist violence, structural racism is coded into the way a community is organized so that the social order privileges white people over people of color. The history of Setauket replays many aspects of the common American experience of structural racism. From its origins in African slavery, African and Native American indentured servitude, and the exploited labor of free people of color to the physical and discursive displacement of spaces and sites occupied by the minority community, Setauket has consistently structured people of color as inferior and superfluous to the main workings of the community. This pattern was codified in the realm of local history when the majority community established three historic districts in the village without any mention or inclusion of the Native and African Americans who have always been in the village (Klein 1986).

Structural racism continues in Setauket today as the historic Native and African American community struggles to survive. Almost the entire community of color lives along a short stretch of Christian Avenue around their historic church, cemetery, and legion hall. This community is declining as families move away, and most new residents in the historic district are white. Higher Ground's work to create the BCALH historic district was an effort to document the significance of the community in order to help to preserve it; this achievement is what led to the A Long Time Coming project. All of these factors are evidence of structural racism and the nonwhite community's response. These people have had to work largely on their own and with occasional support of outsiders (including regionally based archaeologists and preservationists) to persevere and have done so with the extremely limited resources afforded them. They have also had to work under the surveillance of the dominant local community, which remains quite interested—from a distance—in their efforts.

These fraught conditions cannot be addressed by a traditional archaeology focused on contributing new stories to the existing archive. Rather, the research conducted by A Long Time Coming is politically defined so that as we recover new information about the past we also position that material to challenge the status quo by showing how the history of Setauket is also a history of racism and exclusion. This is the point of the critique of the authorized heritage discourse in chapter 1. Chapter 2 builds on this work to develop a counter-narrative that both documents the history of Native and African American people and shows that their role in the community and their exclusion from its dominant narrative is the way racism and white privilege persist.

Creating a counter-narrative that identifies structural racism in the authorized local heritage discourse fosters a deeper reflection on the impact of storytelling and circulation of ideas within the community at large. It is not accurate to claim the majority of white people in Setauket are racist. This is not to say that I have not had conversations where people admitted to being racist in the past or that I have witnessed racism in the village today. Yet personal recuperations and new appreciations of the diversity of local history do not help my collaborators in their struggle to help their community survive. Instead, this book builds a better understanding of the way exclusive, partial, and racist narratives of the local past make the majority community complicit in the erasure of their neighbors. Our expectation is that A Long Time Coming will initiate a complete rewriting of the local narrative to regard the Native and African American people as actors in the development of the village and the majority as complicit in the structural denigration of people of color, even as it benefited from the labor of people of color and the privilege of being ignorant of their neighbors' struggle.

A Stratigraphic Framework

This book employs a stratigraphic framework to tell the story of the historic Native and African American community of Setauket and our expectations for cultural change in the community at large. The first chapters examine the contemporary surface of Setauket. Chapter 1, "How History Controls the Past," is a critical review of the authorized heritage discourse. Most residents and visitors encounter and generally accept this narrative since it derives from local historical societies and is reproduced in the local schools and across the local landscape. This story highlights the minor role Setauket residents played in the American Revolution, focusing on their patriotism and sacrifice for the new nation. A secondary aspect of the discourse adds the effort of twentieth-century preservationists and historians to recover this history and build a landscape supportive of the master tale. There is no place for Native Americans and African Americans in this master narrative except as pathways for the achievements of whites.

Chapter 2 reviews the purpose and content of an online resource called "A Counter-Map of Setauket, New York" (Alemy et al. 2017). This map presents a series of place-based stories to show how the surface of Setauket contains ample evidence of the history and persistence of Native and African American people in the village. These stories are a combination of counter-narrative sites such as Bethel AME Church and the legion hall that are easily visited today as well as places whose current historical narratives need to be brushed aside to reveal the unconsidered but easily documented stories about people of color that they contain. A set of material possessions associated with Ernest Hart, a solitary African American man who lived in a small cabin on the rear part of his sister's property on Christian Avenue, rounds out this narrative. The collection was left behind after Hart died in 1977, neglected, that is, since the time Setauket dominant narrative was put in place. The study of these artifacts provides a humanizing counterpoint to the way the Native and African American community is left out of the local story.

The next chapters explore of the parts of the story not as easily seen on the surface of the Setauket. Chapter 3, "From Creole Synthesis to Racial Modernity," reviews a variety of documentary sources on Native and African Americans that bring to light hidden discursive and material histories related to race and racialization in Setauket and the surrounding region. The chapter lays out a framework for understanding racialization in two phases. The first is the emancipation era (1790–1840) which is designated as a time of flux and hybridity that I term a "creole synthesis" (Smith 2013). By the 1840s hardening racial divisions fueled by the rise of white supremacy shifted the discourse on race to one that I term "racial modernity" (Stewart 1998, 1999). I track these changes across multiple documentary sources, including the artwork of William Sidney Mount, liberal Long Island weekly newspapers, and the shifting residences of people of color in the Town of Brookhaven and Setauket. The last source gives voice to the contemporary community's memories of its struggles with racial modernity since the 1930s.

Chapter 4, "Archaeological Histories of the Silas Tobias and Jacob and Hannah Hart Sites," presents an overview of the archaeological research conducted by the A Long Time Coming project. I review the particular histories of the Silas Tobias and Jacob and Hannah Hart sites as well as the excavation methods and findings that document the sites and their material remains. These sites are vital to continuing the counter-narrative, since they are the homes of important historic Native and African American families. The Tobias site and family help to add to our understating of people of color in Setauket in the nineteenth century, while the Hart site and family tell us more about their experience at the turn of the twentieth century. Both sites present evidence of the consistent displacement of the community. The Tobias site is located in the Old Field section, which has not had a resident of color since the early twentieth century. The Hart site is located on Main Street, a section of Setauket that has not had people of color living in it since the 1950s.

Chapter 5, "Material Histories and the Dynamics of Racism in Setauket," is a detailed analysis of the recovered material culture. Examining artifacts and site characteristics, the chapter tests whether the proposal that racism intensified through time over the course of the nineteenth and early twentieth centuries at the Tobias and Hart sites is sustained. I show that the Tobiases enjoyed the use of good land and access to local natural resources, experienced certain levels of economic autonomy, and practiced long held cultural practices. In contrast, the Harts lived on a difficult property, had to work for wages, and showed very little in the way of a distinct culture outside of their social standing. Certainly, two sites cannot tell a whole community's story, but the diverse sources of data as well as their conformity to the expectations of the model lend it significant support.

Chapter 6, "Conclusion: Resistance, History, and Civil Rights," reflects on the findings from the research in this book and situates them in a framework we can use to look ahead. The discussion centers on evidence that shows how Native and African Americans in Setauket have long refused to forget. Not only is there great value in knowing more about the past and how history leads to present, people of color living in Setauket also demonstrate a form of memory that recognizes, celebrates, and defends their survival for the last three centuries as a minority community. To the main discussion of Setauket's past, the conclusion presents some additional examples of this history-making in recent years that reflect on the power of the community's historical claims as well as the limitations in the ways the heritage field can support these efforts. I urge that a more developed civil rights agenda be instituted in heritage practice. Specifically, I call for adopting a form of affirmative action in the way we define and approach how people and relationships—and not just buildings, documents, and traditions—are preserved. The preservation of people and historic communities requires civil rights activism to foreground the humanity of history and historical experience and the suffering the loss of people and memory causes. We need such affirmative approaches to recognize how relationships are the core of who we are and that we are embroiled in political action in preservation work, whether we realize it or not.

Notes

1. Robert is well known for publishing "The United Voice" from 1993 to 2009, a newsletter containing an assortment of cultural, natural environmental, and political articles.

2. Also see discussions about archaeology, heritage and politics in McNiven and Russell (2005), Liebmann and Rizvi (2008), Stottman (2010), Rico (2014), Gonzalez-Ruibal (2016), Harrison (2016), and Holtorf (2018).

1

HOW HISTORY CONTROLS THE PAST

People are trapped in history and history is trapped in them.

James Baldwin

The *Three Village Guidebook* is the most prominent and popular book on the local history of Setauket, New York. To set the stage for readers, the book opens with these words:

> To travel the Three Village area, to walk its woods, fish its waters, see its restaurants, shops, and museums, is to taste contemporary American life with a flavor of the past. What cannot be supplied to the visitor, or the reader . . . , is the imagination to reinvest the scene with a zest of eras past. Like ourselves, the now long dead labored, sorrowed, laughed, and loved. Houses and clothes, modes of communication and transportation change over the centuries, yet we tend to retain a close kinship with previous members of the species.

From here, the *Guidebook* proceeds to provide an introduction to history in the Setauket area and an inventory of 300 historic sites and structures that lend the landscape a historic character. The amount of work that went into compiling this inventory is very impressive, which makes it surprising that the author would characterize history as a "flavor" or "zest" complementing "contemporary American life." Yet the extract provides insight into this logic in the way the Three Village area is presented as a stage for traveling, walking, fishing, seeing, eating, and shopping. Missing from this long list of activities is work. Historical pursuits such as visiting historic sites and museums like those at Setauket are rather categorized as forms of leisure. This discursive separation of history and work minimizes the possible consequences of historical narratives in contemporary American lives, since their impact supposedly relates to what we do for pleasure rather than productivity.

The *Guidebook* reinforces this construct for readers. We are invited to invest the current scene in Setauket with imagined pasts we can create with the book's help. This invitation assumes anyone, residents and visitors alike, is capable of imagining and appreciating Setauket's historic qualities. There are two problems with this perspective. First, the past is positioned as external to the people who live with it, and anyone privileged enough to understand the value and role of history as a leisure activity can freely know, enjoy, and apply it in the world on their own. Second, as the extract establishes, there is a presumed commonality between the people of the past and present that ignores the transformative effects of history. "Like ourselves," an undefined past people lived in Setauket in familiar ways, as long as "we" also remain equally and essentially undefined. This rhetorical kinship between generic past and present residents of Setauket gives agency to the place where people have labored and died instead of those individuals who actually did the work and suffered their fates. Building a common association across time by virtue of being the same species and living in the same place undermines the humanity of history and hides the violence that makes this proposition seem reasonable. It is as if nothing has actually happened in Setauket that might separate us from those who were there before. This could not be further from the truth in Setauket or anywhere for that matter, since both change and continuity are the result of significant effort.

The historical narratives that circulate in Setauket are based in an unchallenged outlook on the world that developed simultaneously with the construction of the village as a historic place in the mid-twentieth century. The outlook behind these narratives derives from those who see their home as a place of leisure rather than work and their neighbors and community at large as an uncontested collective. In a nutshell, it is a story of modern America seen through the lenses of suburbia and consumerism. This chapter examines and critiques the influence of this suburban outlook on the way the past has been conceived and put to work in Setauket. The premise is the idea that the history people learn there is designed to control the past by promoting narratives that give people the content and a framework for understanding historic events. In Setauket these narratives, while compelling, are largely local adaptations of a manufactured American colonial and Revolutionary War history. An important result is that people of color are ignored and their story is left out of what people learn when they visit Setauket. To explain how the monolithic and monochrome suburban worldview was established despite the consistent presence of people of color in Setauket, I start with a brief overview of local history. I then turn to look closely at the narrative presented in the *Guidebook* to show how people of color are recognized and then dismissed as relics or minimized as insignificant to the narrative of Setauket's past.

A History of Setauket

Setauket, New York, is a village on the north shore of Long Island, situated in the Town of Brookhaven in Suffolk County (figure 1.1). The village of today was founded and settled by English colonists from Massachusetts in 1655, though the original residents were Setalcott Native Americans. Descendants of these first people still live in the region and have contributed directly to the A Long Time Coming project. We know a little bit about the Setalcott people from archaeological sites in and around Setauket. More than 20 precontact archaeological sites dating from 6,000–350 B.P. have been recorded in the area, including shell midden deposits, village sites with burials, small camps, lithic production/workshop areas, and scatters of isolated artifacts (Tweedie 2017:5–6). These sites demonstrate that Native Americans have lived in Setauket for millennia and that they established communities and lived off local resources quite successfully.

Among these sites are two precontact village sites likely occupied until the time colonial settlers arrived. Located on West Meadow Creek in Stony Brook Village, the West Meadow site a small settlement first inhabited 5,000 years ago (Ritchie 1959; Village Times Herald, 8 July 2016; Wellman 2016). It is close to one of the Native and African American community's earliest landmarks, Old Bethel Cemetery. A cultural connection between the ancient site and some of Setauket's more recent residents is thus quite possible. The Late Woodland Englebright site is the remains of another a small settlement defined archaeologically by a series of postholes, storage pits, and an abundant deposit of shells, animal bone, and stone and ceramic artifacts. A radiocarbon date of 1275 AD was derived from archaeological data, though it is thought the site continued to be occupied up to the time of contact (Gramly and Gwynne 1979). Faunal data from the Englebright site suggests a year-round occupation, which is contrary to the dominant interpretation of seasonal occupations discussed below.

Early records and land transactions with English settlers document Setalcott people still living in the area after 1655. These documents detail exchanges in which Indian sachems permitted colonists to use tribal lands for cattle grazing, timber extraction, and settlement. Through such devices and agreements al-

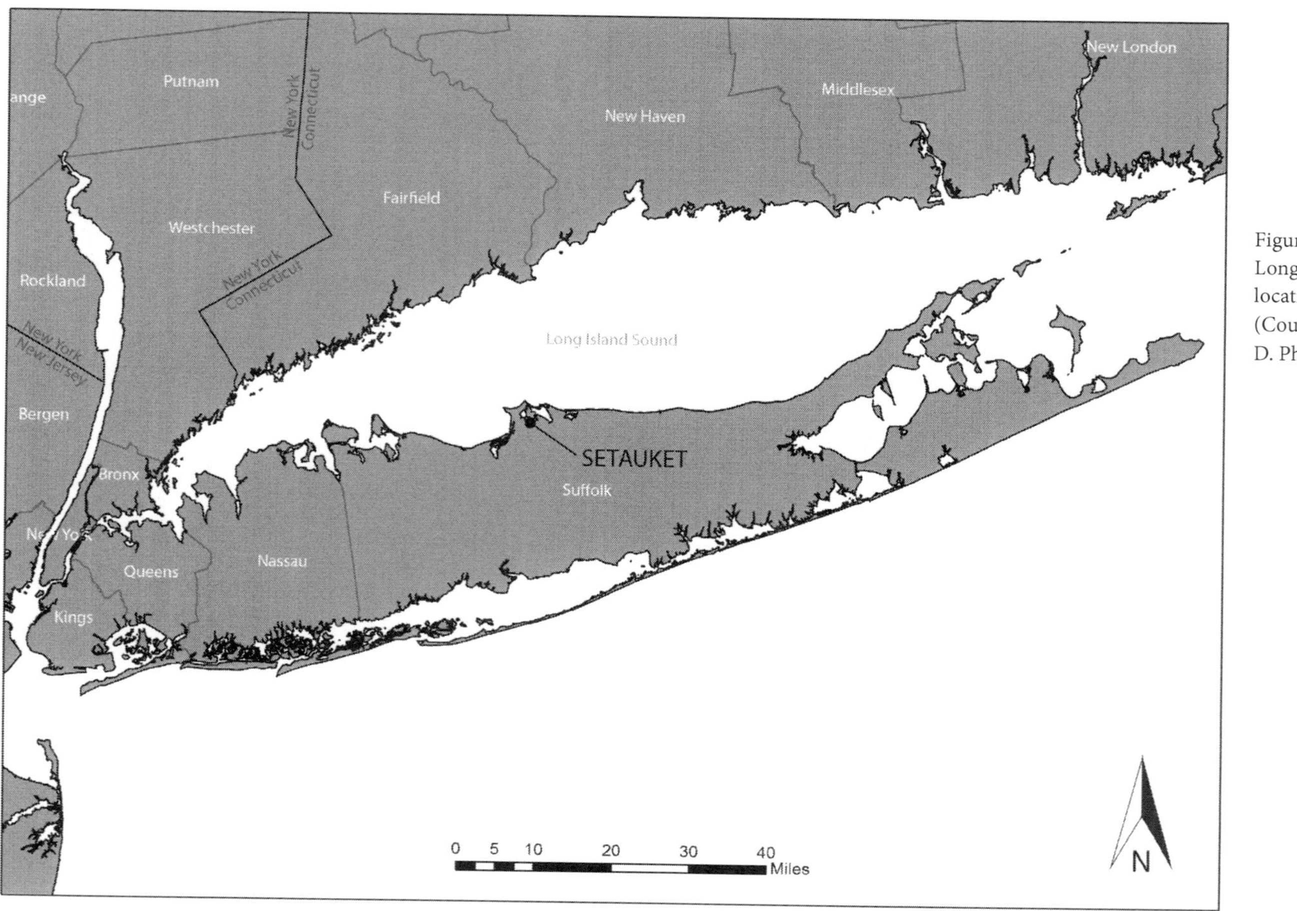

Figure 1.1. Map of Long Island showing location of Setauket. (Courtesy of Bradley D. Phillippi.)

most all of the land in the Town of Brookhaven was brought under English control by 1700 (Ross 1902). With no plan or purpose to expel Native Americans, indigenous people remained in the region, accommodating newcomers while adjusting to the new ways and mores of colonial life. Today, some descendants of these original people are formally recognized by New York State as the Unkechaug Nation, who occupy on a reservation at Poospatuck on the south shore of Brookhaven Township (Strong 1998, 2011). Other indigenous people, including Setalcott descendants, presumably lived in other sections of the township and gave up their formal tribal activities until more recent years.

Survival for Native Americans under English colonial control was more difficult than in the precontact era. Land and other resources that had been available to Setalcott and other indigenous people became increasing inaccessible. They also had to accommodate to new routines of work, including indentured servitude. Examples of indentures in Brookhaven Township include a 1746 record in which Indian Rubin bound himself to work for Richard Floyd as a whaler for three years (Adkins 1980:13). Similarly, Sibel (Sybel) Lott indentured Samuel, her one-year-old son, to Stephen Woodhull. That Samuel's indenture was sold to Benjamin Floyd illustrates the similarities between servitude and slavery for Native Americans (Strong 2011:180).

The struggle for indigenous people to survive is revealed at the early historic Strong's Neck site in Setauket. The site was discovered when human burials were damaged by construction equipment and vandalized by local people who removed remains before and during the archaeological study in the 1970s. The site had a post-in-ground house, several cooking pits, a hearth, lithics and pottery, as well as European artifacts such as "Delft china, a glass rum bottle rim, a metal button, a lead nail, and a fragment of a kaolin pipe" (Werner 1982:208). Six burials—one infant and five adults—were found "thrown in at random with no particular orientation" in a shallow common grave (Werner 1982:207). These people were buried both face down and face up and overlapping with one another, suggesting they were buried in a hurry and with little ceremony. What caused this rushed burial is unknown; however, the fact that the site was abandoned in the early colonial period indicates a disregard for their lives in a time of cultural conflict, a sentiment expressed again in the vandalism of the burials during the excavation. The fate of these individuals matches a general disregard for Native Americans in local history that I discuss in more detail later in this chapter. In fact, until recently most stories about Native Americans on Long Island were based on the idea that they had disappeared. Repeated claims from as early as 1670 were made in which Long Island's "last full blood" Indian passed away (Furman 1874:33; Prime 1845:40, 101; Strong 1992:64–65).

Official township records from Brookhaven show that many of the historically prominent families in the town's history were among the first settlers. Families such as the Woodhulls, Brewsters, Satterlys, Floyds, Hawkins, and Smiths made a lasting impact on Setauket and the rest of Brookhaven. Many of these families also has close relationships with people of color reflected in the records of African American Woodhull, Brewster, Hawkins, and Floyd families. These families were likely enslaved by white families with the same surnames. The first record of slavery in the Setauket area was the sale in 1672 of a man named Antony to Richard Floyd for 48 pounds. Other records document the sales of Samboe in 1677, Jack in 1683, and Dick in 1684 (Brookhaven, New York 1880: 29, 48, 51, 52). The prominence of slavery in colonial Setauket is documented in the 1704 inventory of William Tangier Smith, who lived on Strong's Neck. Smith owned 13 enslaved people: "two old negroes Toro and Oyon, two negroes Tom and Mary, James negro and Mary Tom's, Titus and Phillis at 40 each, Charles negro 60, Toney at 60, Dick at 50 and Diego at ten" (Wellman 2016). There are many other similar records, as well as a high likelihood of transactions involving the enslavement African persons not officially recorded.

The demand for enslaved labor in Setauket was driven by the region's focus on farming. Brad Phillippi (2016:144) notes that in colonial Setauket most property owners practiced "composite farming," which balanced self-sufficiency with production for the market. Phillippi (2016:144–45) explains that

> conventional composite farms possessed several acres of improved fields for sowing and reaping oats, barley, wheat, flax, corn, potatoes, and/or peas. . . . Parcels of unimproved land adjacent to fields provided forests for wood and lumber, and pastures for sheep, goats, cows, and pigs, which supplied families with fresh meat, dairy, and other useable byproducts. Families also maintained smaller plots for gardens and grew comestibles for their kitchen tables.

Farmers processed some of these products, especially wool, flax, lumber, and apples, for sale as well as barter with neighbors to supplement their supplies. Besides productive work and exchange, the structures, fences, fields, equipment, and animals on these farms required a great deal of maintenance.

Since farming was labor intensive, many Long Islanders counted on the "Indian servants and negro slaves" living in their households to do this work. The number of enslaved men and women in Suffolk County grew from 188 in 1703 to 1,452 in 1771 (Hough 1857).[1] Moreover, people of color of both indigenous and African heritage formed a communal intercultural interest in their mutual survival and likely also resistance to enslavement and dispossession. That enslaved Africans and Native Americans, as well as whites, interacted socially in the colonial period is documented in Suffolk County's muster rolls, where people of color are listed as "Indian," "Mustee," "Mestizo," Mulatto," or "Negro," based on the presumed racial admixture of their parents (Strong 2011:136–37).

An interesting document reflecting concerted action by people of color as well as efforts by local leaders to control them is captured in the following declaration recorded in April 1732 by the trustees of the town under the heading "Small Pox":

> Present Justis Brewster, Mr. Woodhull, Mr. Tomson, Mr. Miller, John Smith voteed & agreed upon att this meeteing by the Trustees, that, Whereas, by reson of the small pox, wee are under ye greatest obligation Imaginable to use all possibel endevers for ye speedy & effectual suppressing thereof, the Justises ad Trustees of the Towne, out of a pius senc of their duty, have thought fit, & doe hereby strictly prohibit & fore warn all persons, whatsoever, from selling or otherwise disposeing of to any Indians, Indian servants or negro slaves, any manner of strong drink or likquors on penalty of being peremtorryly obliged to finde suretys for thare good behavior & answering thaire contempt att the court of sessions to present all which disorders. All masters of families are also hereby desiered & required to keep & restrain thare servants & slaves from Absenting themselves by night without sume Extraordinary Occation & Express Token thereof, & to incorage all persons to ingaged herein, wee do allso certifie that whosoever shall apprehend & secure any such Indian servant or negro slave so absenting themselves after it is dark, and ye next morning convay & bring them before Athorty of the sd Justis shall, ass a Reward, reseve from him thre shillings currant money, & also the like recompenc for any other Indian found Drunk att any other time, and being in like maner aprehended. Convayed, & convicted. All which Indians or slave, unles prevented by thair masters, paying six shillings for ye use aforementioned, shall, by said Justis, bee sentenced to be public whipt according to his respective Demerrit, & such persons as shall faithfully execute the same, shall allso be payd by ye said Justis thre shillings more, all & singular, which sumes of mony disburst by the said Justis on this pertickeler ocation, it is unanimusly assented sall be punktually repayd

> them by ye Towne Treasurer on reasonable demand. This Act to continu three month in forc from the publication. All persuns are also hereby strictly forbid pulling down any fences made to prevent the danger of spreding ye smalle pox, ass they will ansuaire ye the contrary at thaire peril. (Brookhaven, New York 1880:124–125)

By 1732 there were enough number of people of color in the region to warrant a far-reaching act of government interest and potential retribution. Local authorities considered controlling the nonwhite population to be a public health concern in part because "negroes" and Indians were interacting, perhaps living and working together, and giving them the opportunity to conspire to create problems for township trustees.

Other economic activities such as tavern-keeping, legal and medical work, and the operation of commercial enterprises were increasingly common in the eighteenth century in Setauket, but none were substantially disconnected from farming until after 1800. The first independent industry in the Setauket area was shipbuilding. Shoreline shipwrights established shops in Setauket and in nearby Northport and Port Jefferson. Hundreds of vessels were launched by these builders by the mid-1800s, and, importantly, people of color found waged work in the trade. Tied to growth in shipbuilding was an increase in coastal and ocean-going trade out of Long Island (Barsh 2002; Bolster 1997). While records are scarce for residents of Setauket, many people of color from Long Island such as Jeremiah Pharoah and Pyrrhus Concer found work and built careers as sailors (McGovern 2015:appendix F) or pursued other water-based work as boatmen, baymen, or oystermen (Welch 1991).[2]

In the late nineteenth century and early twentieth century, Setauket experienced a short-lived industrial boom after a piano factory opened in 1861. This factory was refurbished to produce rubber boots and became Suffolk County's largest employer in 1880 with 125 workers, a number that had grown to almost 400 by 1885 (Stern 1991).[3] The worker community at the rubber factory consisted of both local people and Eastern European immigrants coaxed to Setauket after they arrived in New York City. These workers formed the core of Setauket's first working-class neighborhood known as Chicken Hill, a community with a diverse population of people born in or descended from Ireland, Poland, Lithuania, Germany, Russia, Africa, and America. People of color continued to live in Chicken Hill after the factory closed up until the neighborhood was razed in the 1950s (Wellman 2016; figure 1.2).

Additional changes came to Setauket after the Long Island Railroad opened a

Figure 1.2. Chicken Hill neighbors at the home of Irving Hart, ca. 1934. (Courtesy of the family of Theodore Green, Collection of the Three Village Historical Society, Long Island.)

branch line to the village in the 1880s. The railroad connected Setauket to New York City and supported a summer tourist industry in Setauket aimed at city residents. Several hotels and camps opened to serve these middle-class visitors. Some wealthier visitors invested in property, especially in Old Field, which became an elite summer destination and later a permanent home for the wealthy.

Among the new residents in Old Field were Frank Melville and his son Ward Melville, who had made a fortune together in the family's retail shoe business. The Melvilles made a significant imprint on the local landscape as local developers. In 1925 their Nasakeague Land Company built the planned community of Old Field South (Welch 2015:242), which was developed not only to turn a profit by building homes on underutilized farm land but to serve as a buffer between the elite estates of Old Field, where the Melvilles lived, and more modest communities to the south. Citing a Suffolk Improvement Company pamphlet, historian Richard Welch (2015:240–241) notes that "though profit was clearly one of their objectives, their avowed goal was 'protecting their own shore estates in Old Field' by controlling the extent and nature of development, and selling homes 'to desirable residents only.'"[4] Deeds for lots in Old Field South had restrictive covenants permitting only single-family homes of two stories or less, none to be used for business purposes, and any alterations including the exterior paint color only by approval of the Suffolk Improvement Company. Home owners also agreed that "no part of said premises . . . shall be used or occupied in whole or in part by any person of African or Asiatic descent or by any person not of the White or Caucasian race except that domestic servants, chauffeurs and gardeners of other than White or Caucasian race may live on or occupy the premises when their employer resides at or occupies said premises."[5] Like many other housing developments in the nation (McKenzie 1996), the Melvilles used architectural and racial restrictions to produce a manufactured homogeneity of affluence, housing, and community. Marketed as providing "Small Estates for Country Gentlemen" with an "English Country Atmosphere" (Welch 2015:242, 243), the class status and cultural heritage of the people they sought as buyers is clear.

Built with Old Field South, the Old Field Club provided wealthy residents an exclusive space to build a community of like-minded people. The club gave members private access to Sound Beach, a pool, tennis courts, and an impressive club house. The Melvilles also built a private school for area residents and a summer residence for club staff (NYS Board for Historic Preservation 2015). In 1930 the club added a distinctive U-shaped barn, ring, and grandstand so that it could host the North Shore Horse Show each summer and serve as a base for participants in the Smithtown Hunt. These equestrian activities cemented the elite status of the club and its members, perks attractive to those seeking what Welch (2015:243) calls the "snob factor" desired by people "who aspire to the to join the rank of the socioeconomic elite and sought to demonstrate their status by acquiring the semblance of the affluent lifestyle, including an exclusive address."

Melville's Suffolk Improvement Company was involved in other development projects in Setauket and Stony Brook, as well as land deals that provided the sites for the growing number of schools. The principal result of these new developments was a rapid growth in the local population after 1940. In the Town of Brookhaven, the population grew over 15 times in size from 32,117 in 1940 to 365,015 in 1980 to 486,040 in 2010. In Setauket, Old Field, and Stony Brook, the population grew from 2,135 in 1940 to 29,865 in 2010, though notably Old Field still has fewer than 1,000 residents (Shupe et al. 1982). These changes brought about an entirely different way of life in Setauket and also led some to consider the history of the village.

Melville led this latter interest as a founding member of the Society for the Preservation of Long Island Antiquities, whose 1948 mission was to preserve historic structures in the face of rapid post–World War II suburban development. It is ironic that a suburban developer would be called to work for historic preservation, but his connection to vast stores of capital facilitated the purchase and renovation of several historic houses in Setauket and Stony Brook. Melville also founded the Long Island Museum of American Art, History, and Carriages in 1939, which was part of his redesign of Stony Brook village center into a New England–style colonial revival shopping space. This shopping center is described as "Melville's dream . . . to create a colonial Williamsburg like his friends the Rockefellers had done in Virginia, but his would be a living, working version. To accomplish this, Melville embarked on a $500,000 acquisition and building project. For starters the downtown grouping called 'The Block' was completely razed" (*Long Island Business News*, 9 January 2004). At least one family of color was displaced from Stony Brook (interview with Carlton Edwards, 22 June 2011). The Stony Brook shopping center and other historic properties are now managed by the Ward Melville Heritage Organization, a legacy organization dedicated to preserving the glory of its namesake.

Like the new housing developments, history and historic preservation in Setauket catered to the wealthy in Old Field as well as the rising middle class who settled in Stony Brook and Setauket. Only the homes of wealthy landowners were saved and restored, and the stories told at these sites dwell mostly on the patriotic achievements of people during the colonial and Revolutionary era. The story of the village's diverse historic community has been largely ignored. Yet Native and African American residents are not only still living in Setauket; they were also part of the Melville's world. People of color were domestic servants in the Melvilles' home, and Ward Melville was certainly aware of the families he displaced when he tore down the original Stony Brook village. Moreover, he became directly connected with people of color after he acquired property on Christian Avenue in 1961. This property, known as Kalmia Woods, he planned to develop into several new housing lots. Fearing a new round of displacement, several women in the community, including Ethel Lewis and Caroline Moore, coaxed Melville to sell the lots at reasonable prices to Bethel AME Church and its members. Robert Lewis remembers, "It was my mother, Caroline Moore, and a couple of other people who convinced Ward Melville to intervene on behalf of the community. . . . I remember seeing Dorothy Melville and my mother sitting together in our back yard talking over the situation" (in Wellman 2016; email to Judith Wellman, 19 June 2016). Between 1968 and 1982 eight Kalmia Woods lots were sold to Bethel AME Church, and several of its members like Reverend Joseph and Margaret McKenzie, Theodore and Ella Green, Barbara Treadwell, Harry and Pearl Hart, Sherwood Lewis, and Dorothy and Rodney Certain. Melville also provided affordable home financing loans to other Christian Avenue residents (interview with Michael Calvin, 17 June 2011).

This overview of Setauket history provides two key themes. The first is that people of color have always lived in Setauket. The Setalcott, the first people to live there, survived for thousands of years and are still there today. Their story is not well documented, but we do know that their survival is tied to a similar struggle faced by people of African descent who were brought to Setauket as slaves. Living in similar conditions and at times laboring in the same white-headed households, these people of color formed alliances and unions that gave rise to the mixed-heritage Native and African American community living in the village today. A second theme is that those at the head of society developed a range of economic practices to accumulate and expand their wealth. Originally farmers, settlers expanded into new trades like shipbuilding, factory production, tourism, housing development, and historic preservation. These activities consistently relied on the labor of people of color, though none of the farms or businesses were owned or run by them. Rather, what we see is the appropriation of land and labor from people of color for more than 350 years.

This struggle continues. The suburbanization of Setauket brought an economic assault on the community of color living on Christian Avenue. Only two original owners of the Kalmia Woods lots still live there, and several other lots on Christian Avenue have been sold to newcomers, including the historic R. W. Hawkins house, which was sold and demolished in 2004. While elders remember working on local farms or riding in the back of Harry Hart's truck to find work landscaping, road building, or shoveling snow, such opportunities for earning no longer exist. Similarly, elders also recall that there used to be abundant wild foods available such as berry bushes and fruit trees and fish, crabs, and other shellfish in the stream beds and coastlines. The new housing developments took the resources away when formerly wild lands became the private property of new residents.

This shift in the landscape and the labor market has been matched by rapidly rising costs of living associated with suburban growth and a willingness of well-off suburban Americans to tax themselves to pay for public services and schools. Shifting away from racial covenants, upper-middle-class suburbanites now use high taxes to keep out minority and poor residents and create relatively homogenous communities (Archer et al. 2015; Hayden 2003; Jackson 1987). In Setauket this practice runs against the grain of a historical village community that has always had racial and class diversity. Unfortunately, those in the majority community who know this about their history and could advocate for preserving local diversity prefer celebrating other, less difficult, historical legacies and issues. To the appropriation of land and labor, we have to add then the appropriation of the narrative of local history, which excludes people of color almost entirely. In the following I discuss the preferred historical narrative that dominates knowledge of the past in Setauket. I critique this narrative and show the way it controls how the minority community is represented in local heritage discourse.

Heritage in Setauket

This section examines the way heritage in Setauket is produced. I discuss the content that is the focus of the central narrative and point out how it excludes Native and African American people except in ways their presence supports the main themes. To explain this process I also consider key concepts from the field of critical heritage studies that help to show that neglecting people of color is not an oversight but part of the way the dominant narrative serves other interests. These interests are in the value of property and whiteness, which serve Setauket's majority community at the same time they disempower and further destabilize people of color.

The field of critical heritage studies contributes a range of critical insights on heritage in terms of the meanings of the past in contemporary social life as well as in the industry of practitioners who do the work of preservation, conservation, and heritage education.[6] This scholarship shifted the focus of heritage research from the nature of narrating past events to the critical analysis of how and why specific heritage narratives are selected and by whom.

Laurajane Smith (2006) sees heritage as a discourse or a particular way of thinking, speaking, and acting with the past in contemporary society. Heritage is thus established through boundaries and rules that limit participation and access to those with the power and authority that come from proper credentials and experience. Smith reminds us that heritage happens now and that references to the past are made for contemporary reasons. Most practitioners and consumers do not think of heritage this way, acting instead on the premise that retelling the past is politically neutral and an inherently good deed. Smith's particular contribution is the idea of the authorized heritage discourse (AHD), which "focuses attention on aesthetically pleasing material objects, sites, places and/or landscapes that current generations 'must' care for, protect and revere so that they may be passed on to nebulous future generations for their 'education,' and to forge a sense of common identity based on the past" (Smith 2006:29). An AHD lies at the root of several disempowering effects of history in Setauket.

An AHD rests on a notion of "the past" as a singular and uncontested realm. In place of multiple and conflicting narratives, the past in an AHD is confined to a limited scope of content validated by historians, preservationists, and other professionals. The presence of such objective expertise intentionally detaches the past from contemporary social interests and the potentially spurious claims of competing (and thereby unauthorized) heritage communities. As stewards of the past, heritage professionals stabilize the narrative and ensures its accurate reproduction. There is no room in an AHD for debate regarding the content and meaning of heritage since the focus is on its propagation.

An AHD "constructs heritage as something that is engaged passively" (Smith 2006:31). People who visit heritage sites are seen as "empty vessels" seeking to be entertained or edutained with historical stories. The most active role they can play is to use historical narratives to construct an identity. Typical heritage discourses promote national belonging and patriotism, so sites and events tend to be authorized if they connect and contribute to the narratives of national cultures and help us reinforce our identity as citizens. An authorized heritage is also a securely bounded and managed. Boundaries define the content of heritage in the delimited physical forms of heritage sites, historic buildings, cultural landscapes, and historic districts as well as in the way professionals and stewards are defined as distinct from the public. Most of all, the authorized past is separate and protected from the present.

We see all of these attributes in the AHD in Setauket, where the main focus is the Culper Spy Ring, a Revolutionary War American espionage network that spied on the occupying British army in New York City. The spy ring was organized by George Washington and led by Major Benjamin Tallmadge, who lived in Setauket. Spies gathered information about British military activities such as supply movements, boat construction, or battle plans in New York and then traveled to Setauket where that information was delivered across the Long Island Sound to American agents in Connecticut. The principal actors in the spy ring were Abraham Woodhull, Caleb Brewster, and Austin Roe of Setauket and Robert Townsend of Oyster Bay. Legend also suggests that Anna Strong of Strong's Neck in Setauket used her laundry line to send coded signals about Brewster's movements (Nelson 2011; Rose 2007).

A secondary event was the one-day Battle of Setauket that took place on August 22, 1777. This conflict resulted from an attempt by patriot troops from Connecticut to create unease among a small fortified encampment of loyalist soldiers in Setauket. The patriot troops landed in Old Field and marched to the village green, where they exchanged gun fire. After three hours of shooting and one known injury, the patriots retreated, taking with them a dozen stolen horses and several blankets (Hall 1905; Ward 1952).

Figure 1.3. Promotional image for the 2015 Spirits Tour led by the Three Village Historical Society. Photo by Rhiannon Gupta. (Courtesy of Three Village Historical Society, Long Island.)

These two stories from the American Revolution are the focus of the AHD in Setauket. The local Three Village Historical Society (TVHS) has a permanent exhibit on the spy ring called "Spies! How a Group of Long Island Patriots Helped George Washington Win the Revolution." The society also hosts annually a Culper Spy Day as well as a variety of Revolutionary War–themed walking tours. These events are opportunities for local avocational historians to dress in colonial garb and, for some, to role play as Abraham Woodhull, Caleb Brewster, and Anna Strong (figure 1.3). There is a small business called Tri-Spy Tours that offers biking, walking, and kayaking tours of the spy ring sites. Its founder states that "the Culper Spy Ring is about average people doing extraordinary things. These brave men and women, who risked their lives, have changed the course of history. It's about time they get the recognition they deserve. Tri-Spy is a fun way for people to be active and to learn about the Culper Spy Ring and our Revolutionary War past" (Tri-Spy Tours 2019). From a local perspective, the Woodhulls, Brewsters, and Strongs were far from average people, though pointing out that they were part of the elite class and slave owners would not likely be an attractive selling point for those considering a trip to experience American heritage in Setauket.

Without intending to undermine the validity and meaning of the events at the core of Setauket's AHD, I want to explain that the intense focus placed on the

Revolutionary era in Setauket's heritage has put in place a manufactured history for the community instead of one engaged with the actual qualities and authentic communities of Setauket. First, the narrative makes a direct connection with George Washington and thus employs the mythic trope of "Washington slept here" found at many American heritage sites as well as homes and businesses attempting to promote their brands. While the trope is largely laughed at in professional heritage circles, the presence of Washington in the Setauket narrative is centered and lends it an official and recognizable status. Second, the story of the spy ring provides the narrative with not only intrigue but also an example of citizen patriotism. Visitors are regaled with a story of personal sacrifice and risk in the name of the nation and, since the spy ring was a success, a story of American victory. The spy ring characters as such are proper role models for descendant generations of Americans. With a statue of Benjamin Tallmadge standing at the Setauket elementary school and the Ward Melville High School mascot, the Patriots, the public value of this message is clear.

Another manufactured aspect of Setauket's AHD is a focus on the colonial and Revolutionary eras to the exclusion of other periods in history. Nothing epitomizes this more than Ward Melville's colonial revival rebuild of Stony Brook village, an architectural statement made in conversation with John D. Rockefeller's effort to recreate colonial Williamsburg. The colonial revival style in Stony Brook is repeated in public buildings throughout the region, including the 1951 Setauket elementary school and the 1968 Ward Melville High School. Again, this is not an entirely spurious claim since Setauket was a colonial village with a Revolutionary-era story, but the "colonial" reference here is to a vague time period and a point of origin. Having a colonial history gives Setauket a role to play in the way citizens at large know what it means to be and become American.

Finally, the spy ring is also a story about race and class in America. Given that its agents were white, property-owning men and many, including Washington, were also slave owners, they came from the most privileged social positions of their time. Identified without any mention of their race or class standing, they are instead presented as "average people" who did "extraordinary things." Notably, the spy ring story has a racial component, though it is rarely considered. This is the story of Cato, an enslaved African American who served as a spy and courier along with his owner Hercules Mulligan. Cato supposedly used his enslaved status as cover so he could inform the Continental Army without raising suspicion (Rose 2007). There is no mention in Setauket of Cato nor any of other people of color who might have supported the patriot effort. Their absence makes the spy ring story conspicuously white and limited in its impact as cultural heritage for communities of color.

Arguably, the whole of the current Three Village landscape serves as a stage for transforming Revolutionary-era history into an authorized heritage discourse. What counts as history in Setauket is restricted to a single narrative about a small group of people from a specific time. This simplified history of the village is played over and over in the community's heritage performances. It is evident in multiple restored colonial homes and churches, colonial revival public buildings, and statues of revolutionaries at the public school as well as in the use of the names of spy ring actors and other Revolutionary patriots for street names, subdivisions, and landmarks. There is even a large glacial erratic on the village green known as Patriot's Rock, dedicated by the local chapter of the Daughters of the American Revolution in 1927 in honor of the spy ring story.

Proponents of Setauket's AHD are active in the community through multiple organizations such as the Three Village Historical Society, the Three Village Community Trust, the Ward Melville Heritage Organization, the Frank Melville Memorial Foundation, and the Setauket Neighborhood Association. These organizations manage historical resources for educational and community purposes, almost all of which reference the spy ring and Setauket's colonial origins. They also offer prime board positions which enhance the prestige of prominent Setauket residents. None of these organizations consider the history of Setauket's community of color, nor have any of them ever counted people of color among their leadership.

While the AHD in Setauket is a celebration of the heroic deeds of ancient village residents, little of the story is about Setauket, which itself comes off as unremarkable. The village fades to be a backdrop for the moral and patriotic actions of individual spy ring agents. The absence of local value is also reproduced by the members who play the roles in reenactments. Outside of the Native and African American community, few descendants of the early families still live in Setauket. This means that those invested in telling the spy ring story are mostly newcomers. Their desire to participate in local heritage performances suggests a deeper desire to belong, a status they can achieve by knowing and reproducing uncritically the exclusive heritage stories propagated by the AHD.

Lost in the decision to focus on a singular historical moment is an interest in presenting more authentic histories of the Setauket community. Some efforts have been made to complement stories of the spy ring with those of the painter William Sidney Mount, and a recent exhibit at the TVHS on the Chicken Hill neighborhood is very good and shows an effort to diversify the main narrative. However, the spy ring and colonial Setauket remain the headline act. This minimal interest in other histories is not happenstance. It is a cultivated process the leading heritage organizations pursue both in Setauket and nationwide. To show how this is the case in Setauket, I explore next the role reserved for the Native and African American community in the AHD.

The Terminal Narrative: Authorized Stories of the Native and African American Community

Archaeologist Michael Wilcox (2009a:11) argues that one of the strategies of colonialism is the construction of a "terminal narrative" for Native Americans. These are

> accounts of Indian histories which explain the absence, cultural death, or disappearance of Indigenous peoples. Terminal narratives have had a profoundly damaging effect on popular conceptions of contemporary Indians. Most of the information communicated to the general public about Indigenous peoples is associated with destruction and disappearance. Conquest narratives, disease, cultural and demographic collapse, acculturation, and assimilation are all closely associated with Indigenous peoples.

Terminal narratives of Native Americans are especially common in archaeology, where the approach to abandoned and thus "archaeological" sites is as "a kind of skeleton, the corpse of an evolutionary dead end" (Wilcox 2010:102). Implicit in archaeological research are questions about why the people who created the archaeological record left. What happened? What bad fortune fell upon them? What mistakes did they make? These research questions easily adopt moral implications about the capacities of past people and our responsibility to them today. Writ large, they are mirrored in the idea that "the presence of 4.5 million Indians in the United States today is a complete mystery to most Americans. And how could they be led to think any different when most of the people interpreting Native American prehistory were explaining the disappearance of a people they had not bothered to meet?" (Wilcox 2009b:125). Wilcox (2009a:11) questions this logic provocatively, asking "what if archaeologists were to explain the continued presence of descendant communities five hundred years after Columbus instead of their disappearance or marginality?" Clearly this would require a shift of focus more in line with the ethics of collaboration and political archaeology discussed in the introduction.

The AHD in Setauket situates Native Americans and African Americans in a terminal narrative. The following examines how these communities are represented in local history, especially in the *Three Village Guidebook*, written by Howard Klein (1986) and published by the Three Village Historical Society.

"Humans Are Not Native to Long Island"

The *Guidebook* opens, "Humans are not native to Long Island, or indeed to the Western Hemisphere. The earliest known immigrants were the Indians who might have settled here as much as 10,000 years ago" (Klein 1986:15). This thought sets a tone for the book and the town regarding the place of its people in history and today, though this is an especially pointed statement about Native Americans and the descendant Setalcott community. Establishing that no one is truly native to Setauket any claim to being first or having a special place for Native Americans in the modern community is immediately dismissed. Claiming in essence that "we are all immigrants" strategically also establishes the legitimacy of today's immigrant owners of these ancient lands.

The *Guidebook* next provides a fly-by history of the Setalcotts that further bolsters the legitimacy of the modern landowners. The second paragraph explains that the Setalcotts were named after the village site along the local creek and that this creek later became the first settlement of the English. Despite being "handsome," the Setalcotts were "heathen" and easily succumbed to disease. Ultimately, the book explains that "the Indians bartered away their lands freely and the English for the most part treated the transactions with some honor" (Klein 1986:15). The details of the first "transaction" are transcribed:

> The price paid was recorded as "10 coats, 12 Hoes, 12 Hatchet, 50 Muxes (or mucksucks, small awls used to perforate sea shells in making wampum), 100 Needles, 6 Ketles, 10 Fadom of wampum, 7 Chest of Powder, 1 Pare of Child Stokins, 10 Pound of Lead, 1 Dosen of Knives." Cloth was prized among other goods by the Indians, who prior to the European migration, had never seen it.

While printing the text of this document helps the reader understand early Indian-settler relations, its inclusion also demonstrates the village was justly acquired by the first colonists in a fair exchange. The author also proposes settlers' benevolence and cultural superiority since they in fact bettered the meager Indians in the exchange. Highlighting a quaint interest for things like cloth we are directed away from noticing the clear desire among the Setalcotts for tools, weapons, and cash (in the form of wampum), objects both parties would have recognized as valuable resources to be used in managing their developing relationship.

Having sold their land freely, Indians are not considered beyond such initial exchanges in most local histories. The same story is repeated in many other TVHS publications and other popular histories of the area. Other sources that mention Native Americans further the idea that Indians need not be recognized as part of the community and its history. These include references to the nifty record of their lives found at prehistoric archaeological sites, stories which tend to be paired with the notion that Native Americans were "highly mobile" villagers, so their use of the land they subsequently sold away was seasonal and temporary and thus not the same as if they were removed from more permanent homes. One of the most powerful terminal statements closes out the *Guidebook*'s introduction:

> As the local Indians receded through disease or intermarriage, naught remained of them but the sound of their tongue in the names used every day in the Three Villages. Names that Walt Whitman said, "roll with the venison richness upon the palate"—Comsewogue, Lotowana, Naasakeag, Minnesauke, Nissequogue, Sachem, Poquott, and, of course, Setauket. (Klein 1986:20)

In two sentences Native Americans are denied their contemporary presence by having "receded and intermarried" and then being replaced by modern residents who not only settled their land but also inherited ancient Indian names that they use in their own art and place-making practices.

There is one other indirect reference to Native Americans in the *Guidebook* that also powerfully sustains the terminal narrative. In the text of a walking tour of Setauket's Main Street, the *Guidebook* mentions "Indian Rock," a glacial erratic boulder. The origin of this compelling name is not explained; in fact, its connection to Native Americans is entirely ignored, at least explicitly. Rather, the stone is described as a

> six foot by 15 foot boulder of fine-grained gneiss, a metamorphic rock formed under great pressure and heat from other types of rock, contains the minerals feldspar, quarts, mica, and others. It has been estimated to be about 200-million years old and was deposited here by the Wisconsin Glacier, which terminated along two lines sweeping the length of Long Island and whose terminal moraines formed its topography. Such boulders were carried here by the ice sheets from mountains far to the north. (Klein 1986:44)

Rich geological details replace any sense of the Indian people the rock is named for and at the same time silently associates Native Americans with the

Figure 1.4. Drawing of Indian Rock on Main Street, Setauket. *Three Village Guidebook.* (Courtesy of the Three Village Historical Society, Long Island.)

time and space of geology. As at nearby Garvies Point Museum and Preserve, where archaeologically based dioramas of prehistoric Native American life-ways sit alongside explanations of the region's geologic and natural history, the *Guidebook* fixes Indian people as "prehistoric" and understood best after their remains are excavated from the earth. Finally, despite the construal of Indians and boulders as signs of the permanently past, the *Guidebook*'s description makes sure to note that Indian Rock, like the Indian people and all others who have ever lived on Long Island, is an immigrant.

Indian Rock is illustrated in the *Guidebook* by an evocative line drawing that depicts the boulder amid a tired old tree and a patch of swamp grass and reeds (figure 1.4). If this was all there was to the image it would be unremarkable; however, the drawing includes a white couple strolling by the rock on their way to play tennis. Because this is a drawing, the choice to include the tennis players was a conscious act that reveals the subconscious logic and power of the AHD.

Visitors to Setauket today would not be surprised to see this couple strolling along Main Street toward the tennis courts. An affluent village, Setauket is defined by historical associations with the American Revolution, its prized and well-preserved historic housing stock, and a contemporary community that understands and values these attributes. A more critical reading would also point out that the use of the landscape now is less marked by the effects of development than preservation because Setauket is a place of leisure. While it is a predominantly suburban residential community, there is a noticeable aversion to spaces and memories of work. Factories built in the nineteenth century have been torn down, the shipbuilding industry along the waterfront disappeared before World War II, the area's summer tourist industry disappeared by the 1950s, and the houses and neighborhoods where working-class people lived have been removed or are isolated out of sight of the "historic" sections of town. What passes for work today is confined to a set of strip malls with stores, restaurants, and offices that serve the village's propertied families along a bypass road across town. Instead, the much quieter Main Street is now a residential section where happy couples can stroll out of their historic homes to the local tennis courts. Such actions materialize the proper way to live and enjoy life in modern Setauket. Given this context, the presence of the couple in this drawing is no more exceptional or under threat than the "huge boulder" they are walking by. Like Indian Rock, they reflect the presumed permanence of what Setauket has become.

"Slaves on Long Island Farms Were Few"

If Native Americans serve as a proxy for prehistory in the *Guidebook*, people of African descent are almost (and conspicuously) absent altogether. Enslaved Africans are mentioned just a handful of times in the *Guidebook*. Three refer to structures or spaces that may have been built for use by enslaved people. These include the Edwards "slave" house, a residence that may have been the Thompsons' slave house, as well as the "slave gallery" built at the Caroline Church in 1744. Klein doubts these are actually connected to slavery. Regarding the Edwards slave house, he notes, "although slavery was practically eliminated from this region long before the Civil War, local residents claim it was slave quarters. Its diminutive scale would indicate it was at least a servant house" (Klein 1986:110). He writes that the Thompson "slave" house "could have been a slave or servant quarters but its construction of brick and fieldstone suggest it was intended for more affluent residents" (1986:46). Klein is likely correct that these are not surviving examples of slave housing, though this is because of the very rare occurrence of separate "slave housing" in the northern United States. For the most part, enslaved people were housed under the same roof as their master's family or in barns or other outbuildings (Delle 2019; Fitts 1996; Rava and Matthews 2013). For example, the Thompsons, who enslaved more than a dozen people, housed them in the upper rear floors and garrets of their house.

Alterations to standing houses as well as new construction during the time slavery ended in New York (between 1799 and 1827) indicate the Thompsons and other former slave owners moved spaces devoted to labor, like kitchens and offices, out of the main house. The need for separate spaces for work seems to have become a problem only after emancipation (Matthews 2011a, 2017; Phillippi 2016). While the *Guidebook* devotes seven pages and nine images to the Thompson house site and family, most other sites are given a paragraph and at most one photograph. There is no mention that the Thompsons were slave owners, although the author makes note of Samuel Thompson's diary, which contains vital details about enslaved people and their work (Marcus 1988; Phillippi 2016).

It is curious why references to "old slave houses" are now so common in Setauket and other historic places, even if such structures did not exist. Of course, without these stories the history of slavery would not play any role in Setauket's historical narrative. Attributing small houses and segregated spaces to the enslaved, modern people in Setauket have found a way to deal with the legacy of the human bondage that their ancestors and predecessors benefited from. Moreover, maintaining "ghosts" of slavery, they also distance themselves from these ancestral slave owners and relinquish responsibility for the legacy of slavery in their communities today.

This outlook underwrites the overview of slavery on Long Island in the *Guidebook*. Klein (1986:18) notes that "a 1672 law permitted slaves to be sold in town and, although slavery was never as widespread on the small Long Island farms as it was in southern plantations, it was an accepted way of life in northern colonies." He also mentions that the 1790 federal census for the Town of Brookhaven recorded "a total population of the about 2,600 of which almost 10 percent were 'other free persons' (283) and another 10 percent were slaves (240). The other free persons were undoubtedly bonded servants and other non-whites, probably Indians, and some freed slaves" (Klein 1986:19). On the same page as this statement is a drawing (figure 1.5) depicting several people of color as farm laborers with the caption "Slaves on Long Island farms were few." While it is correct that southern planters enslaved many more people than northern farmers, Klein nevertheless documents that 20% of the local population consisted of either enslaved or bonded laborers in 1790. The drawing of the field workers is also a curious inclusion, since it is not referenced anywhere in the text. The *Guidebook*'s discussion of slavery is so curtailed that it indicates the author perhaps saw an underlying need to give the issue more presence but simply did not have the words for it.

The *Guidebook* ensures readers that slavery in Setauket was comparatively

Figure 1.5. "Slaves on Long Island were few." *Three Village Guidebook*. (Courtesy of the Three Village Historical Society, Long Island.)

mild and was eliminated from the village a long time ago. While the 1790 census shows William Floyd owned 14 enslaved people, most "local farmers owned no more than two each" (Klein 1986:19). More important, "since slavery was not basic to the Long Island agrarian economy, it was easier to abandon the evil practice. . . . In 1799 the Act of Manumission in New York provided a formula for the gradual freeing of slave families by 1827. . . . Slavery was practically abolished long before the Emancipation Proclamation of the 1860s." This statement is factually correct, but the congratulatory emphasis distinguishing Long

Island from the South is overwrought, especially the mistaken belief that "slave families" were freed. Given that owning even one person is a dehumanizing act, noting that there were fewer enslaved people in the North does not excuse the community that tolerated slavery in their midst.

This extremely limited engagement with slavery in the history of Setauket reveals a sense of great discomfort. For almost every statement about slavery, the *Guidebook* minimizes its existence and impact. Like the book's treatment of Native Americans, enslaved Africans are noted and then forgotten. Enslaved people and the enslavers emerge as myths, as ghosts, or as an evil aspect of history that those living now would never consider. Inasmuch as the history of slavery is in the past and all people are now free, readers of the *Guidebook* and the residents of Setauket should have no worries about the legacy of slavery in the village.

The current AHD seeks to remove histories of dispossession and slavery from the landscape. The problem for the heritage industry is that the historical community of color on Christian Avenue is still there, and these people cannot distance themselves from the violent history that is part of Setauket. They know that people of Native American and African descent make history every day in Setauket and have been doing so despite the racial violence perpetrated against them since the 1660s. This includes the fact that their white neighbors today seek to live out a history created to relegate the community of color to the margins.

Eel Spearing at Setauket

Making history every day and having it recognized by others are very different things. In Setauket, this is complicated by the fact that people of color are documented in some of the resources deployed in the authorized narrative. The most well-known of these sources are William Sidney Mount's paintings from the mid-nineteenth century. Mount is considered one of America's greatest genre painters, whose work reflects everyday life as he saw it on Long Island (Frankenstein 1968, 1975; Kaplan et al. 1999; Smith 2013). His paintings include lively and evocative scenes from the Setauket area of "farm workers nooning," "dancing on the barn floor," "school boys quarreling," "bargaining for a horse," and "the rock on the green," as well as many portraits of people of color, such as *The Banjo Player* and *The Bone Player*. Many believe his masterpiece is *Eel Spearing at Setauket* (figure 1.6).

Art historian Meredith Henry (2011) describes the painting this way:

> Painted for a wealthy New York lawyer who wanted a nostalgic picture of his childhood on Long Island, *Eel Spearing at Setauket* is one of Mount's

Figure 1.6. *Eel Spearing at Setauket,* 1845, by William Sidney Mount. Gift of Stephen C. Clark. N0395.1955. Photograph by Richard Walker. (Courtesy of Fenimore Art Museum, Cooperstown, New York.)

> most famous paintings. Painted in the gorgeous morning light, two figures—a little boy and a female slave—fish for eels on the smooth river in Setauket. The manor of the commissioner, the Strong family estate, stands in the background, on the horizon. The slave stands in the foreground and wields a spear as she prepares to spear an eel. . . . The boy sits in the back of the boat, watching as the woman spears the eel. The subtle coloring of the sand, water, and landscape speaks to Mount's fervent study of the Long Island landscape and his use of indigenous pigments. The painting not only represents Long Island, it is Long Island.

This fawning assessment of the painting is shared by many Setauket residents. Many people brought the painting to my attention and pointed out where on Conscience Bay the boat and the painter were located. Among these people is Jack Strong, a descendant of the "commissioner" who still lives in the manor house. Strong very much wanted me to see where the painting hung in his home before it was donated to a museum. The painting is clearly a touchstone for local history, especially its African American component.

I heard one important story about the painting from a member of the Christian Avenue descendant community who is also an active member of the Three Village Historical Society. The society is known for programs in which members dress and act as characters from Setauket's past (see figure 1.3). These include a Spirits of the Three Villages Cemetery Tour during the Halloween season and a Culper Spy Day event at which actors retell the story of the spy ring. At one event a women of color dressed as Rachel Holland Hart, the name attributed to the woman who modeled for Mount in the *Eel Spearing* painting. She was excited to play this role and indeed she did provide a reference to the village's diverse history.

After extensive research, however, I do not think Rachel Holland Hart was the model for the figure in Mount's painting. Her identification is based on oral tradition among the descendant community of color (Green 1999). Yet there is nothing in local archives that identifies her by name and no records of her name in documents associated with William Sidney Mount. The same is true for most other people of color who modeled for Mount's other paintings and portraits, though some were identified after the fact (see Edward P. Buffet, William Sidney Mount: A Biography, 1924, Three Village Historical Society, Setauket, New York). She is thought to have been a domestic servant working in the Strong household at the time. The 1840 census records that Selah Strong headed a household that included five free people of color, including a girl between 10 and 24 years old. This could be a reference to Rachel, but the census does not give names other than the head of the household, so we cannot be sure.

A woman named Rachel L. Holland is identified in a burial permit from 1902 in the TVHS archive. At 73 years old, this woman was born in 1829, which is about the same year community historian Ted Green (1999:64) thinks Rachel Holland Hart was born. The Rachel L. Holland who died in 1902 seems then to be the person Green thinks was the model in *Eel Spearing*. She would have been 15 years old at the time of the painting. Green also notes that Rachel Holland Hart "was born [Rachel Tobias] on Brook Road in Port Jefferson . . . the daughter of Abraham and Clarissa Jones Tobias, but nothing is known of her more distant ancestry." He does not provide sources for this genealogical data, nor do other records help to clarify who these people were. Green believes Rachel Tobias married Andrew Holland and that they had a son also named Andrew. There is no source of an Andrew Holland in the Setauket area, other than a 1900 census entry for a 35-year-old black man by that name. This would mean he was born in 1865, when Rachel Holland Hart was 35 years old. This is a reasonable possibility, except this Andrew Holland's mother is listed as born in Virginia, which does match what Green says about Rachel Tobias. Green also says that Rachel Tobias later married William H. Hart, with whom she had five additional children. One of these children was Jacob Hart, the head of household at one of the sites excavated for this study. Data from the 1865 and 1870 censuses show a home headed by William H. Hart. In 1865 his wife was identified as Rachel L. Hart, and in 1870 she was listed as Lucretia Hart, presumably the same person. It does not seem likely that this woman is Rachel Holland Hart, since she is supposed to have given birth to Andrew Holland in 1865, which is not likely if she was raising a family with William H. Hart that same year.

While genealogical research can easily lead to mistakes and dead ends, there is enough information to conclude that the stories in Setauket about the name of the model in the *Eel Spearing* painting are not accurate. None of the documentation indicates with any clarity the existence of an individual named Rachel Holland Hart in the Setauket area nor that she was a servant of the Strong family as oral tradition suggests. Documentary sources confirm that a woman of color named Rachel L. Hart (née Tobias) lived in the village in the late 1800s but whether this person was previously named Rachel Holland Hart cannot be verified. It may be that these multiple Rachels are mixed up in the community's memory, though that too is something that cannot be confirmed. While some doubt about whether the model for *Eel Spearing* was named Rachel Holland Hart is warranted, no such doubt is evident in the way her story is told in Setauket today.

The *Eel Spearing* painting was commissioned in the 1840s by attorney George Washington Strong to recall "his childhood pleasures" (Green 1999:63). His great-nephew Thomas "Judd" Strong was the model for the boy in the back of the boat. The boy represents the New York lawyer's memory of his own childhood in Setauket. Documentation seems to confirm that the model for the boy was Thomas Strong, but as just discussed, we cannot say who the model was the woman in the front, whether someone like her ever existed, or if she was instead an imagined character that sprang from the minds of Strong and Mount. When current residents act as Rachel Holland Hart in a community event, they are acting out a composite character whose place on the canvas and now the dramatist's stage was created to serve the nostalgia of a wealthy white lawyer for the "simpler" years of his childhood. These were years when enslaved people of color formed a picturesque rural subject for George W. Strong and perhaps a quite distinct image from his everyday urban encounters with free African Americans in 1840s New York City. The *Eel Spearing* painting and the remembered figure of Rachel Holland Hart are a powerful place where the local history of slavery, framed through the lens of elite nostalgia, has taken control of the past so that the violence and racism commonplace at the time is overlooked. Moreover, once a quasi-fictional character takes center stage, especially one whose identity derives from rose-tinted memory of white elites, what room is there for actual people of color to be recognized?

Another example of the way people of color are controlled in the authorized heritage discourse is the image of the Three Village Historical Society (2005) publication *The Setaukets, Old Field, and Poquott*, a volume in the Images of America series (figure 1.7). This photograph of a man leading his boat into the water is meant to capture the feel of the coastal environment of Setauket, which it succeeds at doing. Unlike the more than 400 other images in the book, however, this image is neither captioned nor sourced. This missing detail was likely an oversight but it nevertheless suggests that what is important about the photograph is what it evokes more than what and who it actually documented. Surprisingly, people in Setauket know the man as well as what he was doing.

The subject is Bill Hart, a Native and African American man who made a living as a bayman. "Bayman" is a catch-all term for a small-scale, independent fishermen who worked in close-to-shore waters collecting clams, oysters, fish, and eels (Gabriel 1921:91). Most baymen had small boats like the one in the image and would have used their catch for subsistence or sold it to supplement their income. This photograph presents a very different image of working on the water than Mount's painting, since in this case it is clearly someone going out to earn a living. As Green (1999:64) notes "What would be a simple recreation for Thomas 'Judd' Strong, his [great] uncle and the painter could have been important to the livelihoods of Long Island African Americans. Selling either freshly caught eels or eels that had been cured by smoking over an open fire could supplement the cash income of a family hard pressed to make ends meet." Like the tennis players walking by Indian Rock, we see again a positive historical association of Setauket with leisure, but we also see how this history obscures and removes from the story the presence of labor and, especially, the men and women of color whose work has helped to give Setauket some of its most basic historical symbolism. One last vignette about the place of people of color in Setauket's AHD helps draw this aspect of the power of history over the past in Setauket to a close.

This last story comes from the writings of Kate Strong, a popular and well-known chronicler of Setauket's history, which she shared in *True Tales of the Early Days of Long Island* (Strong 2013). Strong published more than 250 sto-

Figure 1.7. Cover of *The Setaukets, Old Field, and Poquott*, showing bayman Bill Hart. (Courtesy of the Three Village Historical Society, Long Island.)

ries in this series between 1940 to 1976. The first of these tales was titled "An Old Slave's Fiddle." Originally published in 1940, it is nominally about Anthony Hannibal Clapp, an enslaved man whose headstone in the Mount family cemetery in Stony Brook (figure 1.8) caught Strong's attention. The top part of the stone has a violin carved in sharp relief, a representation of Clapp's skill and perhaps livelihood as a fiddle player. Below the carving is a lengthy and laudable epithet. While the carving of the violin is the inspiration for Strong's essay, she abandons Clapp and his headstone after a few sentences to write the rest of the essay about William Sidney Mount. The connection is that Mount knew and remembered "Toney" from his childhood, but this is less important to Strong than the fact that Mount himself played, made, and painted violins. From there the essay recounts some additional historical facts and meanings about Mount's life having nothing at all to do with the fiddle or Clapp.

While Strong was not a professional historian and so may be excused for stylistic eccentricities, she was a member of one of the community's most established and wealthy local families, and she is still recognized as a local treasure decades after her death. If only for the sake of understanding her role in creating the AHD of Setauket, it is worth asking why a tale meant to recount aspects of Mount's life makes any mention of Clapp as a slave owned by Mount's family at all. I think we see again an effort to create a history that takes control of the very troubled role and meaning of slavery and racial violence in the past. In this case, Clapp's enslavement provides a way into the space dominated by a history that for the most part has no place for it. Slavery is not the subject, nor even in the end are those who were enslaved. Rather, slavery and the enslaved reside at the margin of Setauket's AHD. After all, as interesting as Clapp may be to the storyteller, Strong's narrative implies that Mount is someone we actually need to know more about since his paintings are a principle source for understanding Setauket, and we would not want to confuse his portraits and memories of working-class people and people of color to mean that we should pay attention to them when we think of Setauket as a historic place today.

Conclusion

The primary historical narrative in Setauket puts a clear and primary focus on a small part of its history and community to the exclusion of other stories, time periods, and people. The story of the Culper Spy Ring gives the local community a compelling, prepackaged colonial history to propagate. It also promotes a public relationship with history that requires an enjoyable role for interpreters

Figure 1.8. Tombstone of Anthony Hannibal Clapp, 1819. (Courtesy of the Long Island Museum of American Art, History, and Carriages. Melville Collection.)

(often in costume) as intermediaries, fostering history as something abstract and separate from the way life is lived in the community today. The authorized heritage in Setauket also employs a terminal narrative that writes Native Americans and enslaved Africans out of the history of Setauket, despite the fact that their descendants still live there.

Arguably, the desire by both those who propagate the AHD and those who consume it uncritically would not be as appealing if the stories of the Woodhulls, Strongs, Brewsters, Thompsons, and Mounts included their association with the displacement of Native Americans and enslavement of African-descended people. This would require a shift in the discourse by moving history from being a leisure activity to something more akin to labor, where violence and exploitation are more at home. In chapter 2 I examine a counterpoint to the AHD in Setauket. The story remains on the surface of the ground as I discuss multiple sites, events, and people from the Native and African American community that are mostly in plain sight on the Setauket landscape. That they are not more well-known is not because they are not important or hard to find but because their existence does not support the authorized heritage discourse in Setauket.

Notes

1. From Hough 1857: 1698, 558 (20.8%) slaves out of 2,679 total; 1703, 188 (11.4%) slaves of 1649 total; 1712, 244 (5.5%) slaves of 4,413 total; 1723, 975 (15.6%) blacks and other slaves of 6241 total; 1731, 601 (7.8%) slaves of 7675 total; 1737, 1,089 (13.7%) blacks of 7,923 total; 1746, 1,599 (17.3%) blacks of 9,254 total; 1749, 1,286 (13.9%) blacks of 9,284 total; 1756, 1,045 (10.2%) blacks of 10,290 total; 1771, 1,452 (11.1%) blacks of 13,128 total; 1786, 1,068 (7.7%) slaves of 13,793 total; 1790, 1,127 (7.0%) (1,098 according to Slaves table) of 16,094 total; 1800, 886 (4.6%) slaves of 19,464 total; 1810, 413 (2.0%) slaves of 21,113 total; 1814, 339 (1.6%) slaves of 21,368 total; 1820, 323 (1.3%) slaves of 24,272 total.

2. Several people of color are listed as sailors in the 1880 census, all but two of them living in Port Jefferson. This included Jerry Sells from Setauket and Isaac Tobias from East Setauket. In Port Jefferson, sailors of color included Henry Jones, Samuel Sells, Samuel Tobias, Henry Tobias, Charles Tobias, Jeffrey Smith, Washington Phillips, Madison Lewis, Peter Guard, Benjamin Smith, and Jefferson Smith.

3. Several people of color are listed as working at the rubber factory in the 1880 census, including Henry G. Satterley, Margaret Titus, Sidney G. Titus, Samuel C. Buffett, and Benjamin Buffett.

4. The original source is the Suffolk Improvement Company's pamphlet "Old Field South" published ca. 1936, Three Village Historical Society.

5. Suffolk Improvement Co. Restrictions on Old Field South contained in deed of Wm. Tomlins Jr., April 1930, Three Village Historical Society.

6. There are several leading voices in the field of critical heritage studies including David Lowenthal (1985, 1998), Laurajane Smith (2004, 2006), Lynn Meskell (2002, 2018), Barbara Little and Paul Shackel (2014), Rodney Harrison (2009), and Emma Waterton (Waterton and Watson 2014; Smith and Waterton 2009).

2

A COUNTER-MAP OF SETAUKET

> Few of us have thought to ask what truths a map may be concealing, or have paused to consider that maps do not tell us where we are from or who we are. Many of us do not know the stories of the land in the places where we live.
>
> *Adam Loften and Emmanuel Vaughan-Lee*

In 1961 the *Suffolk County News* (20 July 1961:8) reported:

> The Rev. John C. Raines, former pastor at the Methodist Church here, returned from a Freedom Ride in the South this week, and told local residents that things are not much better in the North. Citing the separate Negro and white living areas, separate graveyards and separate American Legion Posts, the Rev. Raines said that the large Negro population of Setauket is crowded into two two-block areas of substandard houses. "There is an unwritten segregation law which forbids Negroes to move into two or three high-class districts in town," he said. "There are no Negroes in the local volunteer fire department or on the school system staff," the minister added. He suggested that "the South send its Freedom Riders to Setauket and let them go down and try to join the Old Field Club." The Rev. Raines said he was trying to pinpoint a segregation pattern that many Long Island communities share with the South.

The paper interviewed John C. Raines to hear some of his personal experiences in the African American civil rights movement. A freedom rider in the South, he was arrested and sentenced to six months in prison for disturbing the peace in Little Rock (Chicago Tribune, 13 July 1961:20). Instead of talking about his experience in Arkansas, though, he focused on what he saw in Setauket that seemed so much like the racist South. For Raines Setauket required a radical intervention like the work being done by the freedom riders in the South to restructure its racially segregated social order. He also highlighted a number of highly visible landmarks of the black community, many of which still exist. This chapter provides a tour of these sites that proves Setauket is a vibrant and diverse community, even if the dominant historical narrative neglects to recognize it.

The framework of the chapter is the idea of a counter-map (Wood 2010). Counter-maps are created to represent people, events, and ideas that have been left out or misrepresented by official maps and related documentations of a place. Counter-mapping is a political act aimed to expose the inherent subjectivities and agendas of official maps as well as provide an opportunity for marginal communities and common people to speak back to the maps that impact their lives. Here I treat the authorized heritage discourse (Smith 2006) of Setauket outlined in chapter 1 as the official map. To develop a counter-map, I redraft the visual representation and experience of history in the village to be more inclusive and critical of the way the AHD controls what we can know about Setauket. The chapter begins with a discussion of the theory of counter-mapping. I then discuss how maps currently function in Setauket, especially regarding the local practice of historic preservation. This is followed by an inventory of several historically significant sites associated with Native and African American people in and around Setauket. This inventory is meant to be taken as an alternative map of Setauket that makes room for critical histories of people of color. I close the chapter with some creative implications of the counter-map, drawing from oral history and contemporary archaeology that provide place and face to the stories of the minority community.

What Is a Counter-Map?

Counter-maps "greatly increase the power of people living in mapped areas to control representation of themselves and their claims to resources" (Peluso 1995:387).[1] An excellent source for understanding counter-mapping is Denis Wood's (2010) *Rethinking the Power of Maps*, especially the essays "The Death of Cartography" and "Talking Back to the Map." For Wood, counter-maps not only illustrate injustice, they also expose how maps can be powerful tools of oppression. We count on maps to be correct, to accurately show us where things are and how to find our way. In this process, the hidden influence of maps lies in the way they inform us about what is really out there, a process that makes maps powerful agents in the construction and experience of space and place.

The key question in counter-mapping is "what makes a fact a fact," which suggests we need to understand that "mapmaking is more like talking [or] writing" (Wood 2010:165) than we normally think. Maps employ and arrange "facts" such that as we move through space we can know where we are and what places mean based on what we see. As most of us are not trained mapmakers, we tend to use maps uncritically to mark out space and place like this: "We are here, because the map says so" but also "here is X (a street, a house, a place, a site) because the *map says so*." The point of concern driving counter-mapping is that we allow maps to tell us what we see, thereby reversing the direction of knowledge and experience from the world itself to a representation of it. This is one of the problems in Setauket, since none of the maps or other authorized heritage resources mention the Christian Avenue community.[2]

Wood (2010:165) argues that maps work because of their presumed objectivity and through the use of "affectless language." Maps supposedly cannot show beautiful old buildings, burned-out abandoned cars, shiny new homes, or shocking degrees of abandonment that mark how some landscapes are occupied and felt. Unable to convey emotion, official maps effectively cover up what is really there and actually happening (Wood 2010:165). Counter-maps seek to recapture this emotional reality by remembering the intimacies of people and place and allowing a diversity of evidence to be employed, displayed, and put into conversation.

Some of the most effective counter-maps were created by indigenous communities who intimately understood the power of official cartography over their use of the land. Native people have long dealt with the effects of outsiders mapping their territories. Maps that were not produced with, by, or for indigenous people reduced landscapes occupied for generations into blank environmental slates defined by waterways, forests, topography, transportation routes, and modern political borders. The implication that people occupied places was present, but nothing on these maps showed how they occupied them, let alone what places might have meant and continue to mean.

Several indigenous communities have created counter-maps of their homelands as a response. The earliest example was the 1976 Inuit Land Use and Occupancy Project. Here, "hunters, trappers, fishermen, berry pickers, mapped out all the land they had ever used in their lifetimes, encircling hunting areas species by species, marking gathering locations and camping sites—everything their life on the land had entailed that could be marked on a map" (Wood 2010:130). Hugh Brody (1981) worked on the project and concluded that "the Indians' maps, like their experiences of them, are clear representations of their use of the land. . . . They represent a reality and have an integrity that social science can rarely achieve" (quoted in Wood 2010:131). Another project, titled the *Maya Atlas*, was "made by the people who live in the maps. The task was to create a way that people who live in their geography could make maps of it: that is, to make their geography visible and accessible" (Maya People of Southern Belize 1997 in Wood 2010:137).

An important result of indigenous counter-maps is the way evidence is marshaled to promote these indigenous understandings of space and place. The Supreme Court of Canada concluded in 1997 that indigenous claimants' reference to oral tradition, song, dance, and other performances that supported their ownership of traditional territories had to be accepted as cartographic and political evidence. "Having been challenged by a song, a dish of sand, a painting, *no state map can ever again be quite the authoritative thing that it was*" (Wood 2010:142, emphasis original). The crux of the issue is that this evidence is made up of subjective material and cultural objects rather than objective cartographic or historical "facts," and, more to the point, these elements were accepted as legitimate evidence of a cultural presence, occupancy, and claim. Herein lies the true impact of a counter-map. It is evidence based and thus reliable, but it also demands that we accept a broader range of what counts as evidence, especially as the evidence changes the criteria and register of what is mapped and how maps are made and read.

Counter-maps created by William Bunge and his colleagues in the Society for Human Exploration and the Detroit Geographic Expedition and Institute show the power of naming the evidence of the map. Committed to scholarship for the public benefit, Bunge trained Detroit residents how to construct their own facts so the maps would "be more relevant to their situation" (Wood 2010:167). In one case they changed the name of a map produced by the city from "Children's Pedestrian Deaths and Injuries by Automobile" to "Where Commuters Run Over Black Children on the Pointes-Downtown Track." Here we see an emotional appeal that shifted blame from the victims to the suburban commuter perpetrators killing black children. Another emotionally powerful counter-map documented the "Region of Rat-Bitten Babies." The key aspect of Bunge's theory of maps was the process of getting "unlost," wherein Detroit Geographic Expedition members were dropped off in Detroit, where they would spend three days becoming found. They were to memorize existing maps, learn local landmarks, and create their own maps to show that they could find their way on the ground. After this immersion members would be known as "founds" (Wood 2010:168).

Unlearning

The ideas of getting unlost and counter-mapping more broadly connect to the concept of unlearning, an idea embedded in the foundation of A Long Time Coming. According to Virginia Lee (2002),

> unlearning occurs in two ways: 1) through a process of "extinction" or the removal of reinforcements (Ever try sticking to a diet when the pounds stop coming off?) and 2) the apposition of "reciprocal behaviors" or the introduction of a stimulus that evokes a response different from the usual response in a given situation (Why do pediatricians wear child-friendly ties?).

In these terms, counter-maps aim to juxtapose reciprocal behaviors showing that what may be important or vital to some is missing from the reality of others who share the spaces created by the map. As with Bunge, so long as commuters are not identified as agents of death or the white majority community is unaware of the incidence of rat bites in poor black neighborhoods, the oppressive and dangerous conditions of the inner city remain abstract ideas and representations rather than concrete material and social forces. Moreover, creating new maps of the places that people already know is a way to identify the complicity of the majority who also occupy the space, despite their ignorance of the minority's struggle to coexist.

Robert Lewis spoke about the idea of unlearning at the outset of A Long Time Coming: "I think as much as there is an obvious demand upon a growing mind to 'learn,' there is an equally big demand to '*unlearn*,' but I am of the opinion that the demand to unlearn gets drowned out as we unknowingly, (and almost irreversibly), structure our lives to prepare for the realities of our living circumstances" (Matthews 2011b:50). Lewis explains here that the struggle in his home community has been ongoing since the origins of colonialism, racism, the slave trade, and the emergence of African American and Native American emancipatory and postcolonial intellectual traditions (e.g., Douglass 2003; Du Bois 1935; Kelley 1996; Morrison 1992; Robinson 2000; Woodson 1990).[3] In a nutshell, Lewis describes the problem of maintaining a critical perspective on the world while working hard to survive day to day. For African American and Native American communities, these needs are often at odds, since there are bills to pay and radical theory does not generate much income. Yet to lose this edge is to capitulate and potentially lose their community, their identity, and with these their history. The critique emergent in unlearning

> aims less at persons or class practices than at the process through which persons, communities, and class groups are established in civil society. The underlying thought here is that this knowledge comes only through a radical social and personal transformation such that one's identity is strikingly destabilized. While lofty and hard to demand in full, promoting an imagination of substantial change is one way to reveal and potentially undo the influence of oppressive dominant ideologies. (Matthews 2011b:50)

Counter-maps make good examples of how to imagine substantial change, though to be effective they should be juxtaposed with existing maps. In the following I return to the *Three Village Guidebook* (Klein 1986) to discuss and critique the maps that define Setauket's historic districts. I show that despite being profiled as neutral documents, these maps reinforce one of the key features Klein includes in his undefined notion of "contemporary American life."

The Authorized Historic Maps of Setauket

The original edition of the *Three Village Guidebook* was published to make a case for establishing a historic district classification in the zoning code. This goal was met the year of the first edition's publication in 1976, though it was also tied to the bicentennial fever of the year, which of course prized stories from the American Revolution. The work that went into establishing these historic districts is praiseworthy because the preservation of historic structures as part of the local planning process has enabled a great deal more reflection on local history than would have occurred otherwise. A close look at the author's language as he describes the significance of the history of the Three Villages in the preface to the second edition of the *Guidebook* shows important underlying interests and assumptions about the history he has in mind when speaking of Setauket.

Celebrating the creation of the historic district classification, the *Guidebook*'s "1986 Afterthoughts" includes two maps detailing the boundaries of the four historic districts created in the Three Village area in the 1970s (figure 2.1). These maps delineate the historic districts with over-bolded black boundaries, shading, and hatching that separate the historic sections of town from the surrounding undesignated neighborhoods. I highlight this illustration for two reasons. First, the heavy bold lines clearly devalue other places by allowing them to fade into a generic space of historical insignificance. Second, it is in these undesignated areas that we find the historic and present residential sections of the Setauket's minority community along Christian Avenue and in the former working-class neighborhood of Chicken Hill. With the stroke of an artist's pen in a widely used book, the community of color and their history are thus formally excluded from the town's authorized historic spaces.

It was in part because his Christian Avenue neighborhood was excluded from these official historic districts that Robert Lewis worked to establish the Bethel–Christian Avenue–Laurel Hill Historic District in 2005. The BCALH was the first historic district in the Town of Brookhaven to recognize a minority community and the first established based on the survival of significant cultural rather than architectural resources. This was a novel decision in a region that has long preserved its architectural treasures for their aesthetic value with little concern for the social histories these buildings contained. As I have shown, the Native and African American communities have always been a part of Setauket, and especially given their Native American ancestry, their history predates the modern town's founding. Nevertheless, this community was not included when the time came for history to be put down on a map, and then only after a transformation in the way historic designations were determined 30 years later was this oversight addressed.

The book's "1986 Afterthoughts" adds depth to this discussion with its programmatic description of the Town Historic Districts Advisory Committee (Klein 1986:7):

> The Town Board appointed a citizen's Historic Districts Advisory Committee. Membership included non-elected or appointed at-large members, one representative of each Historic District, and the Town Historian, ex-officio. At least one member must be a registered architect. Approval must be obtained for proposed changes made to buildings within a Historic District or Transition Zone. The following require permission:
> new construction or external changes
> moving or demolition of a structure
> erection of a sign for which a permit is required
> any variance from the provisions of the zoning code
> changes in design, materials or outward appearance of a structure
> Forms and information for obtaining approval to make changes are available from the Brookhaven Town Board.

This outline demonstrates the traditional architectural approach to preservation, but its "affectless" style differs significantly from the more congenial tone found throughout the rest of the *Guidebook*. The legal formality in this statement introduces the authority lying behind historic district designations and simultaneously identifies the communities that historic districts act on and presumably for. Specifically, these rules outline the responsibilities of property owners in historic districts. As in most property law in the United States, historic district designations detail the rights and responsibilities that tie autonomous owners to the larger communities and agencies that provide services and regulate their activities. In this way, historic districts are special as much for their regulation of property as for their designation of history.

It seems then that the local prominence of the *Guidebook* derives in part from its use as an important resource for gathering the propertied community in Setauket around a common understanding that their town is historic, that it should remain that way, and that they are fortunate to own a piece of it. Historic district boundaries establish the special places where property ownership binds people, families, and businesses together in common pursuit of the preservation and enhancement of their way of life. Ultimately, property ownership is what Klein (1986:6) means by "contemporary American life." What else in this context can be flavored with the zest of the past than the particular properties that stood through the many years of Setauket's history and stand now as prizes for those wise and wealthy enough to acquire and appreciate their historic qualities?

The construction of history as a component of private property excludes those who do not own property, such as renters, boarders, or residents in group homes. While some members of the Native and African American communities in Setauket are not property owners, many do own their homes and have for generations. Certainly they also are aware of the value of the past, the character, and quality of the village. The exclusion of their homes from the historic district designation suggest instead that they are not architecturally distinguished or were built and altered in more recent years and not eligible for inclusion in the historic districts zones defined by specific architectural characteristics (figure 2.2). However, the fact that many nonwhite property owners did not acquire and build their homes until recent decades is itself part of the historic development of the area, which historically devalued their contributions and thus kept them at an economic disadvantage well into the twentieth century. Following this sort of historic district–driven thinking, that some minority families found success, invested in property, and created the community of color now living on Christian Avenue is not part of Setauket's official history, which is focused on much earlier years and restricted to the achievements of its white property-owning citizens and their followers. By this reasoning, when the community of color joined the ranks of the propertied and made history in the mid- and late twentieth century, they got around to these things too late.

Research Methods

The counter-map of Setauket is a view of the current landscape that allows the Native and African American community to come more clearly into view. Although most of their historic and contemporary places are left off the authorized maps of Setauket's history many are in plain sight. Most of the others are hidden only because of a lack of attention and questioning about who and what are constituted as historically important. To document these sites I worked with Higher Ground to collect stories from current residents about their knowledge and experience of place in Setauket. We researched archival sources such as censuses, maps, historic photographs, deed records, and other documents to locate and flesh out stories of places connected to people of color. I also used archaeology to document aboveground and underground historical and material culture resources connected to the community.[4]

Counter-Map of Setauket

To populate a counter-map with sites that tell an alternate history of Setauket, I turn back to John C. Raines's observations on the parallels between the segregated South and what he knew of Setauket as a minister there in the 1950s. He observed that there were "separate Negro and white living areas, separate graveyards and separate American Legion Posts" and that "the large Negro population of Setauket is crowded into two two-block areas of substandard houses." I provide details of these sites and sections of the town and guide us through several other sites that are likely to have escaped Raines's eye since they are hidden by new development and preexisting controlling narratives (figure 2.3).

Landmarks of the Native and African American Community

The first site is the Irving Hart Legion Hall, Post 1766 (figure 2.4), located on Christian Avenue in the heart of the BCALH historic district. The history of the legion hall starts before its construction in 1949 (Suffolk County News, 28 October 1949:14). In earlier years, another legion hall in Setauket (Post 417) served local veterans. We know from oral history (Longjohn and Flajnik 2011) that Post 417 was not officially segregated, but when people of color attempted to join after World War II they were made to feel unwelcome. During this time, race relations in the United States were in flux and the military was a key arena of struggle, especially after President Harry Truman ordered the integration of troops in 1948. Truman was pressured to deal with segregation since many of his peers and civil rights leaders promoted the inspiring Double V Program: a victory for democracy against its enemies both abroad and at home, a reference to Jim Crow segregation and the idea that African Americans sacrificed equally but earned only half a victory on their return home.

It is hardly ironic that the Irving Hart Legion Hall opened to serve the community's "colored" veterans one year after the troops were integrated. The story of the founding of Post 1766 also notes that Ku Klux Klan members in Post 417 rejected the inclusion of people of color as members after World War II. This was also true for the women of color who wanted to join the ladies auxiliary. As a result, Setauket's nonwhite vets and their wives organized the new post by meeting the minimum of 15 founding members plus one. The last member was Ralph Lyons, a white man who left Post 417 in solidarity with his African American friends. When the founders drafted bylaws for the new post, they included a rule not found at most other legion halls: "every race is included" (Longjohn and Flajnik 2011). As Pearl Hart remembered, "we were fortunate to have a building erected in honor of our soldiers of World War I and World War II by Mrs. Rachel Hart Midgett—dedicated in the name of her brother Irving Hart. Thus, the Irving Hart American Legion, Post 1766. This really was a blessing for we needed a place for our activities through the Legion as well as for the Bethel AME Church, Setauket" (Longjohn and Flajnik 2011).

The legion hall was indeed built on land donated by Rachel Midgett, a leader in the community who owned several properties on Christian Avenue. Deed histories show she acquired the lot she later donated for the legion hall in 1928 while married to her first husband, William Young. It is likely the Youngs moved to Christian Avenue to be close to Bethel AME Church and Laurel Hill Cemetery, two ancient landmarks of the community of color in Setauket. Other families of color also settled on Christian Avenue at that time, creating one of the "colored" enclaves John Gaines described in 1961. The other was Chicken Hill, which has since been razed to make way for a strip mall.

The Irving Hart Legion Hall was built across the street from Bethel AME Church of Setauket, which still serves the community as a place of worship (figure 2.5). The current church building was erected in 1909 and has been used continuously since for services, marriages, baptisms, funerals, and other events marking vital moments in the community's life. Moreover, the church has always been an institution maintained by community members, allowing them refuge and a place to gather and engage as a community with the larger world.

The Bethel AME congregation dates to as early as 1845. The earliest surviving documents, from 1848, record that community members acting as the trustees of the African Methodist Episcopal Society of Setauket and Stony Brook obtained a small plot of land on Christian Avenue in Stony Brook to build a church and establish a cemetery. One record is a deed that states the trustees will only use the site for a place of worship. The second is an agreement that the trustees will erect a fence along the property boundary at their own expense. Both documents indicate a certain lack of trust by the seller, William Bayles, that the society would keep its word. The signatories of this document were the trustees of the African Society: Richard Ackerly, Jacob Tobias, Abraham Tobias, and David Tobias. Only Ackerly signed his name, while the three Tobiases signed with their mark (figure 2.6).

In 1871 the congregation moved the church to the current site of the Bethel AME Church on Christian Avenue in Setauket. While they likely moved the original church building at that time, they left behind a set of beautiful nineteenth-century headstones, which stand now in what is known as Old Bethel Cemetery. Markers are present for David, Jacob, and Abraham Tobias, as well as members of other historic families of color who lived in Setauket and Stony Brook (figure 2.7).

It is not known why the trustees wanted the particular original site. It could be simply that the Bayles family welcomed the trustees to build on a corner of their property, but the landscape at the site suggests that there may be more to the story. For one, the site was built between Stony Brook and Setauket villages rather than in either of them, revealing perhaps a desire to worship in a place apart from the white-dominated villages. It may also be that the founders wanted to lay claim to a space outside of town that they had long used for gatherings, rituals, and perhaps even burials. The site is located on a upland rise above the shore of the Long Island Sound near the mouth of a spring that feeds into Aunt Amy's Creek. Elevated locations such as these were often used by precontact Native Americans for burial sites for more than 3,000 years (Long Island Genealogy 2019; Ritchie 1965:175–178; Tweedie 2014:82–83).[5] Moreover, the precontact Native American Stony Brook Site is located where Aunt Amy's Creek empties into West Meadow Creek at the shore line (Ritchie 1959). It is reasonable to consider that the site selected for Old Bethel Church and Cemetery may have been part of a tradition of ritual land use by the community from long before European settlement.

The community's oldest documented landmark is Laurel Hill Cemetery, founded in 1815 (figure 2.8). According to a document filed in 1853 the Town of Brookhaven authorized Setauket residents Colonel Isaac Satterly (1765–1859) and Benjamin F. Thompson (1784–1849) to "lay out a negro burying ground in the Village of Setauket known and called by the name of Laurel Hill" (handwritten affidavit, May 16, 1853, in Liber E, Records of the Town of Brookhaven, Three Village Historical Society, Setauket, New York; also see Wellman 2016:4). Why these men were charged to create a cemetery in 1815 and why they chose the spot they did are not answered by this document. The timing is conspicuous, given that slavery in New York was coming to an end. By 1815 the state's Gradual Emancipation Act of 1799 had long been in place and had inspired many slave owners to free their captive laborers. The Thompson family had been slave owners since early in the 1700s, and town records document that Samuel Thompson manumitted at least four individuals between 1813 and 1826 (Phillippi 2016). The Satterlys are not documented slave owners, though they did employ people of color as domestic servants. The decision to establish the cemetery may be in part the result of their relations with people of color. During the time of slavery, it was common for enslaved persons to be buried in their master's family plot. The Thompson family plot is still maintained, though there are no markers identifying enslaved members of the household. That said, graves of enslaved persons were commonly marked by fieldstones rather than engraved markers, so the remains of captive laborers may be located in what are now unmarked graves in the Thompson's plot. As slavery declined, newly free people likely had no interest in being buried with their former master's family, preferring instead an independent burial site. Laurel Hill would have met this demand.

The location of Laurel Hill mirrors that of Old Bethel Cemetery in that both sites are located on hilly terrain that drops down toward a waterway feeding into the Long Island Sound. Both are also situated near precontact Native American sites. In the case of Laurel Hill, the hilly terrain is along the south side of Christian Avenue. The steepest rise is toward the east end of the ridge where it is closest to the mill pond creek. Laurel Hill is located at the point where the topography (heading east) shifts from a more gradual to a steeper incline. The mill pond creek runs from its source south of Setauket through the center of the village before feeding into Conscience Bay. This is an ancient cultural landscape evidenced by the Englebright archaeological site, located a half a block north of where Christian Avenue crosses the creek. Thus, the peak of Laurel Hill is a highly likely spot for Native American ritual practice and perhaps also burials in the precontact era.

Historic Home Sites

The church, cemeteries, and legion hall constitute the public monuments of the Native and African American community in Setauket. Many homes making up the domestic spaces where people of color have historically lived also survive. The Bethel–Christian Avenue–Laurel Hill Historic District includes 30 domestic lots, each of which has its own meaningful connection to Setauket's Native and African American community.[6] I highlight here a few of the early domestic sites on Christian Avenue that are depicted on the 1917 Hyde atlas of Suffolk County (figure 2.9). The stories of these sites tell us about several important people and more generally how the historic Native and African American community occupied this place.

The first of these sites is the David and Mary Eato house (figure 2.10). David Eato was born in 1854 in Roslyn, New York, a town on the north shore of Long Island, about an hour's drive west of Setauket. His parents, Peter and Charlotte Eato, were born in New York. Census records from 1810 and 1820 show that there were a number of Eto and Eato families, all free people of color, living in Queens County. One household, headed by Venis Eto in 1810, consisted of four "other free persons" in North Hempstead Township, Queens County, which is where Peter Eato lived in later years. The Eato family later moved to nearby Port Washington, where David grew up and later became a pastor in the AME church. After serving congregations in Roslyn, Elmhurst, and Port Washington, he was appointed pastor at Bethel AME of Setauket in 1915. He remained in that position until at least 1920. David Eato passed away in 1925.

Mary Lucinda Baker Eato was born in 1868 on Baker Plantation in Troy, South Carolina, the child of formerly enslaved parents. Mary attended Allen University in Columbia, South Carolina, where she is presumed to have studied music based on her later work as a music teacher. After marrying, having children, and being widowed, she joined others in the Great Migration to the North, moving with her family to Port Washington in 1901. She worked as a cook, gave music lessons, and was the organist at the Port Washington AME church, which is where she met David Eato. David and Mary moved to Setauket between 1915 and 1917. Deed records suggest that they rented the house identified on the Hyde atlas on Christian Avenue until after David died. In 1928 Mary Eato purchased the home from the Hawkins family, who owned most of the property on the south side of Christian Avenue. Mary Eato was one of several women in the community to become legal homeowners in the 1920s. It is important to acknowledge that these women were foundational in establishing the community on Christian Avenue near the church and Laurel Hill Cemetery, and they did so before many of the other areas of the village encouraged people of color to move out. Without these foundations, the community on Christian Avenue would not have survived for as long as it has.

Details about the Eatos' life are documented in an oral history interview with two of their grandchildren in 1985 ("Reminiscences of June Eato Bisserup and Barbara Eato Barrett," interview with Elly Shodell, June 1985, Port Washington Community Oral History Program, Port Washington Library). Several notable stories from this interview feature Mary Eato: "The grandchildren used to call her 'Miss Lucy,' a reference to her middle name Lucinda." "She had just a great sense of humor," remembered Barbara Barrett. "When we'd go down to Setauket to see her, she'd always be sitting on the porch with a corncob pipe and she smoked Prince Albert tobacco, and she just had a smile and a laugh for everything and everybody" (Wellman 2016:90).[7] Mary Eato subdivided her lot in 1945 to create new properties for her children. One of her granddaughters married a member of the local Sells family. Consequently, when Mary died, she left a legacy of property, family, and intermarriage with local families. David Eato was also the first of several AME pastors to remain in Setauket after completing his service to the church. The others were Robert DuVal (pastor from 1922–1926), Joseph McKenzie (pastor from 1958–1967), Paul Morrison (pastor from 1967–1984), and the current pastor Gregory Leonard. There appears to have been something special about the Setauket AME community that attracted these men and their families over the generations; their stories contribute to the vitality of this place.

The 1917 Hyde atlas (figure 2.9) shows a few other houses on Christian Avenue. To the east of the Eato house are two domestic structures on the large lot associated with R. W. Hawkins. Hawkins was a real estate dealer, and neither of these structures are thought to have been his residence. The house closer to the Eato house on the map was rented by James Lewis and Rebecca Hart Lewis, Robert Lewis's grandparents. This home burned down before 1946 (interview with Robert Lewis and Pearl Hart, 24 May 2010). The next house moving east is the early core of the home that Robert Lewis still lives in. His parents, Howard Lewis and Ethel DuVal Lewis, moved into the home soon after their marriage in 1925. While the house has been expanded and altered, the Lewis family still owns the lot.

Two other early homes in the Hyde atlas are across the street on the north side of Christian Avenue. These are the former homes of sisters Lucy Hart Keyes (b. 1900) and Minnie Hart Sanford (b. 1897), the youngest daughters of Jacob and Hannah Hart, whose home site was excavated by A Long Time Coming (figure 2.11). Both women purchased their homes from Jennie Howell around 1920 when they were young adults. Even though Lucy and Minnie were sisters and neighbors, they led very different adult lives. Lucy lived her entire life in Setauket, where she worked as a housekeeper for several affluent families in the village. She married William Keyes who was a laborer and gardener. They had two sons and later one grandson, Ronald Keyes, who lived with Lucy after William passed away in 1967. The home is now owned by Bethel AME Church. Minnie Sanford rented out her home for much of her adult years while she traveled in service to the Pentecostal church. She married Harrison Sanford between 1915 and 1920. Sanford worked in the Setauket shipyards, though he disappears from the documentary record after 1925. It may be that he died and his early death led to Minnie's decision to do missionary work. The Sanford home is now owned by a white family new to the community.

In her old age, Minnie returned to Setauket to live in her home on Christian Avenue, living there until she died in 1979:

> [She] would raise the shade on the west side of her house every morning. Her sister Lucy Keyes would do the same on the east side of Lucy's house, so that each could see that the other was O.K. As neighbor Carlton Edwards remembered, one Sunday morning in November 1979, Minnie Sanford did not raise her shade. Lucy Keyes called neighbors, and everyone looked for her. Carlton Edwards, who had walked to church that morning, as he did every Sunday, remembered that somebody finally found her body in the cistern at the southeast corner of her house. (Carlton Edwards, 21 April 2016; Wellman 2016:117)

Creating a Community on Christian Avenue

Like Mary Eato and Rachel Midgett, Minnie Sanford and Lucy Keyes owned their own property. Even though all of the women were married, they did not share in the ownership of their properties with their husbands. This may have been happenstance, evidence of a matrilineal cultural practice, or more likely a deliberate strategy to protect family wealth. It is notable, however, that Hannah Hart, Lucy and Minnie's mother, was also the legal owner of the property where the women were born, despite the fact that she was born in Virginia and her husband, Jacob Hart, was born in Setauket. In this case, at least, native locality was less important than gender in terms of homeownership. Without doubt, women were important and played leading roles in the social life and success of the community.

By 1920, beside the families headed by Lucy Keyes, Minnie Sanford, and Mary Eato, three other families of color led by Martha Sells Hart Burton, Rebecca Hart Lewis, and Kate Scott lived on Christian Avenue. Except for Mary Eato, all of the women were related by blood or marriage reinforcing their commitment to each other and the new community they were building. By 1930 there were 12 separate households of color living on Christian Avenue and Mud Road. By 1940 this number grew to 16.

Rachel Hart (Young) Midgett (figure 2.12) was among the newcomers in 1930. Between 1928 and 1931, Rachel and William Young purchased the land that constitutes four separate lots today. These parcels are the sites of six separate homes as well as the legion hall today. These homes have been altered and expanded, rented to community members, and passed down to children and grandchildren who still own some of the properties. Like Mary Eato, Rachel Midgett subdivided her property for the benefit of her family and community. Together these two women created one of the special qualities of the Christian Avenue neighborhood. Because of the subdivisions, many of the lots on the south side of the road are crowded with houses that climb up the hillside (see figure 2.2). This landscape is very different from the one-home-per-lot construction typical in suburban subdivisions just down the road. It also shows that women developed successful strategies to protect their families and community and encourage people in their community to share in the benefits of precious family resources.

By the 1930s the Christian Avenue community was in full swing. Evidence giving insight to life on Christian Avenue from this time is found in the events and activities reported in a weekly social report on many of Long Island's communities of color published in the Brooklyn-based *New York Age*. For example, the column from Setauket on April 7, 1933, noted that

> Mr. and Mrs. Charles A. Sells are the proud parents of a baby son, born Saturday, March 18, at a Brooklyn hospital. Jacob Sells made a business trip to Philadelphia one day last week. Mrs. Williams Smith was tendered a surprise party last Tuesday evening, the occasion being her birthday. Besides the guest of honor those present included Mr. and Mrs. Wm. Keys. Mr. and Mrs. J. H. Bristol, Mr. and Mrs. William Young. Mr. and Mrs. Ed Stewart, Mrs. E. G. Calvin and E. Calvin, Jr., Mr. and Mrs. Daniel Lewis and Mssrs. Isaiah Hart and Walter Thompson. A delightful evening was had by all.

Such intimate yet mundane details of everyday life suggest a self-confidence not necessarily expected from a small community of color, though in the 1930s this sort of social reporting was likely also an antiracist strategy employed by African Americans to assert their presence in public and their right to a common experience of community.

Lucy Hart Keyes's life was an important part of a project led by Glenda Dickerson, a former professor of theater at Stony Brook University.[8] Dickerson and her students interviewed several members of the Christian Avenue community in the late 1980s. Dickerson's final work—a play based on the interviews and called *Eel Spearing at Setauket*—is fondly remembered as an important event in the community. Performances of the play came just before the development of the early stages of an autonomous historical consciousness in the community that led to the creation of the Setalcott Nation tribal council and Higher Ground. In other words, Dickerson's project laid the essential groundwork for the historical research accomplished since, including work presented in this book.

Dickerson's interview with Lucy Keyes for the *Eel Spearing* project provides details about her family and work history, how she came to afford her house, and also her garden. She noted that gardening supplemented her household income with fresh food. She had "a big garden, three pig pens, a chicken coop, and an apple tree." At 87 years old, she continued to plant: "I'm going to plant beans and beets and carrots next week. I don't know why I'm doing it because ain't nobody but me. But I've just got to do it. I've always did it, see? Don't know how to do anything different!" Robert Lewis also recalls gardens and fruit trees in the neighborhood:

> Everybody had a vegetable garden. My Mom and Dad had two of the largest gardens, one on the north side of West Meadow Road, where it intersects with Locust Avenue. Not his property. A lot of it he sold, not even sure what he grew. My mother would bring baskets of stuff from it. And the other huge garden that he had was right here on this property [on Christian Avenue], the entire backyard. From wall by the tenant's house, all the way up the hill into the back, almost 300 feet long by 100 feet wide. Kids had to do the weeding. It was good to be working on the earth, when I look back on it. And Mom canned everything. . . . Many sweet black cherry trees grew randomly along Christian Avenue, without formal cultivation. (Wellman 2016:65)

Landownership enabled the women in this community to find both economic security and the opportunity to provide directly for their families through small-scale farming and gardening. These efforts to provide for themselves certainly lessened the burden for waged work but also allowed them to minimize interactions with local storekeepers which may very well have involved moments of racial tension and conflict.

Alternative Landscapes

Memories of gardens connect to other histories of the local landscape that allow us to understand the sense of place held by the Christian Avenue community. A broader sense of the Setauket landscape is captured in the following statement entered into the town record by Pearl Lewis Hart in 2005:

> The springtime meant getting our gardens planted, with harvest in the fall. The foliage in this area was beautiful. The laurel bushes all in bloom made this place another world. I readily understand our cemetery's name being Laurel Hill. The wildflowers along the road, the roses, the buttercups, added to the beauty. During the summer it was great to walk Christian Avenue. The road was narrow allowing the tree branches from each side of the road to reach each other forming a canopy or shield from the hot sun. It was just beautiful. So nice and cool. . . . The month of August was a time for harvesting of fruits and vegetables, which we canned for the winter. Also, the summer meant getting the family together to enjoy the great outdoors. We had the most delicious food including fish and clams from the bay and a special dessert for our August work, blueberry pie. The berries were plentiful then. (Pearl L. Hart, statement, Town of Brookhaven public hearing, 21 June 2005, Town of Brookhaven Historian's Office, Farmingville, New York)

This memory in particular opens an understanding of the relationship between the community and the land including the forests and the shoreline. Pearl Hart is Robert Lewis's older sister, and his memories are similar. He recalls traversing animal trails, pathways, and bridle paths through the woods with siblings and friends including Aunt Lucy (Hart Keyes) to go to Mahoney's Lot to collect "pails and pails" of wild blueberries and huckleberries. Since the area was so wooded and remote, he never knew who Mahoney was. They would follow animal trails to reach West Meadow Creek, where they gathered beach plums and crabs and played in the cool water. They were in the vicinity there of a private beach used by a newly built gated community. Robert remembers going to school with children from that neighborhood, though he never saw these families collecting berries, plums, or crabs. He also remembers collecting turtles and healthful marsh plants near the mill pond and creek.

These stories each describe how Setauket's community of color enjoyed access to freely available food and medicinal resources that they collected in abundance from the formerly undeveloped lands adjacent to their neighborhood. They also show that this use of the landscape was their own cultural practice, as they knew other families in the area who did not engage in these sorts of activities. From archaeology, we can document as well that this way of life is an ancient legacy inherited from ancestors who also collected resources from the local environment. Finally, these stories show the impact of suburban development, since the wild berry bushes, forests, and shorelines are now either uprooted or no longer accessible.

One part of this suburbanizing landscape deserves special mention. This is the so-called colored beach (figure 2.13) on the shore of Setauket Harbor at the former location of Strong's Neck bridge. That bridge was built in 1878 but torn down in 1938 after it was damaged by the Long Island Express hurricane. After the bridge was removed the town brought in truckloads of sand to stabilize the water's edge. Since the shoreline was not a private space, people of color and poor white families from Chicken Hill took advantage and used the spot for swimming throughout the 1940s and 1950s. Carlton Edwards and Helen Sells have fond memories of the beach, which they went to with their families and friends (interview with Carlton Edwards and Helen Sells, 18 June 2018). Besides swimming on hot days, families also collected fresh water from a tapped spring and cherries from the trees that grew at the beach. Sells also remembers that the beach was a place to go when she and her friends left school. At low tide they collected clams, crabs, and other seafood that they would roast on the beach in small firepits dug into the sand. People also came to the beach for larger gatherings like clambakes led by brothers Irving and Bill Hart. These two men in fact organized a crew from the community that wealthy Old Field residents hired to run clambakes at parties (Green 1999:65).

The story of the "colored beach" also speaks about racism on the Setauket landscape. In this case, the segregation of the waterfront is connected to the early twentieth-century development of Old Field as an elite enclave separated by both race and class from the rest of Setauket. Besides owning the large lots and estates, Old Field residents were eligible to join the Old Field Club, a private swimming and tennis club on Stony Brook Harbor that did not accept people of color as members. John Gaines commented on the club when he encouraged "the South [to] send its Freedom Riders to Setauket and let them go down and try to join the Old Field Club." Clearly, the club was more than a segregated elite organization; it was also a well-known site for white recreation that Raines made into a symbol for the antiracist struggle. The Old Field Club was not the only segregated part of the local waterfront. Adjacent to the club is a town-owned stretch of shorefront known as West Meadow Beach. Starting in the 1920s families built small cottages there for daily use. Having a cottage at West Meadow allowed those without the resources to join the Old Field Club to enjoy the waterfront as well. Yet they brought to the beach the same social structure as the club by establishing West Meadow for whites only (cf. Kahrl 2016, 2018; Mullins et al. 2020).[9]

The separation of Old Field from the rest of the community was formalized with the establishment of Old Field Village in 1927. Old Field was designed as an elite community with magnificent homes on large lots. The community was ranked in 2010 as the twenty-fifth most expensive place to live in the United States with an average home value of $1.8 million; its early goals have been met. Separating Old Field from the rest of Setauket directly impacted several members of the town's Native and African American communities. At least as early as 1823, a cluster of small homes occupied by people of color formed along Old Field Road. As many as 10 households of color lived in this area in the mid-1800s, including members of the Silas Tobias household, a site A Long Time Coming excavated in 2015. Until the 1920s, members of these families could walk along Mud Road to visit other Native and African American friends and family as well as to attend services at Bethel AME on Christian Avenue.

This situation changed for the community of color in 1903, when the Old Field Improvement Association cut a right of way for Quaker Path Road to provide a new route between Old Field and the Stony Brook Long Island Railroad Station. Over the next two decades, the community of color in Old Field dwindled and by 1930 was gone. One indication of this change is a sign posted at the intersection of Mud Road and West Meadow Beach Road. On the north side of the intersection, a bright yellow dead-end sign indicates that Mud Road no longer connects with Old Field Road (figure 2.14). In fact, Mud Road was cut off at the Setauket–Old Field line when Old Field Village was established. This act certainly made it clear to people of color that they were not welcome in Old Field, a fact repeated in the racially restrictive covenants of Old Field South. One house remains where Mud Road used to lead before being cut off. This was the home of Julia Hart Ware, another daughter of Jacob and Hannah Hart. Ware lived through this transition, but her family sold the house after she died since by that time there was no longer a community of color in Old Field.

Hidden in Plain Sight

The next set of sites in the counter-map are four well-known historic homes in Setauket, two of which are preserved as house museums dedicated to telling the story of life in the early history of the village. Each of the four sites is associated with a prominent colonial family whose notable contributions to the local authorized narrative are taken at face value, despite, or perhaps because of, the fact that their role as slave owners is not mentioned.

The oldest of these historic homes is the Brewster House in East Setauket (figure 2.15), a colonial relic associated with one of Setauket's founding families. Brewsters were among the first settlers in Setauket in the mid-1660s, and the Brewster House is thought to have been built around that time. While not directly associated with the home, Caleb Brewster was a member of the Culper Spy Ring. The Brewsters lived in their family home for several generations, and the home was later acquired and renovated by Ward Melville. Moreover, the Ward Melville Heritage Organization celebrates the house as "a tribute to the craftsmanship of the first Europeans [in Setauket] and their descendants" (in Gorsline 2015:300–301).

There is a well-documented though entirely silenced presence of people of color at the Brewster House. Both Benjamin Brewster and Joseph Brewster were recorded as slave owners in 1776. Brewsters are also listed as slave owners in each of the censuses taken in 1800, 1810, and 1820. Gorsline (2015:302) reports,

> The Brookhaven Town Records lists a report from John Brewster, Jr., of the birth of a child named Rachel to an enslaved woman in his household on November 3, 1799. A genealogical history written by Leroy Smith (1916), a Brewster descendent, also purports to have recorded from the now misplaced family bible of Joseph Brewster, Jr., the births of Rachel (November 3, 1799), Fanne (February 20, 1802), Rox (December 18, 1805), and Andrew (February 18, 1809) to Nel, a woman enslaved in the Brewster home.

Among the Brewsters born in Setauket, one man's death gives us insight into the family's relations with their enslaved laborers. As we learn from the *New York Gazette and Weekly Mercury* on June 19, 1772:

> About four o'clock last Monday afternoon Nathaniel Brewster Esq. being in the woods with one of his negroes, attempted to correct him for some misdemeanor, which the negro resented, and wounded his master by giving several such heavy blows on his head with a billet of wood, that he

> expired the next morning. The negro was tried the next day, and being found guilty of the murder of Mr. Brewster, was to be executed last Friday.

Concerning a relationship that was neither benevolent nor paternal, this story shows that Brewster expected obedience and presumed to enjoy the freedom to discipline his laborers as he saw fit. Unfortunately for both men, the unnamed laborer was unwilling to obey, a decision that led to their deaths. Of course, the story also shows that the violence we associate with slavery was quite real and certainly not at all confined to the South.[10]

A second site in this group is the Thompson house located on North Country Road in Setauket (figure 2.16). Built around 1709, the saltbox house was home to generations of the Thompson family, who lived there until the 1880s. As with the Brewster house, Ward Melville purchased the home in the 1940s and restored it to its "original condition." The following statement from the Washington Spy Trail website makes a connection between the Thompson house and the Culper Spy Ring:

> A very interesting account of the life in this house is available in the shape of Doctor Samuel Thompson's (1738–1811) Journal or diary where we learn of his work as a farmer and doctor to his neighbors as he prescribed herbs, antimonial purges, and whiskey to treat his patients.
>
> Doctor Thompson's activities were not confined to the farm or medicine, though, as he was also a member of the Long Island Militia during the War for Independence and served on the Committee of Safety of the Town of Brookhaven, a shadow government at the start of the American Revolution. It was during this time that he made surveys of the Setauket and Stony Brook Harbors to determine safe routes that could be used by arriving support troops should the necks of the harbors fall to the British. After the Battle of Long Island in 1776, the militia disbanded, with its members, including Thompson, relocating across Long Island Sound to Connecticut. According to historians, it is probable that he saw service there, but there is no definite proof of this. Later, Thompson would again return to Long Island during the war where his standing as a physician probably absolved him from molestation on the part of the enemy. Doctor Thompson would later be given 1000 acres by the newly formed government following the American victory in the war. (Discover Long Island 2019)

We see in this account how the Thompson house is central to the authorized heritage discourse in Setauket. The home is associated with a patriot family that contributed to the effort to ensure American success in war. A doctor, Samuel Thompson, also provided an essential service to the community at large. This "standing" then translated into release from "molestation" by the enemy and a gift of land from the new government.

The Thompson house could be a site for considering more interesting narratives. Two rare documents—a diary and an account book of Dr. Samuel Thompson—speak about everyday life and relationships at the site and in Setauket. Pages and pages of rich details about running the home and the farm and the family's commercial business are essentially untouched. Included in these pages are repeated references to people of color who lived and worked for the Thompsons.

Brad Phillippi (2016) has studied these documents as well as other archival and archaeological sources related to the Thompsons. This research shows the consistent presence of Native Americans and African Americans at the Thompson house. Phillippi identified 21 people of color who were either enslaved or waged laborers, many of whom were passed along by the Thompsons to their children as an inheritance. From Thompson's journal Philippi (2016:185) derived that

> enslaved women like Priscilla, Sylvia, Dol, and Jenny were responsible for domestic duties in and around the house, including cleaning, cooking, and washing, but also child rearing and the production of home manufactures (candles, linen, dairy products, etc.). Their male counterparts Mingo, Frank, Tony, Sharper, Isaac, and others were primarily responsible for agricultural production, but were regularly called upon for other tasks, like mending fences and roads or maintaining the house garden.

Thompson also hired people of color for temporary work, such as in July 1800 when he hired "three squaws Temp, Sib, and Jude" to pull flax (Phillippi 2016:185).

Phillippi (2016) shows that during the period of emancipation newly freed waged workers performed the same types of work as their enslaved predecessors, but the spatial organization of the site changed. Archaeological excavation uncovered a buried foundation for a detached kitchen built in those years that no longer stands at the site (though this structure is visible in figure 2.16). This outbuilding indicates that the kitchen-related work performed by people of color was moved out of the main house to a separate specialized space. A new wing added to the south side of the house with a separate entrance was likely used to house waged workers of color, a move supported by documentary evidence that fits well with regional patterns of agricultural development. These changes reflect the decision to segregate members of the household who were related by blood from those who were not. Notably, the detached kitchen stood until the 1940s, when Ward Melville tore it down, feeling that it did not fit his idea of a proper colonial home.

On the east side of Setauket Harbor is the small village of Poquott, which is situated on land that had been a single property in the 1700s and 1800s and owned by the Van Brunt family. Originating from an established Dutch family in Brooklyn, Jacob Van Brunt (b. 1747) married Phebe Woodhull (daughter of Nathaniel Woodhull of the Culper Spy Ring) and settled on his grandfather's undeveloped property in Setauket (Bergen 1867). The 420-acre parcel became known as Van Brunt's Neck. The property passed to Jacob's son John Van Brunt and then to John's three sons (John, James, and Jacob), who divided it into three equal parcels. James and John Van Brunt remained in Setauket until the 1870s, as they are listed on the 1873 Beers atlas. On the 1909 and 1917 Belcher Hyde maps, large sections of the middle and south parts of the neck are listed as belonging to James and William Van Brunt. Notably, the census does not list either man as a resident of Setauket in those years. In 1931 Van Brunt's Neck was incorporated as Poquott, a summer and now a year-round elite community.

We know a little bit about the early Van Brunt households from the census records for Setauket. In 1776 Jacob Van Brunt is listed as the head of household for one adult man, two adult women, two boys, and six black residents (two men and four women). In 1790 the household contained two adult men, two adult women, two boys, three enslaved laborers and one other free person. In 1800 John Van Brunt is identified as the head of a household with three men, two young women, one boy, two girls, one enslaved person, and three other free persons, and in 1810 his household included two men, one woman, three boys, two girls, three enslaved persons, and four other free persons. In 1820 and later, the Van Brunt households no longer included people of color as resident laborers. Interestingly, the census records two other Van Brunts in later years, both people of color. S. Van Brunt headed a household of five people of color in 1830, and Charity Van Brunt headed a two-person household of color in 1850. These data suggest formerly enslaved laborers of the Van Brunts adopted their owner's name, though it may also indicate a more intimate relationship connecting the black and white branches of the Van Brunt family.

The story of Van Brunts is important as a site on the counter-map because of their family's enslavement of people of color. Yet even though the family gave up slavery during the emancipation era, their connection to people of color continued. Documentation for this comes from three visual sources. The first is the 1909 Hyde Map, which identifies two houses on the property of William Van Brunt as the homes of "colored families." One or both of these homes are also depicted a photograph from the early twentieth century showing the "Old Van Brunt Slave Cabin" (figure 2.17). The last image is a hand-drawn map of the neck by a descendant from the 1910s showing "Jimmie Van Brunt's" home with a "slave cabin" set in the back of the lot, in roughly the same place where the 1909 map indicates the homes of colored families. The hand-drawn map has a quality of intimacy and nostalgia built in as it identifies the "Original Homestead of our Van B. ancestors" as well as the names the families given to various landscape features such as Sassafras Rock, Van Brunt's Pond, Green Hollow Rock, Lost Ed, Stony Hill Fort, and Ol' Kits Grave. Including the slave cabin on the map suggests that the home, whether occupied at the time or not, was part of the familiar local landscape and, like the other features identified, was nothing to be ashamed of.

The last site in this section is St. George's Manor (figure 2.18). Once the largest single property in the Town of Brookhaven, St. George's Manor was the 1693 land patent of Colonel William Tangier Smith. The manor consisted of two parcels. A northern portion in Setauket known today as Strong's Neck and a southern section centered in Mastic stretched over most of the southern half of the Town of Brookhaven.[11] The first manor house was built on Strong's Neck sometime after 1693. This early house is not well documented, as it was demolished and replaced by the current Greek Revival home built by Judge Selah Strong in 1844.

The property passed into the Strong family through the marriage of William Smith's granddaughter, Anna, to Selah Strong II (Lockwood 1999). The Strong family's roots in Setauket date to 1699, when Selah Strong I settled in the village. The family originally lived near Setauket Harbor but later acquired a large plot at Mt. Misery in what is now Belle Terre. After the Revolutionary War the Smith family abandoned their Setauket property, and in 1785 Selah Strong II purchased it at auction. The property has remained in the Strong family since. Selah Strong II's son George Washington Strong grew up in the original manor house and later became a successful lawyer in New York City. He was the commissioner of several paintings by family friend William Sidney Mount, including the well-known *Eel Spearing at Setauket* (figure 1.6).

Thomas Shepherd Strong inherited the property in 1815. Thomas Strong was married to Hannah Brewster, making a connection between these two historic

Setauket families. Family lore tells of an unnamed slave who saved a trunk with valuable family papers from a fire in 1796 at the Mt. Misery estate. Thomas reportedly freed the slave for his devotion to the family. The home in Setauket passed next, in 1840, to his oldest son, Selah Strong III, who built the still-standing Greek Revival manor house. Selah III is known as "Judge Strong" for his service on the New York State Supreme Court. He was also elected to the US Congress in 1844. In more recent years, the Strong family has been associated with the local historical treasure, Kate Strong, and for the current owner, Jack Strong, who has maintained the property and contributed much to documenting local history.

The Strong home is also connected to the Culper Spy Ring. In this case, it is through Anna Smith Strong, who is said to have used her laundry as a coded signaling device. While this claim is not verified, it is accepted locally as a generally good story worth repeating on local tours and through costumed reenactments. Of course, the Strongs are also intimately connected to the Rachel Holland Hart story from the *Eel Spearing* painting, which has also prompted costumed reenactments derived from the authorized heritage discourse.

Other sources provide a clear and lengthy association of the Strong site with people of color. In addition to the unnamed slave set free by Thomas Strong, the 1776 census of Brookhaven records that Selah Strong II owned four slaves. In 1790 Selah II is listed as owning one slave as well as having four "other free persons" in his household. Likewise, his son Thomas is listed as owning four enslaved laborers as well as one "other free person." Both men were recorded again in 1800 as owning seven enslaved persons, with Selah also having two other free persons and Thomas one in their households. From manumission records, some of these individuals can be named. Keder and Susan gained their freedom from Thomas Strong in 1804. Seylvia achieved emancipation from Selah Strong in 1808. Killis, Abel, Dorcas, and Unice acquired freedom from Thomas Strong between 1814 and 1823. According to the records of slave births, Unice had several children: Rachel, born August 22, 1805; Tamar, born September 25, 1807; Cealia, born January 15, 1810; and Ellen or Nell, born October 23, 1815 (Brookhaven, New York 1880:2.83). Selah Strong also reported that Sharper, "a male Child Born of a Slave of his on the Second day of February 1807" and Silve (perhaps the same as Seylvia above) was born November 20, 1799 (Brookhaven, New York 1880:2.92–93).

When slavery ended in New York in 1827, people of color continued to live in Strong households. Seven "other free persons" lived in Thomas Strong's household in 1830. In 1840 six free persons of color lived in Rebecca Strong's home, and five free persons of color lived with Judge Selah B. Strong. At the same time, some of the former slaves established their own homes. This included Abel Strong, a person of color, who headed his own household consisting of one man over 55 years, one woman between 36 and 55 years, one girl less than 10 years, and one girl between 10 and 24 years in 1830. This is certainly the same Abel who was manumitted in 1816.

We learn more names of the people of color living with the Strongs from the 1850 Census. Catherine Henry, Nancy Woodhull, and Abigail Tobias lived in Rebecca Strong's household. Isaac Jones as well as two women from Ireland, Margaret Blair and Bridget Cummings, lived with Judge Strong. Abel Strong appears again in 1850 as a 66-year-old man with his wife Margaret and children Vincent, Christiana, Edward, Mary, and Elvira. By 1860 David Tobias, Alice Black, and Abby Tobias (who was listed in Rebecca Strong's house in 1850) are living with Amelia Strong. In 1870 David Phillips, Alice Smith (probably the same as Alice Black in 1860), and Ellen Tobias are in Mary Strong's household. Between 1880 and 1920, Strong households did not include people of color. However, in 1930 two households headed by Strongs each had two people of color. Margaret Gibbons and her six-year-old son James lived in the home of Selah B. Strong IV, and Ida Calvin and Elliot Bristol lived in the home of Caroline R. Strong.

The Calvin and Bristol surnames are long lived in Setauket's community of color. The Calvins trace their origin to the early nineteenth century, when Rachel Brewster's (b. 1796) granddaughter Tabitha Brewster (b. 1855) married her Old Field neighbor James H. Calvin around 1880. Calvins still live in Setauket on Christian Avenue. Bristols lived in Setauket at least as early as 1860, when Angeline and David Bristol lived in Rosanna Brewster's home in Old Field and Solomon and Sarah Bristol lived in their own home elsewhere in Setauket. The Bristols are also connected to the Strong's Neck manor. Current owner Jack Strong recalled that members of the Bristol family lived in the home and worked as household servants during his childhood in the 1940s and 1950s. Henry and Ella Bristol at the time were living on Christian Avenue, and Strong recalled that the Bristols living in his home attended services at Bethel AME and would visit with family in that neighborhood.

Among all of the sites in the counter-map, the Strong site is best prepared for a rich historical interpretation that highlights the presence and contributions of the Native American and African American community. From the long history of the enslavement and employment of people of color by the Smith and Strong families we can easily situate St. George Manor as a site of black and Indian heritage. The homes built on the site and the families credited as their owners are all the result of the work and commitments of people of color. To this we can add the tragic story of the shallow and defaced burials at the Strong's Neck Native American site discussed in chapter 1 and the certainly large number of unmarked graves of people of color in the Strong family cemetery. Of course, we should also consider the branches of the Strong family who descend from the family's slaves such as Abel Strong whose survival through slavery and emancipation are achievements deserving much more recognition.

Faces in History

This chapter has told new stories about old sites in Setauket. The purpose has been to shed light on how the whole of the village has roots and tendrils of underground connections to the local history of people of color during slavery and after emancipation as well as the origins of what is today a historically significant yet struggling descendant community. To conclude the chapter I tell two new stories about Setauket and its community of color. Both make use of the unconventional methods that lie at the core of the A Long Time Coming project. One recasts a geological feature as a meaningful historical and cultural site, and the other employs an unusual collection of artifacts to document a poorly understood life. Both show the power of prosaic events and objects to understanding the value of knowing more about past lives in our effort to preserve our past.

In chapter 1 I discussed the treatment in the *Three Village Guidebook* of the glacial erratic boulder in Setauket known as Indian Rock. Despite the Native American associations of the boulder in its name, the *Guidebook* makes no mention of local Indian history or the descendant community. Instead, the description dwells entirely on the rock's geologic history, including the fact that it was carried to Long Island by glaciers and is thus an immigrant like all other "humans" on Long Island. I also noted that the published images of Indian Rock included a couple strolling by on their way to a nearby tennis club, an image quite fitting for understanding Setauket as an affluent and leisurely suburban community today.

Nevertheless, I have remained interested in the origins of the name given to the rock, but no one in from either the white or black community knew anything about the origins of the name. It seemed indeed that its association with Native Americans was the fact that ancient stones and prehistoric people naturally go together. I did hear one story that changed the meaning of the rock by attaching it to the way it was historically used by people in the village. Pearl Lewis Hart remembered sitting on the rock with childhood friends after purchasing sweets at a small store down the block. Pearl and her friends grew up on Christian Avenue and were part of the Native and African American community in the mid-1900s. Her memory was deeply meaningful since it connected her to a way of life now lost in modern Setauket. This was an era when children roamed freely around the village playing with and on its natural features, doing the things, that is, that built and held her community together and gave them a sense of place.

To commemorate this story, I asked an artist to reproduce the Indian Rock image published in the *Guidebook* but to replace the tennis players with two girls representing Pearl Hart and her friend. This new image (figure 2.19) depicts the same landscape in a new way to show the power of a story to shape what we see in the world. The original image positions the rock in the background, as an afterthought—even though it was the focus of the image—to the way modern Setauket residents ought to live in the village. The new image puts the boulder to work toward a different end, providing a safe and special place for two girls to share a treat and talk. The tennis players in the original drawing are depicted anonymously with their faces obscured by shading. This allows them to be just about anyone, as long as they play tennis and live mainstream, respectable, and presumably heterosexual, suburban, white lives. In contrast, the new image shows two young girls of color who have ventured out of their nearby neighborhood to shop on Main Street and enjoy their takings in clear public view. They are not just anyone at all but rather the products of a long struggle by people of color in Setauket to survive and on occasion assert their presence in the village despite being absent from the narratives and consciousness of most people living there.

From other stories collected by the A Long Time Coming project, we know that children of color would have been commonly seen in other public spaces such as streambeds and shorelines, the forests, working on local farms and gardens, and walking to school. These stories are generally accepted as accurate historic portrayals about the way people of color lived in Setauket. The unfortunate fact is that these mundane activities have no place in the AHD of Setauket shared with the wider world. My sense is that these sorts of stories are not more widely told because they are not exclusive. They are the same sorts of stories that could be told about most places on Long Island. Yet perhaps this is the source of their power, especially for understanding rather than selling local history and therefore for making active meaningful historical interpretations versus repeating the master narratives. The result would be a greater recognition by all people of their place as historical actors rather than as passive witnesses to a history that has no connection to them.

A second site that creates an unconventional counter-narrative in Setauket is the Ernest Hart cabin that stands in ruins on the lot formerly owned by Lucy Keyes (figure 2.20). Ernest Hart was Lucy Keyes's younger brother and the youngest of Jacob and Hannah Hart's 12 children. He was born in the family home on Lake Street in 1904, and he is listed as a resident there in the censuses taken in 1910 through 1940. It is likely that by 1940 he was only a temporary resident, since the home was damaged by the Long Island Express hurricane in 1938 and was abandoned and torn down soon after. Hart was a laborer at a trucking company in 1930. In 1940 he reported that he was a handyman working for an "institution." There is no evidence that Hart ever married or had a family. The documentary record does not offer anything more about Ernest Hart until his death in 1978, when he was buried in Laurel Hill Cemetery.

Elders in the community remember that Hart lived in Bridgeport, Connecticut, before returning to Setauket in the 1960s. With the old family home gone and the lot sold, Hart built his own small place behind his sister's house on Christian Avenue. This cabin was 6 ft wide by 9 ft long, with walls made of 2-by-6-in planks covered with tar paper. It had one small room with a door, a single window, and an enclosed loft space for storage under the peaked roof. People who have seen this image of the cabin often admit they would have assumed it was a shed used for tools or other items, not a home. Elders in the community remember that Hart lived there but that for the most part he kept to himself. When Robert Lewis and I inspected the cabin in 2010, we found it still contained a number of objects that belonged to Hart. We collected these objects for analysis, and they show in various ways how Hart made the small cabin into a home. The story of the cabin sadly came to an end in 2012, when a large tree limb fell and crushed it as Superstorm Sandy passed through the area. This was in a way a repeated event for the Hart family, whose original home was also damaged by a powerful storm.

The objects in Ernest Hart's cabin are mostly common household items (figure 2.21). They include a set of mismatched silverware in a red plastic utensil holder. Utensils ranged from a set of forks and knives with yellow bakelite and fancy sterling silver handles to a set of plain stainless steel forks to a novelty spoon from the Beam Quality Cereal Company. There were a number of small (6-in diameter) shallow glass bowls that could have served as his table wares. There are two matched sets of sugar and creamer dishes; one is mid-twentieth-century Santa Anita Ware ceramic and the other is pressed clear glass. There is a salt and pepper shaker set along with a can of McCormick Black Pepper. There is also a novelty Japanese-made cat-shaped salt shaker with the phrase "I'm Salt" stenciled on its tummy. We also found a mincing knife, can opener, potato masher, three spatulas, melon baller, potato peeler, a butter dish, a glass juicer, tea strainer, coffee measure, a soap dish, several mixing spoons and large mixing bowls, a wooden salad bowl with matching tongs, mason jar lids, a jelly jar, and a jar for "Grandma's Unsulphered Molasses." There was also a tin Bundt cake pan and a percolator coffeepot. Finally, there were two stove grates, a frying basket, and a Sterno stove. He also had a chicken feeder, which suggests he kept chickens in the yard. Essentially, there was enough in the cabin to prepare and eat some basic foods.

Other items show how Hart made the cabin into a home. There were two oil lights, one lamp of pressed glass and one lantern made of metal, along with a spouted kerosene storage can. There was a candle holder and an ashtray, a German-made stoneware beer stein, two large washbasins, and two vases. He had a chair, a cot, and a bar for hanging clothes, as well as a small bookshelf used for storing his kitchen items and a unique corner-mounted, coffeepot-shaped storage shelf. A door handle and face plate suggest that Ernest also had a lock on his door. Lastly, a few personal items were recovered including a canvas purse with a sequined sea life design and a hairbrush with a rose motif on a mother-of-pearl backing.

Overall, these items confirm that this was a home used by a single man to live a life of his own close to but not in his sister's household. We did not excavate around the cabin, so I cannot say if there was a cooking area or additional materials that could tell us about his foodways, but from the collection we can see he was prepared to cook and eat his meals in and around the cabin. It is also apparent that he saw this cabin as a home that deserved nice things and decorations. His sterling silver knife set, coffeepot-shaped shelf, decorative vases, blue and gray beer stein, and novelty salt shaker show an effort to beautify and personalize the small space. This may have been complemented by decorative contact paper, some shreds of which were found adhered to the bookcase and on the cabin floor. Perhaps most interesting are the feminine personal items, the origin of which is probably complicated. These could have been items left behind by his sister or another female relative, or possibly a female friend or girlfriend. They may also have been Hart's own possessions. Ernest Hart did not marry, and a single man from a small community of color in rural Long Island may have had few chances to express his sexuality. These items may have allowed him to understand and express who he felt he was. Of course, though compelling, any claim to know of his sexual orientation is purely conjecture.

These mundane items recovered from Ernest Hart's home provide a capstone for the counter-map of Setauket. They humanize the way the community took care of their own. Ernest Hart was the youngest member of his family and the last to leave home. While he seems to have left the area in the 1940s, he returned to Setauket to find refuge from the larger world in a small cabin on the back of his sister's property. The cabin and the protection and support of his sister and other relatives and neighbors allowed this man to live a long though mostly solitary life. Elders do not remember much about Ernest Hart other than that he lived in the cabin. That he was known—yet undisturbed and protected—by his community is the sort of story that marginalized communities in Setauket and elsewhere need now. A mundane story of family, community, home, and care, Ernest Hart's cabin and possessions provide a counterpoint to the dominant heritage discourse in Setauket based in war, espionage, wealth, and leisure. His life reminds them of the ways they are connected to one another by blood, neighborhood, and history, a story that perhaps is more useful not only to Native and African Americans today but to others in Setauket who are passively letting one part of their history disappear.

Conclusion

The point of this counter-map is to show that stories like Pearl Hart's memory of Indian Rock or Ernest Hart's cabin are present across the Setauket landscape. Wherever people of color can be documented, we find new ways of understanding that not only acknowledge their presence and about how they lived but we reframe what matters about these historic places. It is in Aunt Lucy's house and her garden; in the gatherings at Bethel AME Church, the Irving Hart Legion Hall, and the colored beach; and in the small spaces afforded to those enslaved by the Strongs, Thompsons, Brewsters, and Van Brunts that we will find the way people fought to persist despite racism, violence, and inequality. We see this is the work they did, the memories they kept, the institutions they built, and the families they made and cared for. While the freedom rider John Raines was right to point out that Setauket appeared in 1961 eerily similar to the racially segregated society of the South, we must recognize that Setauket included then and today stories of the those who survived these limitations and left their impact on the land and in the places where they lived.

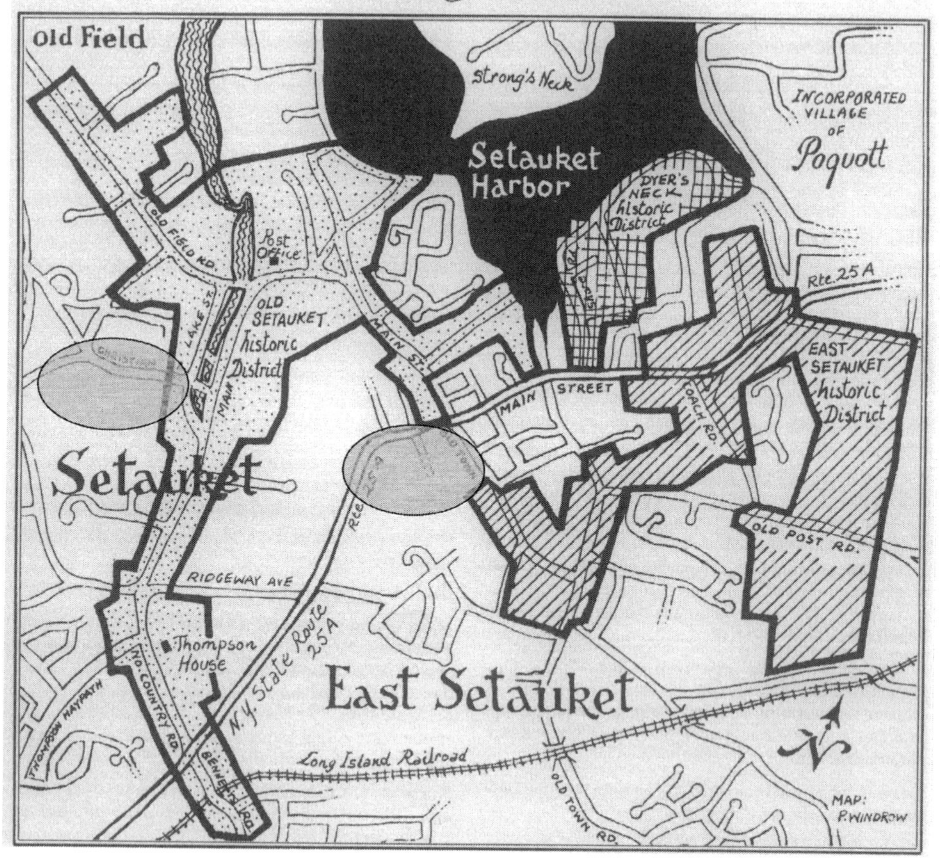

Figure 2.1. The historic districts of Setauket. *Three Village Guidebook*. The shaded areas mark the location of historic neighborhoods associated with Native and African Americans. Christian Avenue is on the left, Chicken Hill is on the right. (Courtesy of the Three Village Historical Society, Long Island, New York.)

Figure 2.2. Typical homes on Christian Avenue in Setauket.

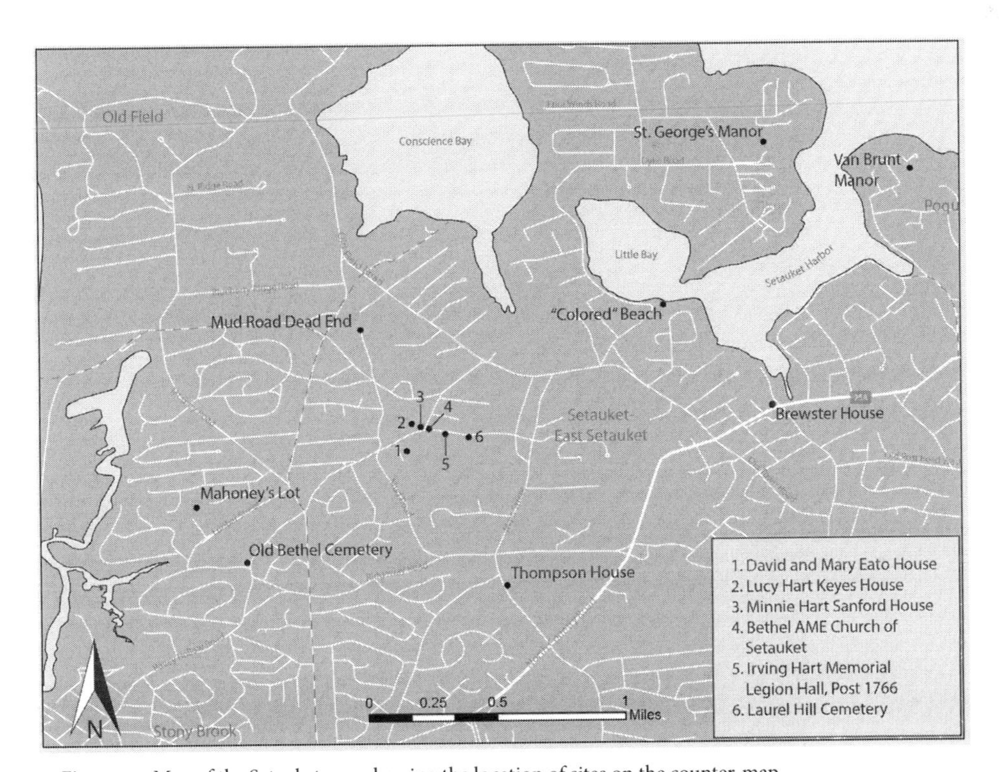

Figure 2.3. Map of the Setauket area showing the location of sites on the counter-map.

Figure 2.4. Irving Hart Memorial Legion Hall.

Figure 2.5. Bethel AME Church of Setauket.

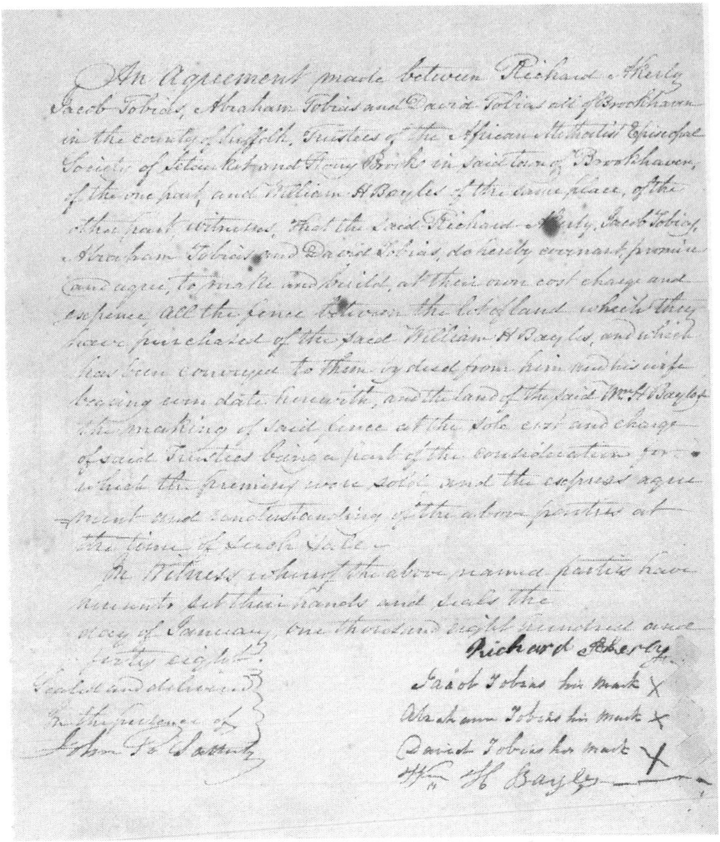

An Agreement made between Richard Akerly Jacob Tobias, Abraham Tobias and David Tobias all of Brookhaven in the county of Suffolk, Trustees of the African Methodist Episcopal Society of Setauket and Stony Brook in said town of Brookhaven, of the one part, and William H Bayles of the same place, of the other part witnesseth, that the said Richard Akerly, Jacob Tobias, Abraham Tobias and David Tobias, do hereby covenant promise and agree, to make and build, at their own cost charge and expense all the fence between the lot of land which they have purchased of the said William H Bayles, and which has been conveyed to them by deed from him and his wife bearing even date herewith, and the land of the said Wm H Bayles the making of said fence at the sole cost and charge of said Trustees being a part of the consideration for which the premises were sold and the express agreement and understanding of the above parties at the time of such sale.

In Witness whereof the above named parties have hereunto set their hands and seals the day of January one thousand eight hundred and forty eight.

Sealed and delivered in the presence of
John R. Satterly

Richard Akerly
Jacob Tobias his mark X
Abraham Tobias his mark X
David Tobias his mark X
Wm H Bayles

Figure 2.6. An 1848 agreement regarding a house of worship to be constructed by the African Methodist Episcopal Society of Setauket and Stony Brook. (Courtesy of Three Village Historical Society, Long Island.)

Figure 2.7. Old Bethel Cemetery.

Figure 2.8. Laurel Hill Cemetery.

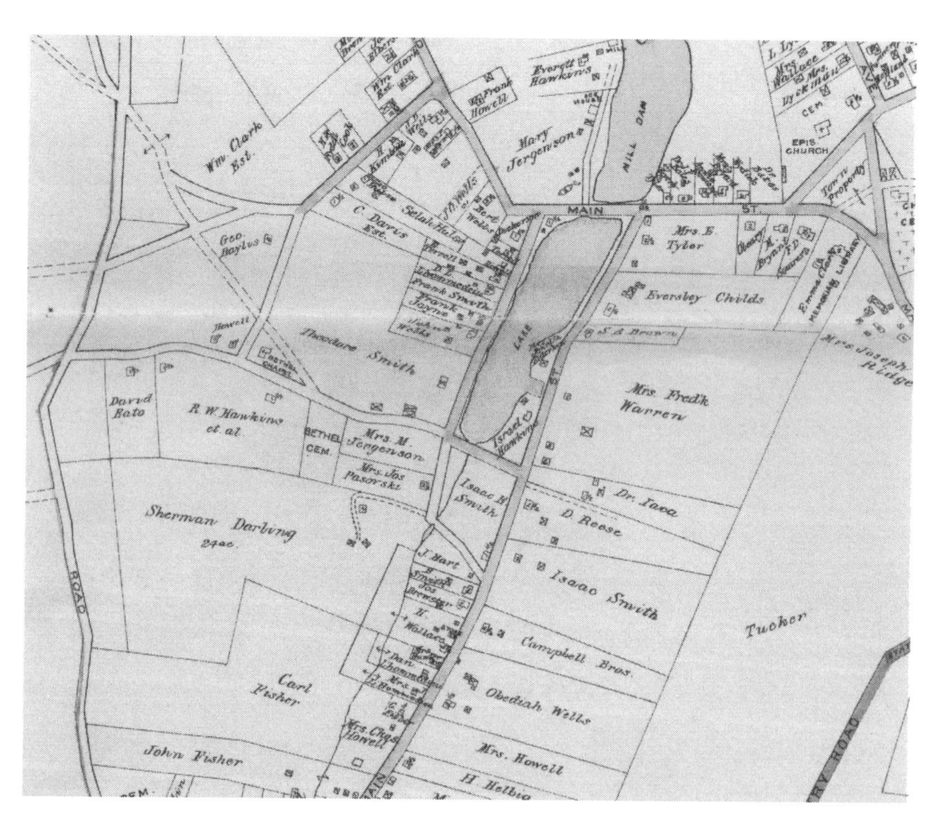

Figure 2.9. Detail of Setauket inset, *Atlas of a Part of Suffolk County, Long Island, New York. North Side—Sound Shore,* 1917. E. Belcher Hyde. Lionel Pincus and Princess Firyal Map Division, New York Public Library.

Figure 2.10. David and Mary Eato House. (Courtesy of Robert L. Lewis and Higher Ground Intercultural and Heritage Association.)

Figure 2.11. Lucy Keyes and Minnie Sanford homes.

Figure 2.12. Rachel Midgett. (Courtesy of Ron Keyes and Higher Ground Intercultural and Heritage Association.)

Figure 2.13. Several members of Setauket's Native and African American community pose for a picture during a clambake. William and Irving Hart organized crews to run clambakes for wealthy families in the region. Pictured are Sarah Hart, Irving Hart, Rachel Midgett, William Hart, Isaiah Hart, and Audrey Henderson. (Courtesy of the family of Theodore Green and the archives of the Three Village Historical Society, Long Island.)

Figure 2.14. Sign showing that Mud Road is now a dead-end street.

Figure 2.15. Brewster house. (Courtesy of the Three Village Historical Society, Long Island.)

Figure 2.16. Thompson house, Historic American Buildings Survey photograph, 1933. (Library of Congress Prints and Photographs Division, Reproduction Number: HABS NY,52-SETA,3-4.)

Figure 2.17. Old slave cabin at Van Brunt Manor. (Courtesy of Longwood Public Library, Thomas R. Bayles Local History Room.)

Figure 2.18. *A View of the Seat of the Hon. Selah Strong, Esq. St. George's Manor, Suffolk County, Long Island, New York,* 1792, Cornelius Tiebout after Alexander Anderson. This original manor house stood at the site until 1844. (Courtesy of Preservation Long Island, Accession #2010.9.)

Figure 2.19. Indian Rock reimagined. (Courtesy of Noah Fontana.)

Figure 2.20. Ernest Hart cabin.

Figure 2.21. Artifacts from the Ernest Hart cabin.

Notes

1. The term "counter-map" was coined by Nancy Peluso (1995) to describe maps created by forest-users in Kalimantan, Indonesia.

2. A great example of the way maps create reality is the story of Agloe, New York. Located in the Catskills region, Agloe was a mapmaker's "copyright trap." This means that there was no place known as Agloe. It was invented by the mapmakers Otto G. Lindberg and Ernest Alpers, who created it from their initials and added it their map. If any other mapmaker included Agloe on their own maps, Lindberg and Alpers would know it was a forgery. By the 1950s, however, a small store opened at the spot where Agloe was depicted on the map and the owners called it the Agloe General Store, making the "trap town" real in a way never intended. As of the 2010s, Agloe is no longer a place, though it was featured in John Greene's novel *Paper Towns*.

3. For African Americans, Robinson (2000, xxx–xxxi) dubs this revolutionary consciousness and history as the Black Radical Tradition. It is "an accretion, over generations, of collective intelligence gathered from struggle . . . in its most militant manifestation. . . . The purpose of the struggles informed by the tradition became the overthrow of the whole race-based structure."

4. Several sites are presented in this tour of African American and Native American history in Setauket along with the way the sources that provide the details we know about each site. I leave out a few sites that we know from archaeology since these will be the focus of chapters 4 and 5. Many of the sites discussed in the following can be found in an online resource, also called "A Counter-Map of Setauket, New York," http://www.arcgis.com/apps/MapSeries/index.html?appid=6c19b6a5d9784f2397297811 16151969. This website employs ESRI's Story Map platform which offers a variety of ways to tell stories with maps. A explanation of how to work with story maps is in Alemy et al. (2017).

5. There is an old slave and traditional Indian graveyard in the woods on the south side of Sugar Loaf Hill, about 100 ft north of a small clearing on the top of the hill on the old Oakwood property in Brookhaven (Long Island Genealogy 2019). Ritchie (1965:175–178) discusses the burial ritualism observed on older (3,500–2,500 B.P.) hilltop burials on eastern Long Island. Mark Tweedie (2014:82–83) notes two "massive hilltop" burial complexes at the Orient #1 and #2 sites which overlook the Long Island Sound. Historic indigenous burial grounds in East Hampton (Pantigo) and Montauk (Fort Hill) are also on hilltops (Tweedie, personal communication).

6. A full inventory of these sites is available in Wellman et al. (2016).

7. The family was very impressed that Mary Eato had been to college, and her mother would always remind her, "Remember, you're an Allenite," a reference to Allen University in South Carolina. Mary Eato was "a very stately lady, very proud. She stood very straight. She also prayed regularly. When she said grace before Sunday dinner, granddaughter June Eato Bisserup remembered 'getting so tired because . . . the blessing lasted so long, and we'd be sitting there looking at hot biscuits, chicken meat, besides the bacon and eggs. . . . My grandmother would preach about all the countries of the world like Europe, Asia, but then when she got to the United States and President Roosevelt, I knew it was time for the blessing to stop.'"

8. Transcripts of this and other interviews collected by Glenda Dickerson and her students are on file at the Three Village Historical Society, Setauket, New York.

9. This racist legacy is not mentioned in the National Register of Historic Places documentation prepared for the cottages, which were added to the National Register in 2004 on the merit of being examples of vernacular resort architecture (*New York Times,* 27 June 2004).

10. I was made aware of this incident by Meg Gorsline. The source is the Hamlet People Database (2011).

11. Colonel Smith is known as Tangier Smith because of his service as mayor of Tangier in Morocco. While this service in Morocco is in dispute, the moniker has been maintained since it helps to distinguish the Tangier Smiths from other Smith families in the region.

3

FROM CREOLE SYNTHESIS TO RACIAL MODERNITY

> In that part of the Union where the Negroes are no longer slaves, have they come closer to the whites? Everyone who has lived in the United States will have noticed just the opposite. Race prejudice seems stronger in those states that have abolished slavery than in those where it still exists, and nowhere is it more intolerant than in those states where slavery was never known.
>
> *Alexis de Tocqueville*

In 1939 William Oliver Stevens published *Discovering Long Island*, an evocative travel guide and historical overview of the region. A whimsical portrayal of Long Island's myriad wonders, the book took a sudden, disturbing turn when the author described the Shinnecock reservation. Stevens wrote:

> Today in the Shinnecock region there is a small reservation for the remnants of the Long Island red men. . . . If the traveler is curious to see one of the most pathetic spectacles of racial decay in all the eastern section of his country, let him turn down this dusty washboardy lane. . . . There are a few cabins here and there, most of them looking dilapidated with broken window panes and patched sides. The scene reminds one of a Negro settlement in the back country of Georgia, except that even there the cabins would have vegetable and flower gardens around them. . . . The scene looks still more like the deep South when we pass the inhabitants of the reservation for these "Indians" have kinky hair and African features. They are palpably negroid. . . . The children might well have come straight out of Harlem or Alabama.

Given this description, readers were not likely to follow Stevens's path down the "washboardy lane," yet I doubt his goal was to encourage people to visit to the reservation. Rather, the point was to establish a presence on Long Island of people fitting racist and demeaning stereotypes. Racializing the Shinnecocks as "palpably negroid," Stevens was not objectively describing Shinnecock people but denying the legitimacy of their Native American heritage, their presence on Long Island, and their status as American citizens. By detailing their homes as "dilapidated" and neglected, he connected their poverty to supposed "racial decay" in a way that blamed the Shinnecock people for their impoverished conditions while conveniently ignoring the long history of racial violence against Native Americans in New York.

By 1939 this kind of racist discourse was commonplace and, for most white Americans, a normal and accepted part of the social order (Dippie 1982; Dixon 1913; Kendi 2017; Smedley 2011). It would take a massive antiracist movement to begin to undo this thinking in the United States. While antiracist thinking can be traced to the eighteenth century, the most promising signs of the movement's success in the United States appeared only after World War II, when the horrors of the Holocaust became widely known (Burkholder 2011; Fredrickson 2002). As this example shows, even just a few years before the civil rights movement took hold, whites on Long Island tended to view African American and Native American residents with fear and loathing inspired by the ideology of white supremacy. What is more, this blunt racism was arguably more potent in 1939 than it had been a century earlier. In other words, race relations had deteriorated on Long Island, and anti-black and anti-Native racism had been steadily increasing over time.

This chapter explains how and why racism against people of color increased over time as a result of economic, social, and cultural transformations at the local and national levels. It challenges commonly held assumptions that racism was a problem rooted in slavery and that it got better over time through the eras of emancipation and the long black civil rights movement. Additionally, this chapter reveals the potency of anti-black and anti-Native American racism in the supposedly progressive North. This escalating racial antipathy allows us to fully grasp the extent of the challenges people of color in Setauket faced and appreciate the strategies they developed to survive under incredibly arduous circumstances (Fitts 1996; Hall 2005; Matthews and McGovern 2015; Melish 2000; Stewart 1998; Sugrue 2008).

The history of racism on Long Island begins in the colonial period, when people of color were denied citizenship by virtue of being enslaved or because of their African or indigenous heritage. Race was the key basis for disenfranchisement, which included not only exclusion from political life but also exclusion from most aspects of the social, cultural, and economic order, such as churches, schools, social clubs, and employment. This situation changed in the years after the Revolution, especially during the era of emancipation post-1799 as the population of free people of color steadily increased. These men and women actively sought social recognition and civil rights, and, while the majority of whites continued to reject them, some progressives embraced a multiracial America and the cultural contributions of a diverse population. The rise of scientific racism combined with a growing abolitionist movement and fears of black economic competition set the stage for increasing white hostility as the nineteenth century progressed. As anti-black actions and sensibilities, including mockery and violence, became more common, the rights and the life chances of people of color were significantly curtailed well into the twentieth century. We see one manifestation of this racial dynamic in Stevens's description of the Shinnecock Indians, whose very existence is treated as a blemish on "civilized" society.

Living through these hostile and constantly evolving conditions people of color certainly struggled, but they also survived—and thrived. Communities across Long Island spent decades developing their families, communities, and cultural lives. The counter-map detailed in chapter 2 provides a view of cultural development and antiracist strategies of people of color in Setauket. Chapters 4 and 5 deepen this narrative by presenting historical and archaeological evidence of how people in Setauket worked against the dynamics of racism in the nineteenth and early twentieth centuries. My task in chapter 3 is to build a bridge to these studies by giving a broader sense of the regional historical context of racism on Long Island and in Setauket.

The chapter starts with a review of the history of slavery and emancipation in New York State to explain the emergence of a creole synthesis in the early nineteenth century. Initially proposed by musicologist Christopher Smith (2014), "creole synthesis" refers to a process of intercultural exchange between diverse communities in early New York. Creole synthesis describes a fluid regime of racial thought that emerged out of the intercultural exchanges between whites, Native Americans, and African Americans during the emancipation era. This creole synthesis was superseded by a hardened racial ideology of white supremacy in the 1830s, which I refer to as "racial modernity," a term coined by historian James Brewer Stewart (1998, 1999) to demonstrate the emergence of our contemporary racial formation. Racial modernity first developed in the 1830s and took a firm and lasting hold in the 1850s.

To ground this story in Setauket, I examine the life and artwork of painter

William Sidney Mount, whose career straddles the eras of creole synthesis and racial modernity and whose work captures central ideas in both eras. To complement this reading of Mount's art, I also consider the dynamics of the local racial discourse evident in nineteenth-century Long Island newspapers. This analysis shows that local media perpetuated racist ideas about people of color and that the nature of this discourse worsened over time, especially as newspapers portrayed people of color as violent, uneducated, and an increasing danger to the social order. I then review census data and local oral histories to document the changing contours of community life for people of color in the Town of Brookhaven and Setauket. This analysis demonstrates a continuous displacement of people of color in Setauket until they were confined to a narrow strip of residential property along Christian Avenue, where they have lived exclusively since the 1960s.

Slavery and Emancipation in New York

In 1799 New York's Senate and Assembly passed the Act for the Gradual Abolition of Slavery. This act set the terms for the end of slavery in New York, stating that

> any child born of a slave within this State after the fourth of July next, shall be deemed and adjudged to be born free: Provided nevertheless that such child shall be the servant of the legal proprietor of his or her mother, until such servant if a male shall arrive at the age of twenty eight years, and if a female at the age of twenty five years. And be it further enacted, that such proprietor his, her, or their heirs or assigns shall be entitled to the service of such child until he or she shall arrive to the age aforesaid, in the same manner as if such child had been bound to service by the overseers of the poor. (Laws of the State of New York 1799)

Gradual emancipation in New York provided a partial and negotiated solution for ending slavery and granted slave owners a generation of labor from unborn children, effectively stealing the most productive laboring years of these supposedly free "servants." Moreover, the law did nothing for the mothers of these children or others who were already enslaved at the time it was passed. The state amended this oversight in 1817, when it established that all slaves born before 1799 would be freed in 1827, though this later act confirmed that the children of enslaved mothers would remain servants to their masters extending for many a "slavery for term" (Gigantino 2015) for years to come.

New Yorkers' interest in preserving bonded labor stems from the state's long history of enjoying the benefits of slavery. The first enslaved Africans were brought to New York (then New Amsterdam) in 1626. By 1700 there were more than 2,000 enslaved Africans in New York, a figure that dwarfed the few hundred enslaved persons in the other northern colonies. This was true despite the fact that New York's investment in slavery was only just starting to take off. By 1750 there were more than 11,000 slaves and in 1770 more than 19,000 in the colony. These figures kept pace with overall population, as enslaved people consistently counted between 11% and 15% of the total population, another figure that dwarfed those for other northern colonies (Phillippi 2016:98). Enslaved African people lived throughout the colony, serving as field and domestic laborers in rural counties and in a variety of capacities from servants to stevedores in New York City. No matter the trade, if there was a need for labor enslaved Africans were used to meet the demand. Moreover, auction houses relied on the slave trade, and smaller parties such as brokers, retail merchants, printers, lawyers, and scriveners attached their livelihood at least in part to the flow of the trade. Furthermore, there was no tax collected on the sale of slaves internally (McManus 1966). Given this widespread investment in the economics of slavery, it is no surprise that New York State slowly wound down its reliance on captive labor.

This situation did not change even as a prominent discourse about freedom took hold during and after the American Revolution. An early effort to end slavery in the state in 1777 was abandoned when the governor discovered a general fear that freeing the enslaved would be "productive of great dangers" (quoted in Gellman and Quigley 2003:26). Emancipation was defeated for the same reasons again in 1785. In fact, in 1786 the legislature passed an act that protected the economic advantage of New York slave owners and confirmed the legality of slavery. Over the next decade, antislavery activists such as the New York Manumission Society stepped up their efforts, though they saw additional emancipation bills fail to be passed in the 1790s. During the Revolutionary era and after, slavery in fact expanded in New York reaching a peak population of more than 21,000 enslaved persons in 1790. Phillippi (2016:126) notes that emancipation came even more slowly on Long Island than elsewhere in the state, such that as late as 1820 more than one in four African Americans remained enslaved, compared to only 5% of African Americans in New York City.

Emancipation on Long Island was not only slow, but it also brought little effective change in the daily routines for the formerly enslaved. Most people of color remained servants or laborers doing domestic or agricultural work.

Phillippi (2016:129) notes that "even if they owned and occupied an independent household, chances are they journeyed to and from white farmsteads that served as places of employment." Nor did the political landscape change in their favor. In 1821 a new state constitution established that

> no man of colour, unless he shall have been for three years a citizen of this state, and for one year next preceding any election, shall be seized and possessed of a freehold estate of the value of two hundred and fifty dollars, over and above all debts and incumbrances charged thereon; and shall have been actually rated, and paid a tax thereon, shall be entitled to vote at any such election. (New York Courts 2017)

Since no such rules applied to whites, who were actually relieved of any property requirement at the same time, this statute established a barrier to citizenship for people of color because of race.

The impact of this ruling was profound. In New York City for example, only 68 (0.5%) of the more than 13,000 free African Americans met the qualifications to vote in 1825 (Independence Hall Association 2017). The law was still felt as late as 1865 when the New York State census recorded that people of color still struggled to meet the requirements to vote. In the first electoral district of the Town of Brookhaven which included Setauket only two out of 47 men of color met the qualifications to vote that year. These two, 61-year-old Jacob Tobias and 50-year-old David Tobias, were among 10 men who met the $250 minimum property requirement. However, it appears the other eight could not meet the burden of having the value of their property "over and above all debts and incumbrances" required to vote. The Tobiases were the only people of color among 632 eligible voters, according to the census, in the first electoral district. This means that the people of color there accounted for 0.3% of the total vote. Until this statute was repealed in 1868, virtually all black New Yorkers lived without direct legislative representation and were thus afforded little political opportunity to address the factors underlying their struggle to survive as racism intensified around them.

Based on this history, it is natural to suspect that other documentary records related to people of color in Setauket and the rest of Long Island and New York would reflect racial bias and struggle. In large part this is correct. However, an innovative reading of the era by a series of researchers suggests emancipation was not simply a new means to reproduce the oppression of slavery in different circumstances. Rather, as I show in this chapter, an argument can be made that the emancipation era was itself a brief but distinct moment of racial ambiguity and progressive politics in which key aspects of the racism, though familiar to us today, had yet to coalesce.

Creole Synthesis

Smith (2014:117) depicts some of the key aspects of the world that Micah Hawkins and his nephew, William Sidney Mount, experienced every day on New York City's Lower East Side in the early nineteenth century:

> In December of 1824, at the Chatham Theater in New York City, a few blocks from the streets and docks of the Catherine Slip where Long Island blacks, their hair tied up in eel skins, were "dancing for eels" to attract trade; where he maintained a grocery store and tavern with a piano built into the shop counter; where his sensitive, artistic, and musical teenage nephew boarded as he the learned the craft of sign painting and dreamed of success as a portraitist, Micah Hawkins took the swirl of ethnicities, accents, linguistic and musical dialects he saw out front of the shop and put that creole gumbo on the stage. And his nephew took note. (Smith 2014:117)

This environment is paramount to this study because it provides insight into some of the most powerful documents of early the African American community and race relations in New York and Long Island. These are the compelling paintings of William Sidney Mount who was born and lived the bulk of his life in Setauket and Stony Brook. As Smith states, however, his time in New York City was influential in his later artwork.

After his father died in 1813, six-year-old Mount moved from Setauket to live with his maternal grandfather, Jonas Hawkins, in Stony Brook. Hawkins, a member of the Culper Spy Ring and head of one of the region's oldest families, ran a tavern as well as a large household of "relatives and dependents, including African American slaves soon to be manumitted" (Smith 2014:88). Included in the household would have been the formerly enslaved Anthony Clapp, whose fiddle and dancing skills are known to have influenced to William Sidney Mount's own musical and artistic work. In 1819, 12-year-old Mount was apprenticed to his older brother Henry to learn the art of sign painting on the Lower East Side of New York City. Mount lived in New York until his painting career took off after 1830. He probably lived with his brother, but he also spent a great deal of time with his uncle Micah Hawkins, who ran a shop near the famous Catherine Slip on the East River.

By the time Mount moved to New York, Micah Hawkins was an established grocer having operated a store there since 1798. He moved his store to Catherine Slip around 1810, where he also operated a hotel and bar. Catherine Slip was a cultural and regional crossroads serving as a port for East River ferries that trafficked passengers from Brooklyn, Long Island, Connecticut, and Rhode Island. The slip was famous for its market as well as an attendant lively atmosphere captured by Thomas De Voe (1862, in Scott 2004:51–52). In particular, the following description has drawn great interest from historians:

> The first introduction in this city of public "negro dancing" no doubt took place at [Catherine] market. The negroes who visited here were principally slaves from Long Island, who had leave of their master for certain holidays, among which "Pinkster" was the principal one; . . . then, as they usually had three days holiday, they were ever ready, by their "negro sayings or doings," to make a few shillings more. So they would be hired by some joking butcher or individual to engage in a jig or breakdown, as that was one of their pastimes at home on the barn floor, or in a frolic, and those that could and would dance soon raised a collection; but some of them did more in "turning around and shying off" from the designated spot than keeping to the regular "shake-down," which caused them all to be confined to a "board," (or shingle, as they called it,) and not allowed off it; on this they must show their skill; and, being several together in parties, each had his particular "shingle" brought with him as part of his stock in trade. . . . Their music or time was usually given by one of their party, which was done by beating their hands on the sides of their legs and the noise of the heel. The favorite dancing place was a cleared spot on the east side of the fish market in front of Bumel Brown's Ship Chandlery. The large amount collected in this way after a time produced some excellent "dancers;" in fact, it raised a sort of strife for the highest honors, i.e., the most cheering and the most collected in the "hat." Among the most famous in their day was "*Ned*" (Francis,) a little wiry negro slave, belonging to Martin Ryerson; another named Bob Rowley, who called himself "*Bobolink Bob*," belonging to William Bennett, and *Jack*, belonging to Frederick De Voo, all farmers on Long Island; . . . the Long Islanders tied [their hair] up in a cue, with dried eel-skin; but sometimes they combed it about their heads and shoulders, in the form of a wif, then all the fashion. After the Jersey negroes had disposed of their masters' produce at the "Bear Market," which sometimes was early done, and then the

> advantage of a late tide, they would "shin it" for the Catherine Market to enter the lists with the Long Islanders, and in the end, an equal division of the proceeds took place. The success which attended them brought our city negroes down there, who after a time, even exceeded them both, and if money was not to be had they would dance for a bunch of eels or fish.

We read here a vivid description of a cultural phenomenon that clearly made an impact on most observers. The black dancers were hired by shopkeepers to attract a crowd to their stores, but they also collected tips on their own by passing a hat. Historian Kevin Scott (2004:54) notes that "with little to sell, of course, they sold themselves, and they found eager buyers." One of the attractions was dancing which was accompanied by a partner who kept time by "patting juba" on his legs or other body parts. This performance was a stark contrast to what most white onlookers would have known as dancing in their own experience. Instead of "vertical and upright European stances" the dancers on Catherine Slip displayed "angular bending of arms, legs, and torso; shoulder and hip movement; scuffing and stamping, and hopping steps; asymmetrical use of the body; and fluid movement" (Glass 2006; Smith 2014:189).

Often paired with De Voe's description is one of several illustrations entitled *Dancing for Eels* (figure 3.1), the earliest of which dates to 1820. Together, De Voe's description and these illustrations allow us to imagine the vital scenes that would have played out on Catherine Slip during the years Micah Hawkins and William Sidney Mount knew it. Yet we can also see why many authors cite these performances as an origin point of the racist tradition of blackface minstrelsy that dominated stage routines in later years (Lhamon 2000; Lott 1995; Roberts 2017; Straughsbaugh 2006). As Scott (2004:50) concludes, "Mount found a world in which music, dance, economics, and slavery were the subject of complex racial negotiations that, while certainly present on Long Island, were concentrated in a way that provided the agar for the acceleration of a developing minstrel culture."

Yet many researchers (Smith 2013; also see Matthews 2011a; Roediger 1999; Scott 2004; and Stewart 1998) argue these descriptions of dancing, music, commerce, and race on Catherine Slip do not themselves reflect the racism of blackface minstrelsy but rather an American creole synthesis whose influence on William Sidney Mount was profound. The spectacle of the dancers was not only their difference from contemporary norms but also the evidence they provide for a coherent creole art form. That dancers competed for tips suggests a structure and form of performance was in place that could be judged. Similarly, and

Figure 3.1. "Dancing for Eels, a Scene from Baker's new play 'New York as it is . . . ,' performed 1848," by James Francis Brown (1862–1935). The earliest known version of this drawing dates to 1820. (Yale University Art Gallery, Mabel Brady Garvan Collection.)

important to this study, the dancing was considered a "Long Island" type or style. For example, in 1807 Washington Irving described one dancer this way: "No Long Island negro could shuffle you, 'double trouble' or 'hoe corn and dig potatoes' more scientifically" (in Scott 2004:59). A playbill for Master Diamond (a minstrel dancer famous in the 1840s) also noted that the Long Island Breakdown was among his signature pieces (Scott 2004:60).

Capturing this expression truthfully rather than in caricature was the goal for some artists of the time. This included Micah Hawkins, who, in addition to running a grocery, wrote music and works for the stage (thus the piano built into the shop counter). Hawkins's most well-known song is "Backside Albany," which became later a minstrel standard. Performed in 1815, it was "the first dialect song written by an American and performed on stage in blackface" (Scott 2004:62). According to Smith (2013:105, citing William Mahar 1988), the dialect in "Backside Albany" reveals a "sincere attempt to render early nineteenth-century African American-inflected, working class speech as it sounded." So while the legacy of the song fed the racism of blackface minstrelsy, its origin belies a greater intimacy between the author and his sources and the likelihood of a greater respect for their humanity and the conditions of their lives than was ever depicted on the minstrel stage.

Hawkins's last work was a full-length ballad opera titled "The Saw-Mill, or, A Yankee Trick," which included an entr'acte written in black vernacular dialect called "Massa Georgee Washington and General La Fayette." This short piece emphasized within the show the opera's overarching theme of the trick. The story is centered on two young scoundrels who pretended to be Yankees to convince an old Dutchman to allow them to marry his daughters so they could acquire his land upstate. Deceptions like this ran throughout the show showing that Hawkins wanted to highlight the trickster theme perhaps as a reflection of the era and a circumstance of the emergent diversity and difficulties of the urban condition. One reading of the performance is that Hawkins saw in blackface and black dialect a performance that reflected the social complexity of the world around him as well as the way acting in disguise provided a chance to highlight, poke fun, and transcend social norms. Notably, the play was harshly criticized by the elite press as "vulgar" and "droll," which Smith (2013:112) thinks may have been one of its main goals. Arguably, this is also what Hawkins saw when Ned, Bobolink Bob, and Jack danced on Catherine Slip: a performance staged to meet the expectations of the audience who were tricked enough by the dance to contribute to the hat.

Embedded in this understanding of Hawkins's works is the essence of Smith's (2013) concept of creole synthesis: that in the multiethnic world of New York as well as other port cities, work camps, and frontier towns—framed as they were by the dynamics of slavery and emancipation in the early nineteenth century—groups previously defined by separate legal statuses began to mix. They then found in each other's cultural traditions, especially their artistic and ritual performances, ways to understand and develop something new. The creole synthesis was one such articulation of a progressive political critique of the tired dominant traditions that no longer applied to life on Catherine Slip or in the multiracial democracy emerging on the Lower East Side that some envisioned as the future of the nation. Since this book is not about New York City, I turn next to build a bridge between William Sidney Mount's experiences there and his life as a young man and a painter in Setauket.

William Sidney Mount

Mount once reflected, "I believe I must have a violin in my studio—to practice upon. To stimulate me more to painting. I remember that when I painted my best pictures I played upon the violin much more than I do now" (Scott 2004:65). This recollection depicts the intersection between painting and music that he strongly believed helped to make him "one of the premier painters in America" (Scott 2004:20). Mount was the progenitor of genre painting in the United States, an art form focused on depicting and celebrating everyday American scenes. For Mount these were the common scenes he witnessed while living in Setauket and Stony Brook. Genre painting, popular in America from 1840 through the end of the century, stood in sharp contrast to the work of portraitists, landscape painters, and especially artists working in the Grand Manner style. Grand Manner was a copy of classical European Renaissance and Baroque styles, whose popularity "is often ascribed to the desire of American elites to create a grand American mythology to offset the nation's youth by emphasizing its European heritage" (Scott 2004:75). The subject matter of genre painting was instead distinctively American, with a focus on "courtship, families, and community life in rural settings that were associated positively with fundamental national values" (Weinberg and Barratt 2009).[1]

Mount was born in Setauket on November 26, 1807. As mentioned, he later moved to live with his grandfather in Stony Brook and again to New York as a young adult. By 1830 he was living again in Stony Brook after studying painting at the National Academy of Design and in 1828 as a student of Henry Inman. He left Inman's studio after only one week, stating that "the desire to be entirely original drove me from his home" (Scott 2004:76). This desire to be original also led Mount to genre painting. One of his first works in the style, *Rustic Dance after a Sleigh Ride* (figure 3.2), was a sensation, winning first prize at the American Institute of the City of New York in 1830. Contemporary reviews and later analysis of *Rustic Dance* show that it captured key notions of American culture by being natural, rural, peculiar, full of everyday drama, and "low" (Scott 2004:79–80).

The painting depicts a crowded room, perhaps modeled after Jonas Hawkins's tavern in Stony Brook, filled with young adults surrounding a dancing couple. The central character's cheeks are red, his clothes are disheveled and, with his hand in his pocket, he is violating "middle-class bodily etiquette" revealing either "his 'rustic' working-class origin, or his state of inebriation—or both" (Smith 2014:198). With one hand extended, he is inviting the woman in the red dress to dance. As she is grasping her dress, it appears she accepts. Behind her is a young man gasping at the site of the other couple in the foreground to the right. There, a nicely dressed urbane man is speaking into the ear of the woman in the white dress. That she is holding her dress in both hands suggests she is also about to

Figure 3.2. *Rustic Dance after a Sleigh Ride* by William Sidney Mount, 1830. (Museum of Fine Arts, Boston, Bequest of Martha C. Karolik for the M. and M. Karolik Collection of American Paintings, 1815–1865, Accession Number 48.458.)

enter the dance. Analysts of this painting suggest that the urbane character represents a slick city "Yankee" looking to take advantage of the simple rustic crowd, especially the central character, who is taken to be coupled with the woman in the white dress. The idea is that the two men and the woman in white are in a love triangle and that the rustic man is about to lose out. Significantly, this dramatic narrative and its characters come straight off the theater stage; thus many analysts think this painting reflects Mount's exposure to the theater in New York, including especially his uncle Micah's productions.

The half-circular-shaped foreground of the painting is completed by the African American violinist on the far left. Here we see a connection between *Rustic Dance* and Mount's admission that he painted with a violin in the studio to stimulate him to work. Kevin Scott (2004) has established that Mount was not only an accomplished musician—he played multiple instruments, as did many other members of his family—but that he believed in the power of music to reach beyond the surface of people and situations, if not also change them. Mount recalled that he "stopped a fight at an Election, by playing a hornpipe on my violin—from shoulder hitting they went to dancing" (Scott 2004:40). In 1860 he repeated this thought, suggesting that "Congress install a band in both Houses to interrupt and heal all divisive speech with the harmonious strains of patriotic music" (Robertson 1998:105). Music builds *communitas*, as people find physical and spiritual commonality in melody, harmony, rhythm, and, especially, dance. Historian Bruce Robertson (1998:105) concludes that for Mount "music and Democracy work hand in hand." Notably, dance and music are key themes in many of Mount's paintings.

Of course, the violinist in *Rustic Dance* also stands out for being black and one of three African Americans in the painting. The others are the man standing with bellows by the hearth on the left and the man straining to see into the room through a door in the back. Holding a whip, this man is the sleigh driver in the story. Like these men, the violinist holds a tool that defines his role as a servant of the whites around him, but knowing Mount's feeling about the power of music, it is quite possible to reverse this relationship: that the dancers were under the control of the musician and the other black men.

This idea finds support in the epitaph Micah Hawkins wrote for Anthony Clapp's headstone, which formerly stood in the Hawkins family cemetery (see figure 1.8):

> ENTIRELY TONE . . . LESS
> *Honor and shame from no condition rise,*
> *act well your part, there all honor lies.*
> ANTHONY HANNIBAL CLAPP
> of African descent
> Born at *Horseneck Conn.* 14, July 1749,
> came to *Setauket* in 1779,
> Here sojourning until he died 12, Oct. 1816.
> *Anthony,* though indigent, was most content,
> Though of a race despis'd, deserv'd he much
> respect—in his deportment modest and polite,
> Forever faithfully performing in life's drama
> the eccentrick part assign'd him by his Maker.
> His philosophy agreed with his example to be
> happy Himself, and to make others so, being

selfish, but in the coveting of his acquaintance
an undivided approbation, which he was so
Fortunate as to obtain and keep__
Upon the *Violin,* few play'd as *Toney play'd.*
His artless music was a language universal,
and in its Effect most Irresistable! Ay, and
was he not of *Setauket's dancing Steps*__
a *Physiognomist,* indeed; he was.__
Nor old nor young, of either sex, stood on
The Floor to Jig it, but he knew the gait,
Peculiar of their *Hobby,* and unasked,
Plac'd best foot foremost for them, by his *Fiddle*
This Emblamatick Lachrymatory, and
Cenotaph's, the grateful tribute of a few
of either sex who knew his worth.

This text presents a great deal to consider, but a few main points stand out. First, Hawkins describes Clapp as happy, which can be seen as a way of justifying his servitude. Yet he also gives Clapp a great deal of credit for his skill. Despite his playing "artless music," his tunes spoke a "universal" language that was "irresistible." He also describes Clapp as a "physiognomist," or a person who is able to judge another's character or predict the future, usually from facial expressions. Clapp could supposedly watch those who "stood on the Floor to Jig" and be able to play the music that would fit their "gait, Peculiar to their *Hobby*." With his violin he would place their "best foot forward *for* them" (emphasis added) leading to their "grateful tribute." Scott (2004:43) suggests "Clapp's spectators and dancers not only . . . enjoy[ed] his music but . . . [gave] themselves up to his control."

Hawkins's epitaph matches Mount's own thoughts about the power of music, and it may be that both uncle and nephew cultivated and shared this appreciation of music and dance together with Anthony Clapp. Clapp was a servant in their family home and likely performed music for and with their family many times. This intimacy is what permitted Hawkins to write such a flowing epitaph and also commission the violin-shaped "Emblamatick Lachrymatory" carved in high relief on the head stone (figure 1.8). It is also likely why William Sidney Mount inherited Clapp's fiddle after the former slave died. Mount recorded his fondness for Clapp after coming across the headstone while walking on his family's property decades later: "I have sat by Anthony when I was a child, to hear him play his jigs and hornpipes. He was a master in that way, and acted well his part" (Scott 2004:44). Mount notes here the power (mastery) of his playing as well as the role he was playing in the performance.

Some have argued that Mount's depictions of the three African Americans in *Rustic Dance* reflect an underlying anti-black racism. Elizabeth Johns (1991:24–25) states that "their role, as Mount represents them, is to serve, and the caricatured grinning faces—like the prints of Jim Crow—suggest the happy childlike black." Considering Mount's feeling about Clapp and the power of music in general, this assessment is likely off the mark or at the very least is too rigid. Kevin Scott (2004:97, n80) suggests a more nuanced reading:

> As for the "grinning caricatured faces" suggesting prints of Jim Crow and the idea of the "happy, childlike black," clearly there is some connection as the blacks in the painting wear the largest grins. Yet, all of Mount's faces in the painting are caricatured, due significantly to the simple fact of Mount's young inexperience. He simply was not very good yet. The criticism also raises the issue of how musicians like Clapp would have conducted themselves physically during their performances for white audiences. Clapp may very well have heightened his appearance of enjoyment in order to confirm and manipulate his audience's expectations and to assure his continued employment, and he may very well have been enjoying himself greatly. The two need not contradict. All this troubles our easy readings of outright racism in Mount's representation of the violinist. Racism clearly is at work in images like these, both in the moment being pictured and in the representation of the moment, but so is the energetic artistry of black musicians.

Bringing a particular critical eye to the painting, Johns saw the fiddler's smile as evidence of racism, when it may in fact just be an attempt to depict the scene as it was. This would have included the likelihood that the musician was likely both performing his contentment for the sake of the dancers as well as actually having good time, especially, perhaps, if he was truly in control of the crowd.

The depiction of enjoyment in *Rustic Dance* is likely why it was so well reviewed, despite the fact that Mount's artistic skills were still developing. The painting fostered a connection between dancing and the sort of carefree happiness of the crowd at the tavern. Part of this recognition relates to Mount's "desire to be entirely original," which led him to break out of the restricted conventions of the Grand Manner–style and high-style portraiture. Similarly, dancing in general was frowned upon by the elite as a sign of low culture. According to Scott (2004:39), Mount collected more than 450 pieces of music, the vast majority of which were "lively, rhythmic, and designed for dancing, an activity that was consistently under fire by Long Island religious leaders." Mount's contemporary George Templeton Strong wrote that Mount "had been living . . . in eastern Long Island, that paradise of loafers, and amusing himself and his friends with his fiddle and his pencil sketches" (Nevins and Thomas 1952:233). Both Scott (2004) and Smith (2014) argue that this elite rejection of dancing was a thinly masked critique of blackness. Originating in colonial fears that music and dancing could lead to slave insurrections as well as later critical and racist view of dancers like those on Catherine Slip, American elites saw in African American dancing evidence of their subhumanity. In contrast, influenced both by his uncle and his own intimate experiences with black people and performance, Mount was drawn to dance just as much as he was to music.

This attraction is clear in his pencil drawing *The Setauket Military Band* (figure 3.3). This piece shows a group of musicians gathered and ready to join a parade such as for the Fourth of July. Not in formation, the musicians were rehearsing in the presence of two African American men. Both men are dressed in fine clothes for the holiday, and one is dancing to the music of the band while the other claps his hands in rhythm. The position of the dancer, with his knee and elbows bent, mirrors the position of the dancer in *Dancing for Eels* and the central character in *Rustic Dance*. Kevin Scott (2004:82) suggests the positions of the couple in *Rustic Dance* indicate they are dancing a jig, which was one of the standard dances of the Long Island African Americans on Catherine Slip. What we see in the painting is thus a white couple doing a black dance or a dance that "though very common at white gatherings, had long been associated with blackness (certainly part of why it was so popular at white gatherings)." Dancing the jig was a common subject for Mount. It is found again in other paintings such as *Dancing on the Barn Floor*, *Dance of the Haymakers*, and *Bar-Room Scene* as well as several drawings where the dancers are both white and black.

The meaning of these images derives from their accuracy. While Mount was clearly impressed and wanted to express the power of music and dance and the role that African Americans played in these scenes, he was not using his democratic or progressive agenda to bend the truth. Rather, he painted scenes from country life as he knew it directly because they expressed his hope to be original and his goal of upending the conservative elite traditions that he felt missed out on what makes life enjoyable. Historian Kevin Scott (2004:84) summarizes this interpretation:

Figure 3.3. *Setauket Military Band* by William Sidney Mount, n.d. Pencil on paper, 10 ½ × 13 ½ in. (Courtesy of the Long Island Museum of American Art, History, and Carriages. Bequest of Ward Melville, 1977.)

> The implication [is] that rural Americans are freer and more natural, and that they love to play and perform. . . . These ideas echo popular stereotypes of blackness and more deeply connect rusticity and blackness, allowing urban viewers to enjoy the merriment of blackness—certainly common in the city—through white, rural substitutes. . . . *Rustic Dance* and *Dancing on the Barn Floor,* then, present [a] black performance that whites could imagine joining.

Mount's work depicts actual scenes in Setauket and other nearby places, and that the people, places, and activities in the paintings and drawings are realistic. So, unlike later Jim Crow caricatures, which appealed to the minds of racist whites, African Americans in Mount's work represent the presence and actions of actual African Americans in and around Setauket. Unfortunately, in most cases, we have no record of who these people of color were, though later recollections did identify one model as Robbin Mills, who lived near Mount's family home in Stony Brook (Edward P. Buffet, William Sidney Mount: A Biography, 1924, Three Village Historical Society, Setauket, New York). Moreover, as Kevin Scott (2004:34) writes regarding Mount's sketch *The Military Band in Setauket*, "while [it] is far from revolutionary in its nominal integration of blacks into white society, it does suggest that much of the [expected racial] separation is a façade. . . . [African Americans] are unquestionably involved."

The idea of racial segregation as a façade in early nineteenth century on Long Island is one to think more about. For one, Mount lays out quite plainly that in addition to being household servants and laborers, African Americans participated in community events like tavern dances, sleigh rides, Fourth of July festivities, or, from another story, ice skating on the mill pond. In this way, as newly freed people they belonged in the community and arguably also in the nation. This is the progressive politics of the creole synthesis. Micah Hawkins showed this by including and accurately representing African American characters speaking in dialect while wearing American military uniforms in his plays. Mount found a way to do this in his art by depicting African Americans as musicians, laborers, onlookers, servants, dancers, and listeners alongside whites and in such a way to remind us that above all else they were part of the larger community and contributed to dynamics of that community in important ways.

Racial Modernity in Setauket

The concept of racial modernity was coined by historian James Brewer Stewart (1998, 1999; also see Roediger 1991, 1999). The idea captures the transition in the way Americans thought about and acted on race in the North in the second quarter of the nineteenth century. Stewart (1998:182) points specifically to the 1830s as the decade of change, stating that

> the North in 1831 stood on the cusp of an unprecedented transformation of relations between races. . . . [It] was rapidly evolving into a modern white supremacist political culture as people in the free states found themselves insolubly divided by pigmentation, invariably governed by biological inequality, and almost exclusively informed by racially self-referential politics and social reform . . . a polity premised on the uniform assumption that nature had always divided black and white as superior and inferior—and always must.

The concept of racial modernity points to earlier decades when race relations, while undeniably unequal, were less defined by the white supremacist sense that people of color were inherently and permanently inferior to whites. Racial modernity thus describes an intensification of racism after a time when racial animosity was actually in decline. This earlier period is what I described as the creole synthesis, based on the evidence of Micah Hawkins's plays and William Sidney Mount's paintings, which reflect the presence of the cultural, social, and status difference of African Americans but do not portray this difference as a sign of an inherent and biological inferiority. Rather, as I argued, these sources reflect on this difference as a largely positive and progressive result of the interactions of the many and sometimes new social communities emerging in the new America.

The reasons for the shift to racial modernity are complex. However, many frame it as a strongly negative reaction to the radical abolitionist movement that, according to the American Anti-Slavery Society, sought "to secure to the colored population . . . all the rights and privileges that belong to them as men and as Americans [so that the] paths of preferment, of wealth, and intelligence should be opened to them as widely as to persons of white complexion" (Stewart 1998:1987). Lofty in its goals, these ideas implied racial integration would be the means to achieve these ends. The idea of integration in the 1830s, however, fostered powerful fears among many whites about the possibility of racial amalgamation, or the sexual mixing of races, which brought to the surface strong anxieties that almost singlehandedly supported the full-blown forms of American racism over the following century. Most threatening, many thought, was the possibility for the defilement of virtuous middle- and upper-class white women by socially and biologically degraded black men.

While these fears were irrational, they drove a rash of race riots in northern cities in the 1830s spurred by public displays of integration within the abolitionist societies. An abolitionist meeting at the Chatham Theater in New York on July 4, 1834, was trebly offensive to rioters because it was promoted as an Abolition Day celebration (July 4, 1827, was the formal date of the end of slavery in New York State), and it was alcohol free. The meeting thus flew in the face of traditional Independence Day festivities and did so while suggesting African American New Yorkers deserved equality with whites and the same political privileges as their fellow citizens. In the days that followed, white anti-abolition mobs burned the possessions of leading abolitionists, stormed an integrated abolition rally, destroyed black and integrated churches, and entered the homes of free African Americans, where they injured people and stole and damaged property (Scott 2004:126).

Riots like this, common in northern cities between 1831 and 1838, were focused on the destruction of neighborhoods and institutions that supported growing and prosperous free black communities. Many interpret the riots as expressions not only of growing fears of amalgamation but of the competition by African Americans in the labor market. One problem with this argument is that most of the rioters in New York were skilled artisans and professionals and not actually competitors with working-class blacks. The whites who lived closest to the black neighborhoods tended to be poorer immigrants who "were more likely to be threatened by the rioters than to be in the mob" (Scott 2004:128). Still, following this rash of riots, anti-black sentiment took root, and by 1840 "whites, both rich and poor, emerged from their wars against the 'amalgamationists' with an unprecedented sense of their interclass power as the dominant race" (Stewart 1998:205). This assessment was not just a celebration of the gains that came from the riots in 1830s but also the adoption of a new belief in the incompatibility of people of color as citizens of the United States.

Evidence for the rise of racial modernity actually appears in the later work of William Sidney Mount. Early critical acclaim of his work led to an increase in commissioned projects which included *Eel Spearing at Setauket* (figure 1.6) as well as *Dance of the Haymakers* and *The Power of Music*, which were each painted in mid-1840s. As these were commissions, Mount would have had in mind the wishes of his patrons as much as what he would have wanted to add on his own. The depiction of African Americans in each counts as among the most compelling and empathetic images in his career, and scholars agree they are shown with a depth of character that reveals the complexities of their inner lives. Arguably, Mount's personal relationships with his models was a factor behind the success of his representations of their character. Critical acclaim for *The Power of Music* led Mount to hire an agent, William Schaus, to sell lithograph prints of his work. Mount subsequently grew increasingly popular in the American South and in Europe, and it seems this success influenced his later depictions of African Americans in ways that reflect the impact of racial modernity.

While Mount previously presented scenes that put whites and blacks together on the canvas in a way that forced a recognition of the presence and vitality of African Americans and black culture in American life, his later works tended to depict African Americans alone. Four of these works, painted as a series known as *The Musicians*, were genre portraits. These were produced in the genre style but as portraits of individuals removed from the settings and other people that made their images attractive in his earlier work. This is not to suggest that Mount abandoned a faithful depiction of African Americans as fully human. For example, the young men in *The Bone Player*, *The Banjo Player*, and *Right and Left* are painted in the midst of performing music, probably professionally, as in a tavern, since they are all dressed in fine clothes. Yet these paintings are character studies, not scenes, so we cannot know the story these men were part of as much as in his earlier works. The paintings reflect southern influence on the lithograph market, since southerners increasingly sought images reflecting aspects of blackface minstrelsy as a way to sustain the racist caricatures they counted on to justify the perpetuation of slavery.

It is Mount's painting *The Lucky Throw* (1851) that shows the lengths he went for the market and the way racial modernity influenced his work. The original work is lost, but a copy retitled *Raffling for a Goose* survives (figure 3.4). The subject is an African American boy holding a goose he won in a raffle. The image captures his joy, but as Scott (2004:169) observes, his

> broad grin, his white teeth, his full lips, his evident happiness, and his innocent joy at winning a goose and at displaying it are all signifiers for a racist type, despite Mount's avoidance of exaggeration. Exaggeration was unnecessary in this instance, for American popular culture, through thousands of jokes, descriptions, images, and stage appearances, had firmly defined even the idea of a black man's grin—and each of the other traits—as inherently humorous.

One review of the painting makes the case clear: "Sale of a Negro—One of the finest specimens of the African race was sold yesterday, in our city. The public, however, ought not to be alarmed, for the subject of this notice is nothing but a *chef d'ouevre,* by our inimitable artist, W. S. Mount, representing the black hero of a 'raffle for a goose'" (Scott 2004:167). Another critic called the boy a "Long Island Nigger," referencing not only Mount's Long Island origin but also a mainstay caricature for performers on the minstrel stage. Matching this external voice, Mount also started using the term "nigger" to describe African Americans more frequently as the Civil War approached. In fact, as Karen Adams (1975:54) writes, "there is nothing in any of Mount's [later] paintings of black people that would offend a slaveholder." Thus, his shift toward a more caricatured depiction of African Americans in his artwork may not have been solely succumbing to the demands of the market or his desire for wealth.[2]

These later works show a shift in style with the hallmarks of racial modernity. As the paintings are not scenes that contextualize race as a relation, we need to reflect on what paintings of solitary African American men tell us. For one, African American alterity was becoming generic, something that did not need to

Figure 3.4. *Raffling for a Goose*, aka *The Lucky Throw* by William Sidney Mount, 1851. (Library of Congress Prints and Photographs Division, Reproduction Number: LC-DIG-pga-01965.)

be set in context since race difference was plain, simple, and hierarchical. Even if Mount's portraits are beautiful artworks, they are also signs of the separations embedded in racial modernity. By the 1850s and after the Civil War, Mount was certainly not alone in depicting African Americans as caricatures:

> The cultural presence of the image of the fugitive slave or freedman had grown steadily since the Missouri Compromise and the publication *of Uncle Tom's Cabin*, but during and after the Civil War the freedman and fugitive slave painting and sculpture became a full-fledged genre . . . with its common portrayals of escaping slaves nearly prostrate in their hiding or, oppositely, full of muscular tension in their running or exultation. (Scott 2004:18)

Adams (1975:55) also argues that Mount's paintings "contributed to perpetuating the stereotypes of the lazy Negro, the happy black, and the black minstrel and buffoon." She concludes that after the Civil War, most genre painters deprived "black figures of psychological complexity" (Adams 1975:58), leaving only caricatures in their place that served political or sentimental white agendas.

While Mount's work is compelling and provides essential insights for understanding the transition from the creole synthesis to racial modernity, his paintings constitute a rather small data set limited to the work of one man. To supplement this interpretation of a change in racial thinking in Setauket and the surrounding region, I also examined archival sources to provide a complementary view on the way African Americans were depicted in popular media in the nineteenth century. The results of this study are discussed in the next section, which describes the transition to racial modernity as well as further developing how racism colored the cultural experience of people of color in and around Setauket.

The Racial Discourse in Nineteenth-Century Long Island

"A Negro, on his own confession, is to be executed at Cahawba [Alabama] on the 15th instant, hired by a white man to assist in a burglary. His evidence was conclusive as to himself, but not legal against his companion and employer in the act. It is thus that great fishes break through, and little ones are caught in the net." This brief report, titled "Equal and Exact Justice," was published in September 7, 1822, issue of *The Corrector*, a Long Island newspaper published in Sag Harbor, about 50 miles east of Setauket.[3] It depicts the injustice African Americans faced before the law in the South, where they were unable to testify against whites. The story is moralized by referring to the difference between African Americans and whites as analogous to small and great fish, the latter of which counter-intuitively escape the net. Given that the story was printed in a Sag Harbor paper, we can surmise that it voices a liberal northern antislavery sentiment. It was shared with readers to illustrate the perspective on the issue held by the newspaper editors, but it likely also reflects the leanings of a good number of readers. The question is how these same Long Island readers would have felt about the African Americans and Native Americans who lived in their town and region. While the newspaper sources discussed here cannot answer this question with certainty, we can gauge from these printed texts a general sense of popular racial sentiments and then track these feelings as they developed through time.

The source for news stories analyzed in this section is the New York State Historic Newspapers project's (2017) online repository of scanned newspapers. I sampled issues from two newspapers for this analysis: *The Collector* out of Sag

Harbor, which started publishing in 1822, and *The Long Islander* out of Huntington, which began publication in 1839. I sampled *The Collector* by reading every issue published over the course of a year in five-year intervals between 1822 and 1837. I then switched to *The Long Islander*, also reading every issue published in a given year in five-years intervals between 1840 and 1895.[4] I used the online database search engine to pull articles that used the term "negro" to identify stories that mentioned and discussed people of color. The idea is that these articles would draw from and contribute to the racial ideologies of literate Long Islanders, which would have certainly also influenced the everyday racial experiences of people of color in the region. The sample of articles is not confined to news stories about events and people on Long Island in the nineteenth century but reflects a broader discourse of race and African American culture and identity that circulated on Long Island via print media. The analysis here shows that the language and conception of African Americans in local newspapers follows the trajectory proposed for this chapter such that people of color are treated with more sympathy and humanity in earlier years than they are later in the century.

The Collector published 13 articles in 1822 that included the term "negro." These articles can be grouped into four types: political articles with antislavery or equal rights messages, articles expressing an abhorrence to racial violence, stories that recognize the humanity and belonging of blacks in American society, and stories that disparage blacks as inferior. The short report "Equal and Exact Justice" falls into the first category. A second example is an obituary published September 7, 1822, for M. Civique de Gastines, a French national who self-deported to Haiti after writing controversial pamphlets in "support of liberty and the maintenance of . . . rights." The article discusses his illness upon reaching Haiti as well as his subsequent death and elaborate funeral. It concludes with this editorial comment:

> These are the people that slaveholders say are different from the rest of the human race, and that they ought not to possess that liberty, which the God of Nature has willed to man. The first assertion is partly true, and they may not only thank, but be grateful to their God, for making them so—for the unprejudiced mind voluntarily acknowledges that they are superior to their culminators!

Certainly, these words show sympathy for African Americans especially in light of the negative assessments of slaveholders. Another example is a report from a Congressman Smith on December 21, 1822, that two hundred free blacks [from Sierra Leone] had been taken by the brig *Camperdown,* and a great number of free negroes from the same place, by the Schooner *Mulatto*. . . . He had particularly adverted to this subject, he said, with a sincere hope to enlist the sympathies of this house, and to lead to such an investigation of the facts, that every effort of the nation may be put in operation to abolish this imperious traffic.

This anti–slave trade statement recognizes the freedom of the blacks from or en route to Sierra Leone and condemns their capture for the slave trade.

Examples from *The Collector* showing an abhorrence to racial violence include the following article from September 7, 1822, titled "Horrible":

At Halifax [Virginia] Superior Court, April Term, Jacob Pope was brought to the bar, charged with having murdered a female negro slave of his by inflicting on her naked body, and limbs, between two and three hundred lashes with a cow-skin. Pope's overseer (says the Halifax paper) deposed that the deceased received at least two hundred and sixty lashes, if not more: that finally the strength of Pope was exhausted, and he (Pope) called upon him to proceed in lacerating the victim of his rage; he declined with entreaties that she had received enough. The witness described the woman to have received the fatal bruises and stripes from which blood gushed, thus: Her clothes were tied over or about her head in such a manner as to admit the suspension of her body by her arms, which were tied to the limbs of an apple tree; then her feet were "lapped" around the body of the tree, and tied some inches from the ground: In this situation she received the whipping which it is presumed caused her death within a day or two after she was released! The jury returned a verdict against the prisoner of MANSLAUGHTER, and the Court fined him in the sum of TWO HUNDRED DOLLARS, and Costs!—Virginia paper.

Vividly demonstrating the brutality of the slaveholder, this article draws sympathy solely for the deceased and those who felt justice was at best lightly served by the manslaughter verdict. Another example printed October 5, 1822, highlights the contradictions regarding slavery commonly published in slave-holding state newspapers. Printed under the biblical heading "The 'Mote,' and the 'Beam,'" the author writes with sarcasm that

In some papers it is mentioned with great indignation and horror, that the Infidel Turks at Smyrna, &c. have offered Greek women, boys, and girls for sale at their shops and bazars. And yet, in the same papers, are to

> be found advertisements, with the names of professing Christians at the bottom, such as this—"For sale, a Negro Family, consisting of a man, his wife, and six children, either together or single, as may suit the purchaser. They are sold for no fault, but to raise money. Inquire of A, B.C.D. &c."

Several other examples show the more subtle politics involved in making claims that African Americans belong in the United States. From August 10, 1822, under the heading "Miscellany," the paper tells the story of a hunter

> who used to allure the Doe within reach of his rifle, by imitating the cries of the fawn—a simple cry like that of a young lamb—and when the mother was led to the spot by the supposed voice of her young, he would kill her. When the fact was known, a general burst of indignation broke forth against the man. From the most elevated in society to the humblest negro on the neighbouring plantations, there was an universal exclamation against the wretch who could treacherously betray to death, by an appeal to that most sacred of all instincts, the affection of a mother for her offspring. . . . The feeling excited, and the interposition, were honourable to humanity.

While the use of the term "negro" reflects the sense that people of color occupy the lowest rung of society, they were nevertheless made equivalent to others in the ability to recognize a betrayal of maternal instinct and condemnation of the hunter. Their feelings (as those of the others) were "honourable to humanity."

The Collector also published a series of "Letters from Fort Braddock" in Upstate New York that depict the everyday scenes of the community in and around the fort. In most of these pieces, "negroes" are listed as among the community in ways that suggest they are neither out of place nor inferior to the others. This statement captures this discursive equality: "From these tales, sometimes marvellous, and generally inconsistent, as they are differently related by the Dutch and the Yankeys, the Negroes and the Indians, I should have neither patience nor curiosity to extract an intelligible narrative, had not chance furnished me with the means at a time when I had no other amusement." Here we see people of color identified as having marvelous tales, equal to those of others in terms of sustaining the author's impatience.

The majority of articles published in 1822 suggest an overall assessment of people of color as low status but also deserving to be seen as human beings and a part of society, so they should not be murdered or executed because of their race. There were only two articles in *The Collector* from 1822 that reflect an anti-black racist bias. On the lighter side an article titled "Singular Longevity" from November 17, 1822, noted

> Henry Brown, now living in Pennsylvania, was born in January 1696. His father was a negro, his mother an Indian. He was a slave 70 years, and has been a freeman 58 years. He was a soldier in Ohio, at Braddock's defeat, in 1755, then aged 59 years. He is now in his 129th year; has long straight black hair; walks about, and enjoys tolerable good health. He never married, and begins to think it too late. He wants to die, but is afraid he never shall.

This character study exemplifies the way people of color are often made out to be unusual and simple. A more damaging assessment was part of a November 17, 1822 story on a protracted duel between William Cumming and George McDuffie in South Carolina: "In the last encounter, McDuffie showed himself a man of courage, and Cumming equally proved himself a poltroon and blackguard. He must have supposed his head was a negro's or a bullocks, in placing it to guard his body, and perhaps with the idea that it was hard enough to glance off a ball, as we have accounts of some other beasts, which it is said will do it." Clearly, this reference to a black person's thick skull is a reference to their supposed intellectual inferiority.

The generally neutral-to-positive assessment one sees in the representation of people of color in articles from 1822 declines after only a few years. In 1827 the year slavery was abolished in New York State, *The Collector* marked that event in an announcement on July 14, 1827, titled "Slavery Forever Abolished in This State" that reproduced key passages from the 1799 Gradual Emancipation Act and the 1817 act ending slavery for all as of 1827. This momentous act was notably mentioned only on the bottom of an interior page between articles on federal politics and how to deal with bugs destroying cucumber vines. Despite minimizing this event, *The Collector* continued to print articles and stories with equal rights, antislavery, and anti-slaveholder messages. For example, on May 19, 1827, an editorial rebuttal of an article published by Mr. Coleman, editor of the *New York Evening Post*, stated that:

> Mr. C. says the northern mind has been abused and deceived in relation to the humanity, loving-kindness, and mercy, of the southern slave-holder towards the object of his paternal care, the slave! who is happy and dances and sings! that he (Mr. C.) has been rightly and fully informed of the happiness of the slaves—for slave-holders, male and female, have assured him that their slaves are happy!!! WHAT PROOF! WHAT TESTIMONY!

Would a man of common sense be satisfied with such proof, where he had one dollar at stake?

If Mr. C. will look into the most loathsome prison, or the vilest receptacle, where, man is found divested of his birthright he may occasionally witness the same strained attempt at mirth and jollity—but does this prove happiness? or rather does it not prove an interval, dedicated by temporary frensy to slacken the elastic cords of the human mind, and hold it for a time, from bustling asunder, by fell and unceasing despair?

Is the negro without feeling?

If he break a bone, will the tinct of his skin shield him from pain?

If on the bed of sickness and consuming with a burning fever, is he more at ease than the white man, or will a drop of cold water less cool his parched up tongue?

If you destroy his property, or plunder from him his money, will he not feel like the white man?

And if on such occasions he feel like the white man—why not when you rob him of his FREEDOM?

Here we see recognition of the essential humanity of African Americans used to counterpose the arguments of an apologist for southern slaveholders. There are a handful of other articles of this sort making the case against the idea of the "happy slave."

In addition to articles like these that supported the rights and humanity of enslaved persons, several other stories expressed abhorrence to southern racial violence. On August 4, 1827, *The Collector* printed an article titled "Horrid Occurrence" that details the lynching of a man in Alabama by a vigilante mob. The man admitted to stabbing a local white man, but the affair got out of hand when the justice of the peace abdicated his authority to the crowd of 70 or 80 people who assembled. After a vote, the mob "decided that he should immediately be executed, by being *burned to death*." The article details the lynching and concludes by noting that "this is the second negro who has been thus put to death, without Judge or Jury in that county."

There were two types of articles in 1827 that did not appear previously. One consists of accounts of runaway slaves. Many of these were printed to expound of the same sense of outrage toward slavery the editors hoped to instill as they did in the article on the Alabama lynching. One story discussed how the punishment of an escaped slave led to that man's death. Another article discussed the deadly gun battle between a "nest of runaways" and their captors in an

Alabama swamp. One more article tells of the enslavement of four free people of color in South Carolina for harboring fugitives.

The second new type of article intentionally paints a negative or insulting image of African Americans. These pieces go further than revealing previously voiced assumptions about low status and intellectual inferiority to levy much harsher anti-black judgments. A story printed on May 26, 1827, and familiarly titled "Horrible Depravity" is about a 10-year-old African American girl accused of murdering both white and black children under her care on a Maryland plantation. Clearly a devastating event, the article confirms the racist suspicions of the reader: "we do not remember ever to have heard of a transaction, in which, at so early an age, such shocking depravity has been displayed." Several other examples of negative representations employ "Negro dialect" to portray African Americans as gullible, superstitious, and simple-minded. Two such stories were printed on the front page of *The Collector* on August 4, 1827, including one where a preacher asked "'What are you made of, Jack?' he said, 'of mud, massa.' On being told he should have said dust, he refused, 'no massa, it won't do, no stick together.'" A very powerful piece of this type was also the only article in this survey of *The Collector* to use the term "nigger":

> EXTRACT FROM SAMBO'S SERMON
>
> Strate is de rode an narrer is de paff which leadeff to Glory
>
> Brederen blevers!—You semble dis nite to har de word, and hah it splained and monstrated to you; yes, an I ten for splain it clear as de light ob de liben day. We're all wicked sinners har below—its fac my brederen, and I tell you how it cum- You see my frens,
>
> Adam was de fus man
> Ebe was de todder
> Cane was a wicked man,
> Kase he kill he brodder.
>
> Adam and Ebe were bofe brack men, an so was Cane and Able. Now I spose it seem to strike you a understandin how do fus white man cum. Wy I let you no,—Den you see when Cane kill he brodder, de massa cum an he say, "Cane whar you a brodder Able ?" Cane say "I don't know massa."—He cum gin an say, "Cane whar you a brodder Able ?" Cane say "I don't know massa." But de nigger noe'd all de time. Massa now git mad, cum gin, peak, mity sharp dis time, "Cane whar your brodder Able, you nigga?" Cane now git friten and he turn wite; and dis is de way de fus white man cum pon dis arth! And if it had not been for dat dare niggar Cane, we'd neba been

> troubled wid dese sassy wites pon de face ob dis ciscumlar globe. Now sing de forty-tenth hymn ticular meter.

This story was certainly not published so white Christians would want to see themselves as descended from a frightened Cane. Rather, its intent was to give white readers something absurd to laugh about at the expense of African Americans, including their religious leaders.

By 1832 stories referencing people of color in *The Collector* became increasing anti-black in tone. No articles expounded the injustice of slavery outside of a story of the unjust murder of a runaway slave. One article mentioned the passing of a new bill regarding freedmen in Maryland, but it did not provide the details that the bill denied them the right to vote, to serve on juries, or hold public office. Instead, almost half of the articles that make reference to "negroes" report on examples of their violence, cunning, or resistance. This shift in representation reflects the influence of racial modernity that followed events such Nat Turner's 1831 rebellion in Virginia and the "Slave Insurrection in Jamaica" reported in the paper on February 18, 1832. Other stories of resistance were smaller in scale including the drowning murder of white woman in Virginia by a "negro woman" who was reportedly jealous of her victim for intending to marry a young man from her master's home (July 14, 1832). Similarly, the paper printed a story on August 4, 1832, of a "negro man" condemned to hang for poisoning an Independence Day feast in South Carolina.

Several articles highlight supposedly humorous caricatures, such as one of a black preacher who claimed he had been to heaven but had not seen any "negroes" there, exclaiming to one man "You brack fool . . . you 'spose I went into the kitchen?" Yet even among these stories the idea of the "cunning negro" appears, such as in an untitled February 18, 1832, story:

> A negro, on a plantation having misbehaved, was sent by his master to the overseer with a note, in which the latter was directed to bestow upon the delinquent divers and sundry stripes. Now Sambo had been sent upon such errands before, and keen were his pangs at being again delegated upon such unpleasant duty. He surveyed the note with a rueful visage, and meditated how he should escape the seemingly unavoidable penalty. At length, a thought struck him: Meeting a brother Abyssian, he shammed sudden and severe illness: "Brodder Jacko," he said, "me got 'mazin pain in 'tomac—prease han dis Ietter to massa, and take a sick brodder's pressinian." The sympathetic Jacko complied with the pretended sufferer's request, and to his amazement was forthwith "posted," and received a

tremendous whipping at the hands of the overseer—a poor requittal, he thought, for doing a brother a favor. Sambo was in ecstaucies at the success of his stratagem. He soon got rid of his pains, and could never see his friend Jacko afterwards without an inward chuckle at the ingenuity of the trick he had placed off upon him.

Over the course of 10 years, mentions of "negroes" in *The Corrector* shifted from articulating concerns for the equal rights of enslaved persons and an abhorrence to racial violence perpetrated by slave owners and southern mobs to also include stories where African Americans are at best humorous stock material for white readers or a cunning, dangerous people ready to take advantage of unsuspecting others, if not revolt or commit murder.

Over the rest of the antebellum era these trends continue. A summary of articles mentioning the term "negro" in *The Long Islander* between 1839 and 1860 is provided in table 3.1. A presumed interest in the politics of slavery and race among the majority white readership remained consistent up to the start of Civil War. This reflects an expected general interest in, for example, changes in the law regarding free people of color in Alabama, slavery in the new state of Texas, and debates over colonization, abolition, and sectional conflict in the antebellum years. "Humor" articles depicting the generic inferiority and simplemindedness of African Americans also continued. The use of "negro" dialect such as in this supposed exchange printed October 19, 1855, between a slave and master regarding shoes purchased for slaves from the North: "'Well, whar do the Yankees get 'em?' persisted the negro. 'the Yankees? why, they pick them trees, Bob.' 'W-w-well,' responded the darkey, holding up his shoes, 'I reckon de Yankee didn't pick dese pair soon enough, massa, I reck'n he waited till—till—*till dey was a little too ripe*.'

Articles published in the 1840s and 1850s suggest readers had an interest in African Americans as dangerous people, though these shifted from being stories of cunning and deceit to focus on crime, especially the murder of whites. One report noted in 1840 that Catherine Hall of Hempstead, Long Island, was murdered by her Negro gardener with a blow of a shovel. Another story tells of a "Negro Plot" to "indiscriminately" murder whites in Princess Anne County, Virginia. Other stories relate lesser crimes, such as theft of a horse in Terre Haute, a watch theft in New Orleans, and the robbery of a white man returning from the New York market by two black men in Hempstead, Long Island. Notably, articles reporting crime cluster in the earlier antebellum years, suggesting the persistence of a greater interest in caricaturing African Americans than fearing them

Table 3.1. Articles from *The Long Islander* by Theme, 1839–1860

Year	Count	Crime and Insurrection	Humor	Politics of Slavery and Race	Runaways	Naturalizing slavery	Slave Trade	Racial Violence	Labor	Positive Stories	Other
1839	15	4	2	3	1	0	2	0	0	1	2
1840	11	4	0	2	0	0	2	0	2	0	1
1845	24	6	1	5	2	1	0	1	1	2	5
1850	14	1	2	4	0	1	0	1	1	2	2
1855	8	1	4	1	0	0	0	0	0	1	1
1860	5	0	1	2	0	0	0	1	0	1	0
Total	77	16	10	17	3	2	4	3	4	7	11
Average	12.83	2.67	1.67	2.83	0.50	0.33	0.67	0.50	0.67	1.17	1.83

on Long Island. That said, the paper published a story in 1855 of the escape of the "negro Conover" from custody in Flushing, Queens. Conover was suspected for the rape and murder of Catherine Quigley. Clearly, according the growing racism of the time, the supposed rape and murder of a white woman by a black man would have realized the greatest fear associated with race in America.

The distribution of the types of articles containing the word "negro" published in *The Long Islander* after the Civil War is detailed in table 3.2. As this period follows emancipation nationwide, articles about slavery or fugitives disappear, though some of the important earlier themes continued. One of these important topics was the legal status and civil rights of free African Americans and the appropriate response to black freedom by whites. A liberal newspaper, *The Long Islander* espoused policies favoring the equal treatment of African Americans, especially their right to vote. In 17 articles published in 1865 that reflect the themes of equality and the politics of race, many were installments in an extended editorial debate with *The Bulletin*, a conservative pro-Confederacy Long Island newspaper. Capturing local feelings about African American civil rights, a report printed July 7, 1865, of a Fourth of July oratory in Huntington argued, "it was very clear and explicit holding that negroes were men in the view of the law, and had come to be so admitted and acknowledged by all men, and as such they had been received into our armies, and fought our battles for the defenses of our government, side by side with our white soldiers, and had earned and were entitled to the privileges of freemen." This concern and assessment for African American civil liberties is a striking contrast to the articles published in the preceding decades.

Articles expressing such racially liberal concerns fell by the wayside quickly. In 1870 and after, *The Long Islander* no longer published any articles supporting African American equality. Instead, the newspaper picked up older themes related to African Americans as criminals, as the subjects of racial violence, and as humorous caricatures for white readers to parody. Articles on black crime were not published in 1865 and 1870, but they appear again in 1875 and remain common until the end of the century. Postbellum crime stories also focus more on Long Island–based events. In August 1875 Chauncey Brewster of Babylon was indicted for abducting the daughter of his employer, Mrs. Balchon. It was later discovered that the two were lovers, so no abduction actually took place; instead, Brewster was indicted "for seduction on the promise of marriage," a statute reflecting efforts to prohibit interracial marriage. In October of the same year, a "stray negro" caused "quite a sensation" in Oyster Bay. In this case, an African American man was suspected of a crime:

Table 3.2. Articles from *The Long Islander* by Theme, 1865–1895

Year	Count	Crime	Humor	Politics of Race	Equality	Racial Violence	Positive Stories	Other
1865	21	0	3	10	7	1	0	0
1870	9	0	4	3	0	2	0	0
1875	16	6	0	1	0	9	0	0
1880	9	4	0	4	0	1	0	0
1885	7	2	4	0	0	0	0	1
1890	11	4	0	3	0	2	2	0
1895	4	4	0	0	0	0	0	0
Total	77	20	11	21	7	15	2	1
Average	11.00	2.86	1.57	3.00	1.00	2.14	0.29	0.14

upon reaching that village, he was immediately arrested . . . and was taken into the barroom of Dickerson's Hotel. Here he was surrounded by a large and excited crowd, who interviewed him thoroughly. He was finally taken before Justice Chipp and told his story. He hailed from Comac, where had been laboring for several years past. He had come to visit the wife of his first love and his boy, from whom he had been separated for many years past, and he expected to return the same night. The hope of the reward grew beautifully less in the minds of our officials after this examination, and the poor negro returned home the following day, after identification by one of his neighbors.

Here, even though no crime was committed, the readiness of Long Islanders to engage in vigilante racial justice and hopefully to profit from it is certainly evident.

Racial violence was also often reported, and many of these stories reflect concern on Long Island for African American liberty and safety in the South. In 1875 alone there were seven different stories of violence by southern whites against blacks that ended in injury and death. Several local stories also fall into this category. An 1870 report reprinted from the *Glen Cove Gazette* notes that "the Town officers of North Hempstead, received the colored men's votes in a separate box 'dressed in mourning.' Eighty one votes were cast, one only straight Democrat. One colored man on his way to vote was assaulted by a gang of half-drunk loafers and badly injured. It is a pity they could not be taught to respect the law and the Constitution by a few years in State Prison." A January 22, 1875, article details the public execution by hanging in front of a crowd of 200 people at the Queens County Courthouse in Hempstead of Jarvis and Jackson (no last names given), African American half-brothers convicted of murdering a white man. Jackson was described as "a full-blooded negro of the soft and sensuous type," while Jarvis was seen as "a less facile subject" who "for a long time expressed a desire to kill his wife." The gory details of their deaths combined with the soft racial profiling of the men make this article among the most disturbing in this analysis.

Finally, humorous stories about African Americans printed for the pleasure of whites were also frequent. These include traditional stories of African American intellectual buffoonery such as the January 7, 1870, story of a "Negro boy in Tallahassee who stole can of [gun] powder, and thinking it contained something good to eat, put it on the stove to warm. He will not eat anything anymore." There is also the September 15, 1865, article describing an African American man at the "menagerie" who discovered a baboon would imitate him but could not speak, leading him to say to the monkey: "You're right; don't open your mouth, kase if you spoke a word the white man have a shovel in your hand in less dan a minit."

Stories reflecting African American humor changed somewhat in the later years of the century. For one, the use of "negro dialect" disappears, as African American humor comes to be described differently. Several articles published in 1885 exhibit this new form as a series of reports from local masquerade balls where, for example, "the characters represented were well sustained; the plumed knight, negro dude, and the old lady with the shockingly bad hat were the most prominent." Another article describes a similar event:

> The plantation song of 'The Lime Kiln Club,' . . . was a little ahead of anything in the minstrel line ever seen in this town, and the audience were fairly convulsed with laughter. The climax came when the bustle dropped from the rear of the dress of the fair African. The address by Julius Collodian, the colored orator, was simply immense, our popular young fellow townsman Douglass Conklin, fairly outdid himself. The plantation song, "Swinging on the Golden Gate," by the same couple, kept the laughter going. In the laughable negro farce "Echo Band" by R.F. Gurney and Geo. Howarth with A.C. Conklin as Ghost, the parts were well taken. As so many were unable to gain admission, the entertainment is to be repeated this evening.

Despite serious debates in local print about African American equality and rights over the previous 20 years, by 1885 the antebellum minstrel show had returned. In this article we see it performed on a stage in Huntington just 20 miles west of Setauket. Moreover, the names of local residents and blackface actors are unabashedly printed along with a notice that the performance was to be repeated due to its popularity.

Another example of blackface minstrelsy brings this story back to Setauket. Stored in the archival records of Red Roof, the first home in Old Field lived in by Frank Melville and his family, is a group photograph from a birthday party that took place at the house in the early 1900s (figure 3.5). Thanks to a list of names written on the back, we know the group included several people in costumes, including members of the Melville family and many of their Old Field neighbors. Three young men in the front row have painted their faces black, two leaving their eyes white, producing the stark contrast common to blackface performance. These three men are Stephen Yates, Arthur M. Quinn, and Edwin H. Thatcher. At the far right of the front row, the young man in the small hat holding his knees is Ward Melville. It is not as easy to determine as the others, but he

Figure 3.5. Masquerade party on the porch of the Melville family home, ca. 1905–1906. Ward Melville is in the front row, far right, wearing a hat. (Courtesy of the Three Village Historical Society, Long Island.)

is also in blackface makeup and was part of the minstrel show they apparently put on at the house. Ward Melville grew up to take over and expand his father's retail and real estate businesses. He was also the founder of the local historical society, a benefactor for several charitable causes, and a direct supporter of Bethel AME Church. The local community has since recognized his prominence by naming the local high school after him. Also important here is that Red Roof stands directly across the street from the Silas Tobias archaeological site, which was occupied by people of color as late as the 1890s. This means that within a decade after the Tobiases left the area, the very same space they had known as their home became the site of blackface performance.

By the later part of the nineteenth century, prominent aspects of racial modernity—a belief in the inherent nature of African American inferiority, a fear of their different and supposedly dangerous tendencies, as well as their suitability for public mockery—was fully ensconced in Long Island. Lacking access to such rich documentary newspaper data from Setauket in particular, I turn next to other sources to round off this analysis of the documentary history of racial and culture change in Setauket in the nineteenth century.

Making a Racially Modern Setauket

The remaining members of the Native and African American communities in Setauket live today exclusively along a half-mile stretch of Christian Avenue, which includes the sites of the historic Laurel Hill Cemetery and Bethel AME Church. I also noted that the survival of this enclave is under a threat by a creeping gentrification. In this section I discuss details of the settlement pattern of people of color in Setauket in the past showing that residential displacement has been a common experience for generations. That they have been confined to one neighborhood and are fighting now to remain is part of a long history of the same struggle for people of color in the region to remain in their homes. The trajectory I describe is one in which racial plurality within larger communities eroded so that mixed households were replaced by mixed communities that ultimately gave way to stricter practices of residential racial segregation that we see in the present. This trajectory reflects one effect of the transition to racial modernity, specifically the way white people in Setauket displaced people of color and decreased the likelihood with each generation that interracial interaction would occur.

To document the segregation of people of color in Setauket and the Town of Brookhaven, I use data from census documents and oral history. The discussion proceeds chronologically, assessing the level of segregation of the community within the Town of Brookhaven as evident in census records between 1776 and 1900.[5] This is followed by a closer look at segregation within Setauket in the twentieth century drawn from oral history. The following discussion examines the distribution of people of color in census records, including the number of households with people of color per page for several early census years (1790, 1800, and 1830). For later censuses (1870 and 1900) other means provided by the census accounts themselves are used to determine geographic location and assess residential racial segregation.

Census Data for the Town of Brookhaven

The starting point of this analysis is the 1776 census of the Town of Brookhaven where 142 "negroes" (6.9% of the population) living among 2,031 whites are recorded (Longwood Central School District 2019). This count documents the highest level of integration in Setauket's documented history, since every person of color was recorded as a resident of a home headed by whites. In this way, the integration for the society the settlers created was essentially 100% for people of color. Such multiracial households reflect the paternalism of slavery and its legacy, which viewed enslaved and free laborers of color incapable of living independent of their white masters (Phillippi 2016). It is likely the 1776 census is a partial count, since it appears to have been a census by subscription. The census did not record Native Americans, even though it is certain Indian people and communities were living in independent households at the time. Native Americans were non-tax-paying residents, so their absence can be explained, yet their exclusion does reveal the thinking of the majority group about who counted as being part of their home community.

Evidence of residential racial segregation first appears in the 1790 Federal Census which recorded 510 people of color, who accounted for 15.7% of the total population of the Town of Brookhaven (US Census, Town of Brookhaven, Suffolk County, New York, 1790), a figure that combines 232 enslaved individuals and 278 "other free persons." The latter group consisted of 48 persons of color living in 13 independent households. This means that almost 10% of people of color lived separately from whites. In both the 1790 and 1800 Federal Censuses, people of color were recorded on all pages for the Town of Brookhaven, suggesting a relatively racially integrated community (US Census, Town of Brookhaven, Suffolk County, New York, 1790, 1800). Additionally, half (49.4%) of the households recorded in 1790 included people of color. This count includes both free and enslaved persons living in white-headed households as well as those living in households of their own. In 1800 only one in four households included people of color, and the number of independent households of color grew to 30. The distribution of households with people of color per census page in 1800 ranged from a minimum of 2.2% (1 household out of 45 on the page) to a maximum 64.4% (29 households out of 45 on the page). Even though people of color are found on every page of the census in 1800, their distribution across the township shows some sections of Brookhaven becoming less racially diverse.

The 1830 census was the first population count taken after the end of slavery in New York in 1827, and by this year residential segregation was even more pronounced. People of color were recorded on only 36 out of 39 pages of the document (US Census, Town of Brookhaven, Suffolk County, New York, 1830). The percentage of households including people of color also dropped to just 17.3%. The distribution of households with people of color per census page in 1830 ranged from a minimum of 0 to a maximum of 59.3% (16 households out of 27 on the page). Changes in residential patterns for people of color are also reflected by the presence of the 13 census pages, one-third of them all, with three or fewer households with people of color. That these were sequential pages suggests a large section of Brookhaven was white by a vast majority. At the same time, people of color were concentrated in fewer sections. Three of four people of color in Brookhaven were recorded on just 13 pages, and these pages record 83% (55 out of 66 households and 244 out of 288 individuals) of the independent households of color in Brookhaven Township. By 1830 it seems clear that formerly enslaved people left their masters' homes but that they were constrained to living in only a handful of neighborhoods in the township that welcomed independent people of color.

By 1870, the first census taken after the Civil War, racial segregation developed further in the Town of Brookhaven as people of color were recorded on just 70 of 262 total pages that year (US Census, Town of Brookhaven, Suffolk County, New York, 1870). This means that nearly three-quarters of all the neighborhoods in the township were entirely white. The 1870 census recorded village names where the data was collected, so it is possible to be confident with the geographic basis of racial segregation. In all, 51 (46.4%) households of color lived in the two north shore villages of Port Jefferson (22 households) and Setauket (29 households). Including 15 other households recorded in neighboring north shore towns (Wading River, Miller Place, Mount Sinai, Fire Place, and Stony Brook) means that 60% of all independent households of color in the township were concentrated on the north shore. Another cluster of 20 (18.5%) households of color were documented in south shore villages of South Haven and Moriches. These districts include people living on the Unkechaug Native American Reservation (Strong 2011) as well as other independent people of color in this immediate area. Together these north and south shore concentrations account for more than three-quarters of the people of color in the Town of Brookhaven, a figure illustrating the racial segregation of people of color into fewer neighborhoods and the fact that the most sections in the middle of the township by 1870 were majority, if not entirely, white.

In 1900 people of color were recorded on just 132 out of the 302 pages of the Town of Brookhaven census that year. This limited distribution across the census pages indicates that well over half of the neighborhoods in Brookhaven were exclusively white (US Census, Town of Brookhaven, Suffolk County, New York, 1900). The 1900 census divided the Town of Brookhaven into 14 enumeration districts (ED), which provide a geographic basis for documenting residential segregation. A majority (53.5%) of all households with people of color are recorded in just four EDs (ED nos. 739, 740, 747, and 748). These districts included the north shore villages of Setauket and Port Jefferson and the south shore villages of South Haven and Moriches. The 115 households with people of color in these enumeration districts accounted for 10% of the overall number of households, both black and white. In the 10 other enumeration districts households with people of color accounted for just 4% of the total. Similarly, 61% (79 of 130) of all independent households of color lived in these four districts, which accounted for 7% of all households in those places. In the 10 other districts, only 2% of all households were headed by people of color. In 1900 the pattern of racial segregation observed in 1870 continued and expanded, as the vast majority of people of color lived in just a few sections on the north and south shores, and the middle section of the township was virtually all white.

The census data from 1790–1900 show a trend of increasing residential segregation in the Town of Brookhaven over the course of the nineteenth century. There are a few reasons for the clustering of people of color. On the south shore the concentration is in part explained by the Unkechaug Native Americans, who lived on and near reserved lands granted to them in 1700 (Strong 2011). People of color were drawn to the north shore by a combination of long-term family residence and opportunities for employment. By 1900 many families of color on the north shore had lived in Setauket and Port Jefferson for a generation or much longer. The Tobiases and Woodhulls, for example, are found in the 1790 and 1800 Federal Censuses, and the Woodhulls, Brewsters, Strongs, and others were descendants of enslaved laborers owned by white families of the same name who lived in Setauket. Port Jefferson and Setauket also had the most developed industries in the Town of Brookhaven in the nineteenth century. Setauket had a piano factory in the 1870s and later a series of rubber factories that employed people of color. Shipbuilding was another vital industry for workers of color in both villages. In addition, there were many white-headed households, farms, and estates that employed people of color as domestics and laborers in and surrounding the village centers.

The 1900 census of Setauket and Port Jefferson shows that people of color held 17 different occupations. One individual was a professional (AME preacher), two were commercial workers (salesman and fish dealer), one was skilled laborer (horse trainer), but the other 84 individuals (95% of the total) held what were considered unskilled occupations, such as day and farm laborers, servants, coachmen, cooks, housekeepers, laundresses, sailors, and teamsters. While these occupations limited the community's socioeconomic advancement, Setauket and Port Jefferson nevertheless provided people of color a greater diversity of occupations and, according to the 1900 Federal Census, a higher likelihood of owning rather than renting a home than any other place in Brookhaven. In sum, in 1900 the opportunities for people of color to live independent lives were much greater in Setauket and Port Jefferson than anywhere else in the Brookhaven Township.

Neighborhoods Displaced in Setauket Since 1900

Even though people of color in Setauket were advantaged as being part of a larger community and having more opportunities for work, they nevertheless faced repeated restrictions over where they could live within the village. The story of the settlement of people of color in Setauket is an example of serial forced displacement (Fullilove and Wallace 2011). It is also one that continues today as the community struggles to remain. Here I discuss three cases of racial displacement in Setauket, all of which were precursors to the community living on Christian Avenue today.

The first instance was the displacement of an enclave of Native and African American families who lived in the Old Field section of Setauket along the west shore of Conscience Bay (figure 3.6). The earliest document referencing any of these households is an 1823 deed between Silas and Abraham Tobias for a half-acre lot with a dwelling house. This site has been located and excavated, and the results of this research are discussed in chapters 4 and 5. That there is not a previous deed to this property suggests Silas Tobias lived there before the deed was executed, and the depiction of a house located roughly where he lived on a township map suggests he may have been living there as early as 1797. In the 1800 census, an individual identified as "Silas, a negro," was the head of an independent household of color (figure 3.7). On the same page are "Abraham, a negro," five other households of color, as well as members of white families such as the Woodhulls, who are known to have lived near the location of the property noted in the 1823 deed. Tobiases are also listed among other families of color in the same area in the 1810 and 1840 censuses (US Census, Town of Brookhaven, Suffolk County, New York, 1810, 1840).

A more detailed record of the Old Field enclave in the 1850 Census shows that it consisted of ten households made up of 47 people of color (US Census, Town of Brookhaven, Suffolk County, New York, 1850). These included the families of Abraham, Silas, and Jacob Tobias. The same families are listed again in the 1860, 1870, and 1880 censuses (US Census, Town of Brookhaven, Suffolk County, New York, 1860, 1870, 1880). After 1870 the households of Adam Brewster as well as his daughter Tabitha and her husband, James Calvin, expanded the number of households of color living in this neighborhood. By 1880 the Old Field cluster

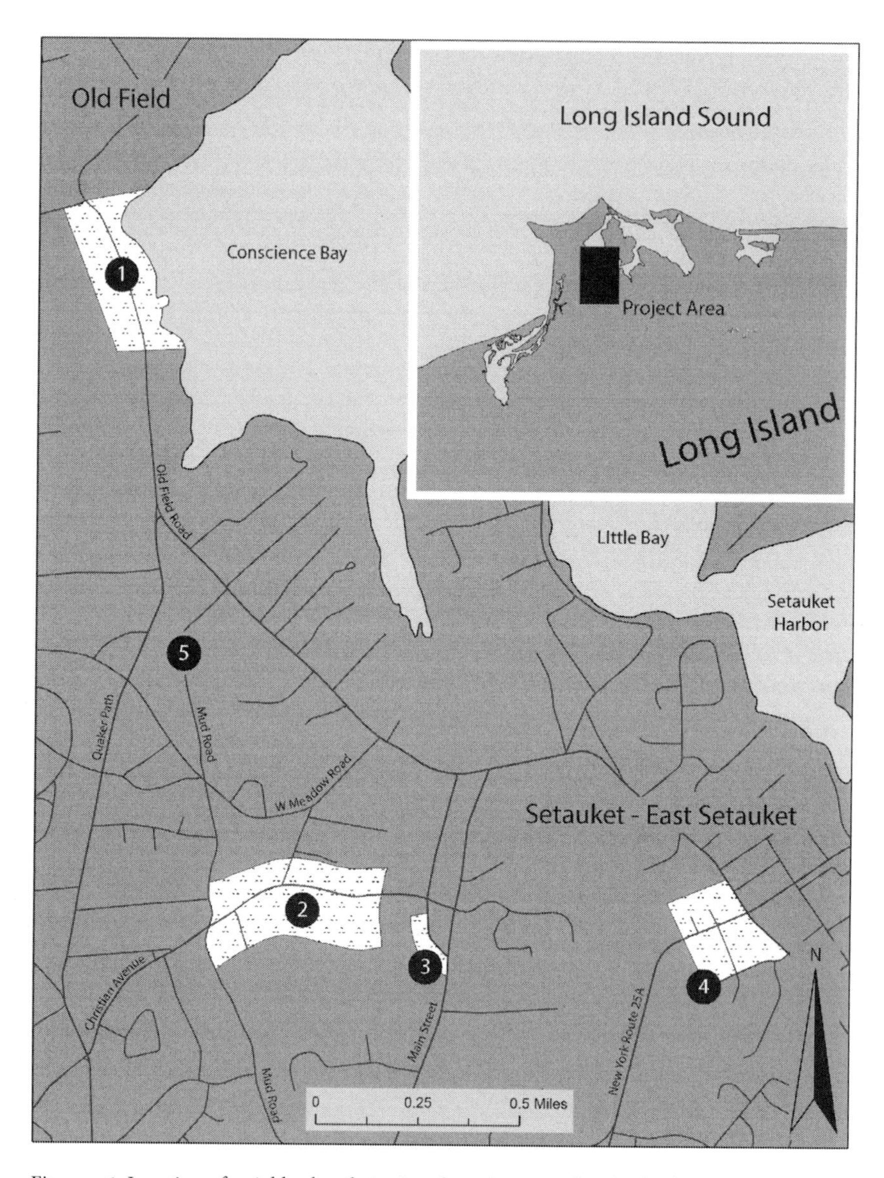

Figure 3.6. Location of neighborhoods in Setauket where people of color lived: 1. Old Field; 2. Christian Avenue; 3. Lake Street; 4. Chicken Hill; 5. Mud Road dead end. None of these is still occupied by people of color except Christian Avenue. (Courtesy of Bradley D. Phillippi.)

consisted of four households, headed by Emeline Tobias, Adam Brewster, James Calvin, and Jerry Sills, and in 1900, 1910, and 1920, the Calvins continued to anchor a small cluster. The enclave was no longer present in 1930 (US Census, Town of Brookhaven, Suffolk County, New York, 1900, 1910, 1920, 1930).

Oral testimony from community elders (interview with Carlton Edwards,

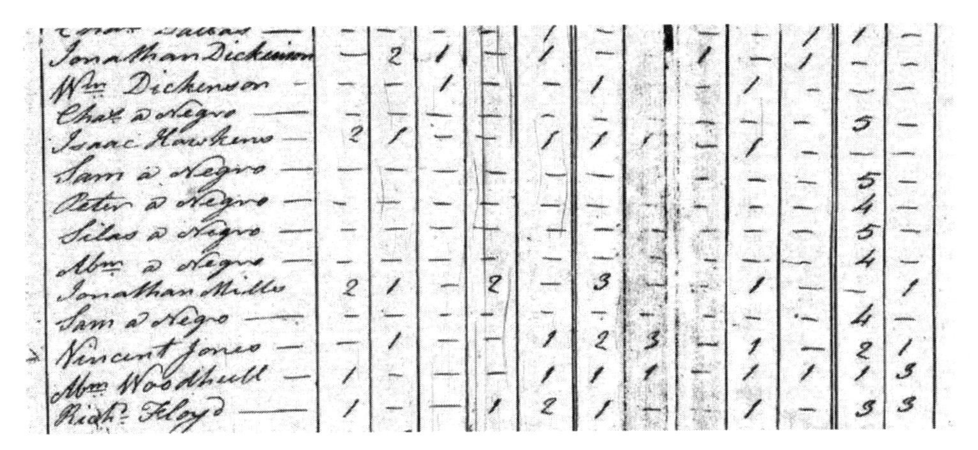

Name												
[illegible]	—	—	—	—	1	—		—	—	1	1	—
Jonathan Dickinson	—	2	1	—	1	—		1	—	1	—	—
Wm Dickenson	—	—	1	—	—	1		—	1	—	—	—
Chas a Negro	—	—	—	—	—	—		—	—	—	5	—
Isaac Hawkins	2	1	—	—	1	1	1	—	1	—	—	—
Sam a Negro	—	—	—	—	—	—		—	—	—	5	—
Peter a Negro	—	—	—	—	—	—		—	—	—	4	—
Silas a Negro	—	—	—	—	—	—	—	—	—	—	5	—
Abm a Negro	—	—	—	—	—	—	—	—	—	—	4	—
Jonathan Mills	2	1	—	2	—	3	—	—	1	—	—	1
Sam a Negro	—	—	—	—	—	—	—	—	—	—	4	—
Vincent Jones	—	1	—	—	1	2	3	—	1	—	2	1
Abm Woodhull	1	—	—	—	1	1	1	—	1	1	1	3
Richd Floyd	1	—	—	1	2	1	—	—	1	—	3	3

Figure 3.7. Detail of page from the 1800 Federal Census for Brookhaven, Suffolk, New York (series M32, roll 27, p. 9, image 132, Family History Library Film 193715).

22 June 2011; interview with Robert Lewis, 23 May 2011; interview with Idamae Glass, 17 June 2011) confirms a small cluster of people of color lived in this area of Old Field in the early 1900s. They recall a house was moved from Old Field to Christian Avenue in Setauket by Tabitha and James Calvin's son Edward G. Calvin around 1930. This happened soon after Old Field Village incorporated as a separate residential section of Setauket in 1927, suggesting white residents of Old Field may have encouraged these families to leave and settle among other people of color on Christian Avenue. At roughly the same time, the Old Field trustees cut off Mud Road, creating a dead end at the village line (figures 2.10 and 3.6). Mud Road formerly provided direct access to Old Field Road, which allowed people of color in Old Field and Setauket to visit each other and attend services together at Bethel AME on Christian Avenue. Cutting off Mud Road at the village line segregated people of color from the new residents of Old Field, which has been entirely white since the 1950s.

A second case of displacing people of color in Setauket is a neighborhood at the south end of Lake Street that was home to a small cluster of households of color during the decades before and after 1900 (figure 3.6). This area includes the former home site of Jacob and Hannah Hart that was excavated in 2011 and 2015 and which is discussed in detail in chapters 4 and 5. An 1873 map shows this area was also home to two households of color headed by W. Harts and A. Tobias. As Jacob Hart's parents were William Hart (b. 1825) and Rachel L. Tobias (b. 1830), it appears he grew up and then chose to live in a house close to other members of his ancestral family. Jacob and Hannah Hart purchased their own lot at the corner of Lake and Main in 1888. They raised 12 children in the home and lived there for the rest of their lives.

After Jacob Hart passed away the home site was abandoned and torn down. While this abandonment created a well-preserved archaeological site, it also begs the question why no one in the family chose to keep the house. Part of the answer lies in a serious environmental concern. Located at the mouth of a spring and adjacent to a creek, the site had access to fresh water, and the family constructed a small well for collecting this spring water. Local memory notes that the creek bed was also a place where children played and where people of color caught frogs, crabs, and turtles and collected useful marsh plants. However, descendants also remember the Harts dealt with groundwater problems. They could supposedly lift a floorboard and see standing water under the house. Another account mentions that Jacob Hart removed the weeds in the mill pond downstream, presumably to create a better flow so that the creek would not back up and flood his property (Green 1999:66). Besides dealing with flooding, the family likely abandoned the house, since by the 1930s the cluster of families of color on Lake Street was gone.

Instead, by 1930, 13 households consisting of 58 people of color lived a half-mile away on Christian Avenue. These included households headed by Lucy Keyes and Minnie Sanford, Jacob and Hannah Hart's youngest daughters (figure 3.7) (US Census, Town of Brookhaven, Suffolk County, New York, 1930). In 1920 this section of Christian Avenue only had five households and 20 individuals of color (US Census, Town of Brookhaven, Suffolk County, New York, 1920). In light of the disappearance of the Old Field and Lake Street enclaves around the same time, the decade of the 1920s can be pinpointed as the time when the contemporary community of color on Christian Avenue coalesced. Its emergence followed the displacement of people of color elsewhere in Setauket, which intensified the segregation of people of color from white households and neighborhoods that had been going on since the early 1800s.

The concentration of nonwhite families on Christian Avenue in the 1920s also correlates with a change in labor practices for women of color in Setauket. In 1930 only 6% of people of color in the Town of Brookhaven were living in the homes of their employers (US Census, Town of Brookhaven, Suffolk County, New York, 1930). This is a substantial decline from 1900, when more than 40% of all women of color were live-in domestics (US Census, Town of Brookhaven, Suffolk County, New York, 1900). The change in residence correlates with a separation of work from home that segregated the community by race, as residences, just like neighborhoods, became increasing constituted by members of a single race. A number of women of color from the Christian Avenue community worked as live-out domestics in the twentieth century. Lucy Keyes was one example. In contrast, Lucy's mother, Hannah Hart, was a laundress worked at her home (US Census, Town of Brookhaven, Suffolk County, New York, 1900). Elders in the black and white communities remember women of color taking in laundry from white families in the community (interview with Carlton Edwards, 12 June 2014; interview with Barbara Russell, 11 July 2013). That white people no longer visited homes of women of color to drop off laundry nor did as many people of color live in their white employers' homes by 1930 shows that blacks and whites occupied increasingly separated spaces within the larger Setauket community.

Postwar development in Setauket also affected people of color when a bypass for Route 25A was opened. The new road led traffic away from the historic village center and promoted the construction of a new commercial strip. The east end of the bypass is where Setauket's former rubber factory operated in the early twentieth century. By the 1950s the factory was long gone, but a small interracial working-class neighborhood adjacent to the former factory site remained. This neighborhood was known as known as Chicken Hill (figure 3.6). The 1930 Census indicates Chicken Hill was home to six households consisting of 19 people of color (US Census, Town of Brookhaven, Suffolk County, New York, 1900). Based on surnames, some families moved to Chicken Hill after being displaced from Old Field. Carlton Edwards (interview, 12 June 2014) remembers that members of his family moved there from Stony Brook after Ward Melville redeveloped the village center there and removed their family's home. Families of color lived in Chicken Hill alongside several working-class immigrant Jewish families, who also formerly worked in the factories. Once the bypass was planned and completed, however, the perception of Chicken Hill shifted from a culturally diverse working-class section to a blighted neighborhood of rental housing that needed to be replaced. Ethel Lewis remembered a rumor that the drinking water in Chicken Hill was contaminated: "They just told them that the water wasn't clean enough, and it would start a disease over there and the whole town would be an epidemic" (Ethyl Mae Lewis, Transcript of oral history interview, 4 May 1987:35, Three Village Historical Society, Setauket, New York). She recalled hearing people saying, "We don't know where to go? Where are we going to go?" and "after that Christian Avenue seemed to be the only part . . . left in Setauket" for people of color (Ethyl Mae Lewis, Transcript of oral history interview, 4 May 1987:36, Three Village Historical Society, Setauket, New York). By 1960 Christian Avenue (figure 3.6) was the only section in Setauket where people of color still lived, and it was at this time that it became known to some as "Nigger Hollow" (interview with E. Cockschutt, 8 July 2013).

Conclusion

This research tracking racial segregation in Brookhaven and Setauket over the last two centuries shows that the displacement of people of color has been an essential part of the way the modern community formed. These data mirror the racial separation exhibited in the other historical sources reviewed in this chapter and together support the broader argument for the emergence and institutionalization of "racial modernity" after the 1840s. From *The Lucky Throw* to newspaper accounts of black crime and local blackface minstrelsy to the removal of people of color from most of the local landscape, we see consistent efforts to privilege white interests and affirm a mainstream sense of the inferiority of people of color. In most cases, these interests are manifest in the privileging of profit over concerns for human rights and a diverse cultural heritage. William Sidney Mount stood to make perhaps the most money of his career by painting genre portraits for the southern market, just as the residents of Old Field could better secure the value of their property if the community was all white. Similarly, racially modern thinking also materialized the white interest in recognizing the inferiority of people of color exhibited in their supposed tendency for violence and crime as well as simple-mindedness. We see this in repeated examples of the way people of color appear in the local press, but we also see it as one of the main ideas behind racial segregation. To identify Christian Avenue as "Nigger Hollow" in the 1960s was to identify the residents as necessarily belonging together and also to mark them as contained. The presence of a person of color, especially one who is out of place like the man from Commack who traveled to Oyster Bay in 1875, was not something that went unnoticed or unpunished.

The diverse data discussed in this chapter also show that essential to understanding Setauket's racial history is the creole synthesis that preceded racial modernity. Perhaps the clearest evidence comes in the convergence of Mount's earlier work, which depicts common interracial experiences at Setauket's "rustic" taverns and farms, with early nineteenth-century censuses that provide objective evidence of multiracial households and neighborhoods in the Town of Brookhaven. Certainly in both cases, people of color—as enslaved and free laborers or musicians and observers—are positioned as marginal and unequal to whites, but they were clearly present and part of the community. From newspapers we also see in this earlier era a much greater interest in the recognition of black humanity, such as in the concerns with the violence perpetrated by slave owners against the enslaved. Unlike in later years, the question "Is the negro without feeling?" was a legitimate concern in the local news in 1827.

From Mount's work especially, we gain a sense not only of the shifting overarching cultural mores but also of a growing nostalgia that comes with the recognition of culture change. This seems most evident in his common depiction of rural life as happy, shown no better than in frequent images of men and women dancing. Dancing offered people a common language in the desire to be content and to celebrate that transcended the boundaries of conventional art and performance of the era. The era of creole synthesis promoted a progressive politics that built on these common sentiments and essential humanity of people of color. To be interested in their welfare, therefore, would be natural, especially if they were suffering under the lash of retrograde southerners. Yet Mount and his peers were well aware of the changing dynamics even in New York, where the deskilling and commodification of labor were ascendant, a shift that was turning middling whites, according to more than a few, into wage slaves. A legitimate progressive reaction at this time would have been to bring out in clear images and words what the threat of wage slavery entailed. What better way to do this than by showing how in the not-so-distant past people of different races and statuses had reveled and frolicked together in common spaces, though arguably following distinct traditions and languages, as they enjoyed "the merriment of blackness" (Scott 2004:84)?

The progressive agenda of "creole synthesis" did not survive. Instead, its source material—African American dance and dialect as well as music written for the stage—became the fodder for blackface minstrelsy, racial modernity's most dangerous and reactionary cultural production. As many have shown, minstrelsy served a clearly racist purpose of soothing the fears of white workers who could be reassured that their society saw in them as something better because they were white. Their reaction, bolstered by all the power that those at the top of society held, reinforced this sense of self at the expense of people of color. We see this in the consistent publication of "Negro dialect" humor in the newspapers and in the racial segregation within small places like Setauket. Of course, we also see it in the continued enjoyment of "black" merriment, though only when performed by whites in blackface and only after the possibility of the cultural transcendence of the creole synthesis faded from possibility.

In the following chapters I apply this understanding of the historical dynamics of race and culture on Long Island to an interpretation of two archaeological sites in Setauket. These up-close studies of households, individuals, and material culture show how people of color in Setauket developed specific ways of life that reflected and challenged the racial sentiments of creole synthesis and racial modernity. These studies allow us to see and track the way people of color in Setauket evaded and resisted the increasingly racist world whites developed in the village.

Notes

1. Genre painting mirrors themes Ralph Waldo Emerson used to describe his writings: "The literature of the poor, the feelings of the child, the philosophy of the street, the meaning of household life, are the topics of the time. It is a great stride. It is a sign . . . of new vigor. . . . I embrace the common, I explore and sit at the feet of the familiar, the low. . . . The meal in the firkin; the milk in the pan; the ballad in the street; the news of the boat; the glance of the eye" (in Scott 2004:107).

2. Another correlation is that during the same era that he produced the genre portraits, blackface minstrelsy itself hardened, a point made by Kevin Scott (2004:163).

3. Thomas Jefferson used the phrase "equal and exact justice" in his first inaugural address in 1801, though he conspicuously avoided suggesting its application to African Americans or across racial lines.

4. The bulk of this reading was completed and compiled by Montclair State University graduate Dante Dallavalle as part of a student-faculty research grant project.

5. More than just a source of population figures, the census can also be a tool for documenting evidence of residential location and segregation. The census was typically collected systematically such that recorders went house to house to collect data. Therefore, it is highly likely that households listed sequentially in the census were neighbors at the time of recording. With this understanding, it is possible to document the distribution of people of color throughout an area based on how dispersed households with nonwhite residents are found to be across the pages of the census for a given year.

4

ARCHAEOLOGICAL HISTORIES OF THE SILAS TOBIAS AND JACOB AND HANNAH HART SITES

One of the most important discoveries of the A Long Time Coming project is a deed to a property in Old Field, New York, a small village adjacent to Setauket (figure 4.1). The deed records the sale of a half-acre parcel with a dwelling house on the west shore of Conscience Bay by Silas Tobias to Abraham Tobias in 1823:

> *To all people* to whom these presents shall come greeting Know ye that I Silas Tobias of the Town of Brookhaven in the County of Suffolk & State of New York for and in consideration of the Sum of Thirty dollars to me in hand paid at and before the Sealing & delivery of these presents by Abraham Tobias of the Town aforesaid have granted Conveyance and confirmed unto the said Abraham Tobias and to his heirs and assigns forever my dwelling house and lot of Land Situated on the west Side of Conscience Bay in the town aforesaid containing by estimation half an acre as the fence now stands. *To have and to hold* the said premises with all the apurtenances there unto belonging unto him the Said Abraham Tobias and to his heirs & assigns forever for his and their own proper benefit and behalf against me my heirs, executors administrators and assigns against the lawful claims and demands of any manner of Person or Persons whatsoever shall and will well and truly *Warrant* and forever by these presents *Defend* the Same In witness whereof I have hereunto set my hand and seal this fifteenth day of September in the year of our Lord one thousand Eight hundred and Twenty Three 1823.
>
> In presence of us Abraham Woodhull Jesse S. Woodhull
>
> Silas Tobias his mark
>
> Liber V, Suffolk County Deeds

We know from other sources that Silas Tobias and Abraham Tobias were people of color. Through this document, we were also able to connect these Tobias men and their families to an amazing archaeological site. This site contains the remains of the home that three generations of Tobiases lived in for most of the nineteenth century as well as thousands of artifacts associated with their everyday lives. In this chapter I compile and explore this and other documents related to the Tobias family and its former home on the shore of Conscience Bay to contextualize the archaeological findings we uncovered.

I also review the documentary record associated with the Jacob and Hannah Hart home site on the corner of Lake and Main Streets in the village center of Setauket. The Harts were also people of color, and the site of their former home was excavated by the A Long Time Coming project in 2011 and 2015. The Hart family moved to this home no later than 1888 and lived there until the 1940s. Living at these sites at different times, the Tobiases from circa 1800 to 1900 and the Harts from circa 1880 to 1940, these families experienced sequential historical eras in Setauket. This chapter establishes an association between the Tobias and Hart families, along with their homes and the overarching themes of the historical moments tied to creole synthesis and racial modernity discussed in chapter 3. This chapter also reviews what we know about the residents and developments at each site from historic documents and archaeological fieldwork that provides a foundation for a more robust interpretation of the excavated materials in chapter 5.

Documenting the Silas Tobias Site and Family

The Silas Tobias site is located on an undeveloped lot between Old Field Road and the west shore of Conscience Bay in Old Field, New York. The lot remains distinct but is now considered a part of a larger property that includes a lot across Old Field Road. The site was identified in research on property deeds on file at the Three Village Historical Society and historical maps as well as in archaeological fieldwork completed in 2015.

Deed History

Because of gaps in the documentary record, the history of who owned and lived at the Silas Tobias site is difficult to nail down. The following considers various source material in detail and offers a proposed ownership sequence for the lot during its occupation by the Tobias family. The deed history of the property indicates the lot was first owned by Silas Tobias, who on September 15, 1823, sold it to Abraham Tobias for $30 (Liber V:104–105, Suffolk County Deeds). This deed indicates the lot was a half-acre in size with a dwelling house and a fenced enclosure. The deed was actually filed May 5, 1835, after Silas Tobias acknowledged the sale on April 30, 1835, and was witnessed by Abraham Woodhull and Jesse S. Woodhull, members of the prominent white Woodhull family who lived nearby. The 1823 deed is the first known for this property, suggesting that Silas Tobias was already living there without having registered a previous deed. It is possible the 1823 deed was registered in an effort to formally establish a claim of ownership of this property. The exact relationship between Silas and Abraham Tobias is not known, though it is suspected that they were either brothers or father and son.

The property history of the lot is undocumented until the 1890s when two new deeds were filed with Suffolk County. In 1893 the lot was sold by the heirs of Abraham Tobias to Edward Ostrom, a white landowner (Liber 404:71, Suffolk County Deeds). In 1894 the "North 34 Square Rods" of the lot were sold by David and Solomon Bristol to the Town of Brookhaven (Liber 411:224, Suffolk County Deeds). Bristol family members were also people of color who lived in Setauket well into the twentieth century. While David Bristol is listed as a resident of Setauket in the 1880 census, it is not known how the family came to own part of the Tobias lot, though it is possible that a member of the Bristol family married a Tobias. In 1895 the heirs of Abraham Tobias also sold the neighboring lot (15-3-2) to John A. Moss (Liber 433:532, Suffolk County Deeds). This is the first known transaction associated with this lot, suggesting either that Lot 15-3-1 was originally larger and subdivided or that the Tobias family acquired the neighboring lot sometime in the mid-1800s, a transaction for which there is no known documentation. The original Tobias lot, 15-3-1, is now part of a property that includes Lot 15-2-11.1 across Old Field Road. Frank Melville merged these lots into a single property in 1900.

The 1823 deed appears to be the earliest document identifying landownership by a person of color in Setauket.[1] As property owners, the Tobiases stood out from their peers, and later I discuss other evidence of the way the Tobias family left their mark in Setauket. For now the task is to establish their association with the archaeological site on this property. An excellent and unique source to be noted is the wealth of historical information about the Tobias family compiled by genealogists Simira Tobias and Vivian Nicholson, both descendants of Silas Tobias. I reference their findings here, and I encourage other researchers to locate their work to help answer other questions about the family (Tobias n.d.).

Historic Maps

Several historic maps also lend details to the story of the Silas Tobias site. The earliest to show the site is the Isaac Hulse Map of 1797 (figure 4.2), which shows a small house between the west shore of Conscience Bay and Old Field Road just south of the intersection with another road that approximates the current route of Mt. Grey Road. This house is in just about the same place as other depictions that help to locate the Silas Tobias site. This early source for the house also correlates closely with the 1800 Federal Census entry for "Silas, a Negro," who has been hypothesized to be the same Silas Tobias mentioned in the 1823 deed (figure 3.7). The site is also depicted on the 1837 US Coastal Survey (figure 4.3). This map of Crane Neck (now Old Field) indicates a house surrounded by a fence, as the lot was described in the 1823 deed, between Conscience Bay and Old Field Road.

The Tobias house is also identified on the 1873 Beers atlas of North Brookhaven, which identifies a house occupied by S. Tobias, presumably referring to Silas Tobias (figure 4.4).[2] Based on the date of the map, the S. Tobias on the Beers atlas is not likely the person referenced in the 1823 deed. The last map that connects the lot with the Tobias family was published in 1896 by Hyde and Company (figure 4.4). Like the Beers map, it shows a house occupied by S. Tobias in roughly the same location as the known site. The date of the Hyde map coincides with the dates of deeds documenting the transfer of the Tobias property from the heirs of Abraham Tobias to people outside of the family. Maps of the area published after 1900 do not show any structures on the site where the Tobias house stood, suggesting that the house was removed after the Tobias family sold the lot.

Tobias Family History

Federal and state census records provide additional information about the likely residents of the Silas Tobias site in the nineteenth century. The earliest census record of Silas Tobias is the 1800 federal census, which listed "Silas, a negro," as the head of an independent household of five individuals (figure 3.7). Listed on the same census page are "Abraham, a negro" (head of a four-person household) as well as five other households of color. Based on this record, it is reasonable to think Silas and Abraham Tobias were brothers representing members of the first generation of the family to be documented in Setauket.

Tobiases are listed among other families of color in the Old Field area in the 1810 (Charles Tobias) and 1840 Federal Censuses (Abram, Jacob, and David Tobias) (US Census, Town of Brookhaven, Suffolk County, New York, 1810, 1840). The more detailed 1850 Federal Census lists the families of Abraham, Silas, and

Jacob Tobias. Based on those listed as neighbors, these households most likely lived at or near the Tobias site in Old Field that year (US Census, Town of Brookhaven, Suffolk County, New York, 1850). Many of the same families were also found in close proximity to each other in the subsequent 1860, 1870, and 1880 censuses (US Census, Town of Brookhaven, Suffolk County, New York, 1860, 1870, 1880) as well as the 1865 New York State Census (Census of the State of New York, 1865). The 1880 census, for example, shows a cluster of people of color in Old Field consisting of four households, headed by Emeline Tobias, Adam Brewster, James Calvin, and Jerry Sills (US Census, Town of Brookhaven, Suffolk County, New York, 1880).

Census data specific to the household of Silas and Emeline Tobias in Setauket is reproduced in table 4.1. These people are the later residents of the Silas Tobias site. The census data presented shows the remarkable subjectivity and mutability of racial designations during this era. Silas Tobias was identified as black in 1850, 1860, and 1865, but he was recorded as white in 1870. Emeline Tobias was recorded as mulatto in 1850 and 1865, black in 1860 and 1880, and white in 1870. Their son Benjamin was identified as mulatto in 1850, while his siblings were identified as black. Benjamin was then identified as black in 1860, as were all his siblings. Silas and Emeline's daughter Emma Tobias was identified as white in 1870 and mulatto in 1880. These variable designations likely mean that at least some members of the Tobias family had relatively light skin color, perhaps as a result of their mixed heritage of African, European, and Native American ancestry.

The census also indicates Silas Tobias was a farm laborer or farmer. In both 1860 and 1870 he owned $300 worth of real estate, likely referring to the site under study in Old Field, which the family may have worked as a small farm. The census also documents that Silas and Emeline had five children: Charity A. (b. ca. 1842), Lucretia (b. ca. 1845), Benjamin (b. ca. 1848), Abraham (b. ca. 1853), and Jane/Emma J. (b. ca. 1858). Silas Tobias's absence from census records after 1870 suggests that he died during that decade. Simira Tobias notes that Silas Tobias died in 1874 at 60 years of age (Barber 1950). Assuming the census documentation that Silas Tobias was 30 years old in 1850 is correct, his age at death in 1874 was indeed close to 60 years. This would then mean that he was born around 1814, not likely old enough to be the man selling the property referenced in the 1823 deed.

Based on this indirect evidence, I suggest the 1823 deed was between a different Silas Tobias, who belonged to an earlier generation than the Silas Tobias documented in the 1850–1870 censuses. As such, the 1823 deed references the transfer of the property from this older Silas Tobias (I) to a new owner and head of household, Abraham Tobias. The theory then is that the Abraham Tobias ref-

Table 4.1. Occupants of the Silas Tobias Site between 1850 and 1880

1850 Federal Census	Age	Sex	Race	Occupation	Value of Real Estate
Silas Tobias	30	M	B	Laborer	N/R
Emeline Tobias	28	F	M		
Charity A. Tobias	8	F	B		
Lucretia Tobias	5	F	B		
Benjamin S. Tobias	2	M	M		
1860 Federal Census	**Age**	**Sex**	**Race**	**Occupation**	**Value of Real Estate**
Silas Tobias	40	M	B	Farm Laborer	$300
Emeline Tobias	40	F	B	Washerwoman	
Benjamin Tobias	12	M	B		
Abraham Tobias	7	M	B		
Jane Tobias	2	F	B		
1865 New York State Census	**Age**	**Sex**	**Race**	**Occupation**	**Value of Real Estate**
Silas Tobias	47	M	B	Farmer	N/R
Emeline Tobias	47	F	M		
1870 Federal Census	**Age**	**Sex**	**Race**	**Occupation**	**Value of Real Estate**
Silas Tobias	45	M	W	N/R	$300
Emeline Tobias	44	F	W		
Emma J. Tobias	12	F	W		
1880 Federal Census	**Age**	**Sex**	**Race**	**Occupation**	**Value of Real Estate**
Emeline Tobias	60	F	B	Keeping House	N/R
Emma Tobias	20	F	M	Laborer	

Note: N/R = not recorded.

erenced in the 1823 deed was the father of the younger Silas Tobias (II) recorded later in the nineteenth-century censuses and the son of the older Silas Tobias (I) who sold him the property. As mentioned, in the 1800 federal census there is a record of an "Abraham, a Negro," the head of a household of four people. Abraham Tobias appears again in the 1840 census as the head of a six-person household. This family consisted of an adult male 36–55 years old (most likely Abraham Tobias), an adult female 36–55 years old (probably Ellen, his spouse), a young man 10–24 years old, a girl less than 10 years old, and two boys less than 10 years old. It is likely the younger Silas Tobias (II) mentioned above was the oldest child in this record, a young man about 20 years old.

The 1850 federal census recorded two individuals named Abraham Tobias as heads of households that year. A young Silas Tobias was also listed as a laborer living in the home of Richard L. Woodhull (table 4.2). It is likely the 50-year-old Abraham Tobias in 1850 is the same man recorded in 1840. It is also likely that he was head of household at the Silas Tobias archaeological site in from the 1820s to the 1850s and that he was the father of the younger Silas Tobias (II) recorded as the head of household there in later decades. These data suggest that the Abraham Tobias documented in the 1840 and 1850 censuses passed away in the 1850s, and at that point Silas and Emeline Tobias took over the household at the archaeological site under study. This helps to explain why the household was identified belonging to "S. Tobias" on the 1873 and 1896 maps. Additional support for this claim is that a Silas Tobias living in Old Field was assessed a tax by the Town of Brookhaven in 1862. Based on these data, I have listed the likely residents and dates of occupation of the Silas Tobias site in Old Field in table 4.3.

The 23-year-old Abraham Tobias listed as a head of household in 1850 and the 13-year-old Silas Tobias living in the Woodhull home are likely nephews of the 50-year-old Abraham Tobias who lived at the site under study. This conclusion correlates with data from the 1840 census that shows Tobias households headed by Jacob Tobias (consisting of 11 individuals, including four boys under 10 years old) and David Tobias (consisting of six individuals, one boy under 10 years old). Households headed by David Tobias and Jacob Tobias are documented in detail in the 1850 and 1860 federal censuses (tables 4.4 and 4.5). These data notably suggest these two men had very different life experiences since in 1860 members of David Tobias's family were living and working in several dif-

Table 4.2. The 1850 Census Records for Select Tobias Households and Individuals

1850 Federal Census	Age	Sex	Race	Occupation
Abraham Tobias	50	M	B	Laborer
Ellen Tobias	35	F	B	
Alma Tobias	11	F	B	
Abraham Tobias	23	M	B	Laborer
Laura S. Tobias	19	F	M	
Abraham L. Tobias	10 mo	M	M	
Silas Tobias	13	M	B	Laborer in Richard L. Woodhull household

Table 4.3. Likely Occupants of the Silas Tobias Site, 1790–1890

Dates	Head of Household	Other Occupants	Relationship
Ca. 1790–1823	Silas Tobias (I)	Unknown	n/a
1823–1850s	Abraham Tobias	Ellen (spouse), Silas, Alma, 2 other boys (children)	Brother or son of Silas Tobias (I)
1850s–1874	Silas Tobias (II)	Emeline (spouse), Charity, Lucretia, Benjamin, Abraham, Emma (children)	Oldest son of Abraham Tobias
1874–1890s?	Emeline Tobias	Emma J. Tobias (child)	Spouse of Silas Tobias (II)

Table 4.4. Census Data for Households Headed by David Tobias

1850 Federal Census	Age	Sex	Race	Occupation	Value of Real Estate
David Tobias	39	M	B	Laborer	$500
Lucretia Tobias	37	F	M		
Jacob Tobias	15	M	M	Farmer	
Abigail Tobias	13	F	M		
Emma Tobias	2	F	M		

1860 Federal Census	Head of Household/Race	Age	Sex	Race	Occupation
David Tobias	Amelia M. Strong/W	50	M	B	Servant
Lucretia Tobias	Stephen S. Roe/W	24	F	B	Servant
Jacob Tobias	Jeffrey Smith/B	24	M	M	Boatman
Abby Tobias	Amelia M Strong/W	20	F	B	Servant
Emma Tobias	Jeffry Smith/B	12	F	M	

ferent households, while Jacob Tobias's family maintained its independence and the value of its real and personal estate.

Several other people of color with the Tobias surname are recorded in nineteenth-century censuses for Setauket, but there is not sufficient evidence these individuals resided at the site under study. Even so, knowing more about them helps give us a clearer picture of the larger network of the Tobias family. Two sets of documents in particular are quite important. The first are the deed and agreement filed in 1848 regarding the property for the Bethel AME Church in

Table 4.5. Census Data for Households Headed by Jacob Tobias

1850 Federal Census	Age	Sex	Race	Occupation	Value of Real Estate
Jacob Tobias	43	M	B	Farmer	$400
Rachael Tobias	41	F	B		
David Tobias	16	M	B	Farmer	
Samuel Tobias	15	M	B	Farmer	
Silas Tobias	11	M	B		
Abraham Tobias	8	M	B		
Isaac Tobias	3	M	B		
Charles Tobias	22	M	B	Farmer	
Hannah Tobias	20	F	B		
Charles R. Tobias	1 mo.	M	B		
Alice Smith	43	F	B		
Eunice Tobias	58	F	B		
1860 Federal Census	**Age**	**Sex**	**Race**	**Occupation**	**Value of Real Estate**
Jacob Tobias	60	M	B	Waiter	$330
Rachel Tobias	50	F	B		
Samuel Tobias	24	M	B	Boatman	$250 (personal estate)
Silas Tobias	21	M	B	Boatman	
Abram Tobias	20	M	B	Farm Laborer	
Isaac Tobias	14	M	B	Farm Laborer	
1860 Federal Census	**Age**	**Sex**	**Race**	**Occupation**	**Value of Real Estate**
Eunice Smith	75	F	B		
Hannah Tobias	27	F	B		
Charles Tobias	8	M	B		
Henry Tobias	7	M	B		
Julia Tobias	1	F	B		
Walter Tobias	7	M	B		
Linda J. Tobias	9	F	B		
Charles Tobias	28	M	B		

Stony Brook. This lot is now at the corner of Christian Avenue and Woodfield Road, the site of the Old Bethel Cemetery mentioned in chapter 2 (see figure 2.6). These documents show that Abraham Tobias, David Tobias, and Jacob Tobias were founding trustees of the African Methodist Episcopal Society of Setauket and Stony Brook. Based on the genealogical and census data, the Abraham Tobias mentioned in these documents is thought to be the head of household at the Silas Tobias archaeological site when these documents were signed.

As founding trustees of the AME church, the Tobias men would have been a prominent in Setauket's Native and African American community. It is worth noting that the creation of an AME society and its capacity to raise the funds to purchase land for a house of worship and a cemetery reflects the strength and organization of the church association. Of course, this also reflects a certain disaffection among the community members for attending church with their white neighbors. Several early nineteenth-century church records of marriages, baptisms, and burials show that people of color did attend white-headed churches in Setauket before 1848.[3] Arguably, the decision to establish a new church solely for people of color may reflect an increase in the overarching racial tensions that came with the developing racial modernity after the 1840s in Setauket.

A second set of nineteenth-century material documenting the Tobias family is military service records from the Civil War. One family member who served was Charles Tobias. He was born in Setauket around 1828 as a son of Jacob and Rachel Tobias. He registered for the Civil War draft in June 1863, noting that he was 35 years old and worked as a waterman. He was assigned to the 3rd US Colored Infantry and in 1864 was admitted to the Colored Ward at the US General Hospital in Beaufort, South Carolina (National Archives and Records Administration 2010). After eight months in the hospital, he returned home, where he was counted in the 1865 New York State census of Brookhaven (New York State Archives 1865). Charles Tobias appears again as a resident of Setauket in 1870 and then Port Jefferson in 1880 (US Census, Town of Brookhaven, Suffolk County, New York, 1870, 1880). A second family member to serve was Abraham Tobias, Charles's younger brother. Abraham Tobias also registered for the draft in June 1863, identifying himself as a 24-year-old laborer. He was assigned to the 26th Colored Regiment in January 1864. His enlistment papers state that he received a $300 bounty from the Town of Oyster Bay, perhaps a public incentive. These funds may also reflect a recognition of certain skills or abilities, since he was promoted to corporal after serving less than two months on February 29, 1864 (National Archives and Records Administration 2010). Like his brother, he returned to Setauket by the time of the 1865 census (New York State Archives 1865). In 1870 he was a laborer in the household of Benjamin Jones, and in 1880 he is the head of his own household along with his wife, Tamer (US Census, Town of Brookhaven, Suffolk County, New York, 1870, 1880).

In sum, this survey of historic documents shows that members of the Tobias family lived in Setauket as early as 1797 with perhaps one family, if not the original branch in Setauket, living on the west shore of Conscience Bay in the home headed by Silas Tobias (I). Over the course of three generations, the family grew in size and prominence. The first generation most likely consisted of Silas, Abraham, and Charles Tobias, all listed as heads of independent households in the 1800 census. In the second generation, born just after 1800, Abraham, Jacob, and David Tobias were three of the four original trustees of the AME church. Jacob and David were also the only people of color with sufficient property to vote 1865. Jacob's sons, Charles and Abraham Tobias, served and survived campaigns in the Colored Regiments during the Civil War. Both veterans returned and remained in Setauket or close by for the rest of their lives. Similarly, their older cousin Silas Tobias (II), after taking over the ancestral property on Conscience Bay, maintained that home for the rest of his life. The property passed in 1874 to his wife, Emeline, who lived there with her daughter Emma in 1880 and probably into the 1890s.

From the deed history we know the family sold the lot in the 1890s. Not listed in the deeds, Silas and Emeline's daughter Emma may have married and moved elsewhere by that time. A widow in the 1900 census named Emma J. Seaman was born at roughly the same time (1860) as Emma J. Tobias (US Census, Town of Brookhaven, Suffolk County, New York, 1900). These are likely the same person, suggesting that Emma indeed married and moved away from the site. Records from 1910 and 1920, however, suggest she may have lived close by (US Census, Town of Brookhaven, Suffolk County, New York, 1910, 1920). In 1910 she lived on West Meadow Road, and in 1920 she is listed as living in Old Field, locations that situate her as a member of the Old Field cluster that lasted until about 1930. These sources suggest she most likely lived at most only a half-mile away from where she was born.

After 1900 the Tobias name recedes from local records. In 1900 Hannah Tobias, daughter of Civil War veteran Charles Tobias, was head of a household in Port Jefferson consisting of herself, two daughters (Emma and Julia) and a son-in-law (US Census, Town of Brookhaven, Suffolk County, New York, 1900). In 1910 Hannah's daughter Julia Tobias was the only Tobias in local censuses. She was a live-in domestic servant working for a single white woman in Port Jefferson (US Census, Town of Brookhaven, Suffolk County, New York, 1910). Hannah had the same job but with a different employer in 1920 (US Census, Town of Brookhaven, Suffolk County, New York, 1920). In 1920 Hannah Tobias's brother Henry and his wife, Anna, were servants in a white household in 1920. Finally, Hannah and Henry's brother, Charles Tobias, was a 68-year-old widower living in Port Jefferson's "Colored Town," though in 1930 he is listed as living in the Suffolk County Almshouse (US Census, Town of Brookhaven, Suffolk County, New York, 1930). Seventy-nine-year-old Henry Tobias was the last Tobias to remain in Port Jefferson. He is listed there again in 1940, by then an 89-year-old man (US Census, Town of Brookhaven, Suffolk County, New York, 1940). It does not appear that Henry, Julia, or Charles had children, so the Tobias line in and near Setauket seems to end with them.

While it is certain that some Tobias family members remained and in fact may still live in the area, the name disappeared due to marriage and people moving away. Some Tobiases moved to New York City, where job prospects for people of color were better around the turn of the twentieth century. We also see in the last generation of Tobiases a social decline that likely reflects the influence of racial modernity on their lives. Whereas their ancestors owned land, worked as farmers and in other positions, and served as leaders in their community, Tobiases living after 1900 had fewer opportunities to acquire these resources and positions. Most did not own land, and while Henry Tobias eventually owned a home, it was located in what the census identified as the presumably low-status "Colored Town" in Port Jefferson. Lacking the solid capital base and working unskilled jobs, it is possible that the last generation of Tobiases in the Setauket area chose not to have children because they feared not being able to provide for them. That Charles Tobias, the son of a Civil War veteran and grandson of a founding trustee of the AME, ended up in the almshouse clearly illustrates the downturn in the family's trajectory.

We can document another cause of their difficultly by looking at what happened at the Silas Tobias site after the Tobias family moved away. For a few years the property was owned by Edward Ostrom, though he did not appear to do anything with it. In 1900 Ostrom sold the Tobias lot to Frank Melville, Ward Melville's father and the founder of the Melville Shoe Company and the Melville Corporation, a conglomerate of retail chain stores. The Melvilles came to Stony Brook for vacations for many years before purchasing the property on Old Field Road. Notably, when Melville purchased the former Tobias lot, he attached it to the larger lot across Old Field Road, where he lived in a home known as Red Roof, originally built in the 1860s. Melville moved that house up slope and expanded it to a six-bedroom mansion (*Newsday*, 5 July 2012). One of the great assets of Red Roof is its two-story porch that provides a beautiful view of Conscience Bay. Of course, from the porch, the Melvilles would have seen the old Tobias home across the street, if it was still standing after they purchased the lot. One has to wonder if the Melvilles purchased the former Tobias lot so they could not only tear down the Tobias house but also ensure that no one could build something there that would impede their waterfront view. The privileges of wealth are evident here in the way that a century of life on one property was eliminated from the surface so that others could see past it to enjoy the view. Fortunately, the displacement of the Tobias family from the site did not damage the underlying archaeological deposits.

Archaeology at the Silas Tobias Site

The Silas Tobias archaeological site consists of two sections. There is a low-elevation coastal section on the east side of the site that the current property owner noted was commonly flooded by waters from Conscience Bay. There is also a higher-elevation terrace on the western part of the lot that rises steeply from 3 to about 20 ft above the low-lying coastal section. Fieldwork at the site involved two phases of study. A initial shovel test survey of the entire upland section of lot assessed the potential of the site for further more intensive study. The lower coastal section of the property was not tested because of wet soils on the surface and the unlikelihood of a historic occupation of ground just a few inches above the water level. In a second phase of fieldwork, further testing involved the excavation of 11 one-meter units in an area of high artifact concentration identified in the shovel test survey (figure 4.5). The following discussion provides a detailed review of these phases of field research.

Initial Survey

The first phase of field research at the Silas Tobias site was a shovel test survey of the property to identify the presence of undisturbed archaeological deposits and to assess the distribution of materials across the site.[4] Thirty-four shovel test pits (STPs) were excavated in this phase of work yielding 3,259 artifacts. STPs with the highest concentration of artifacts were located toward northern end of the site. Artifacts included an abundance of shell and other food remains, nineteenth-century domestic and architectural artifacts, and a handful of larger artifacts suggesting a primary historic deposit in one area. The survey also identified a secondary scatter of artifacts, many of which were precontact quartz lithics in the area closest to the highest elevation at the site. This finding suggests an occasional use of the site by Native Americans before the colonial settlement. The dense concentration of artifacts in the northern section of survey warranted further excavation and study. This work was completed with the assistance of Montclair State University students and local volunteers over the summer in 2015.

Unit Excavations

The second phase of fieldwork involved the excavation of 11 test units (see figure 4.6). Unit excavations were designed 1) to determine if the STP survey results were accurate and 2) to establish the stratigraphic sequence of the site both to determine whether the historic artifacts recovered came from undisturbed contexts and to understand how the site formed over time.[5] All units at the Silas Tobias site produced a large quantity of historic artifacts, and none exhibited any evidence of significant historic disturbance at the site other than by roots and rodents. The results therefore were quite positive and exciting for the possibility of learning more about the Tobias family members who lived at the site in the 1800s.

The Tobias site has a basic subsurface structure with some exceptions related to architectural features unearthed at the site (figure 4.7). The stratigraphy consists of three layers. The uppermost is the ground surface, representing a topsoil accumulation during the twentieth century. That this layer is relatively thin indicates a sparse level of activity on the site since the house was removed. Below the topsoil there is a buried historic deposit associated with the Tobias household. This layer is dark in color and loamy in texture, reflecting the impact of human and other organic activity. The layer is clearest on the east side of the excavated area, which was formerly the backyard of the house lot. The bottommost layer is sterile subsoil consisting of a yellow sand.

Excavation also exposed features and deposits associated with remains of the house structure. A series of stone and brick concentrations that represent the back wall of the house ran across the site north to south. The ephemeral nature of these features suggests this part of the house stood on piers rather than a full foundation. In the northwest part of the excavated area a dense concentration of larger stone and brick are the remains of the chimney. Brick debris found on the surface north of this concentration is thought to be the fallen chimney. Finally, in an area that would have been under the central section of the house, we unearthed a set of large artifacts, including two broken ceramic vessels and two barrel rings (one crushed). It is not known if this feature was a subfloor storage area or perhaps larger objects disposed of below the upraised house. Figure 4.8 provides a plan view of the Silas Tobias site showing the unit locations and a projection of the house footprint.

In all, 10,655 artifacts were collected as well as 58,607 grams of shells. Table 4.6 shows how these materials were distributed among the different excavation units (EUs). The uneven distribution of artifacts prompted analysis of the materials to be separated into three groups, each reflecting different activity spaces at the site. Group 1, consisting of EU4 and EU7, represents an area of the site formerly under the Tobias house. These adjacent units contained no architectural features and many fewer artifacts and shells than the other units. Group 2 consists of EU3, EU6, EU10, and EU11 and includes exposed remnants of architectural features from the Tobias house. These units are distinguished by a comparatively low number of artifacts and shells, though there are slightly more shells in Group 2 than in Group 1. Units in Group 3, EU1, EU2, EU5, EU8, and EU9, represent the area behind the Tobias house. These units are distinguished by a layer of dark organic soil containing a high density of shells and historic artifacts and no architectural features. Group 3 can be broken into two subgroups. Group 3A consists of EU2 and EU8, which have lower artifact and shell counts than the units in Group 3B. These results reflect that these Group 3A units are in an intermediate position between the units in Groups 1 and 2 and the much denser concentrations found further to the east. Group 3B consists of EU1, EU5, and EU9, which have the highest number of artifacts and shells at the site. These units are the furthest east of the excavated sections of the site. Historic deposits from Group 3B represent a concentrated area used for the disposal of household refuse and debris including food remains (shells and bone) and material culture by the Tobias household.

Table 4.6. Distribution of Artifacts and Shells by Excavation Unit at the Silas Tobias Site

Excavation Unit	Total Artifacts	Percentage of Total Artifacts	Shell Weight (g)	Percentage of Total Shells
EU1	1,474	13.8%	13,666	23.3%
EU2	747	7.0%	1,046	1.8%
EU3	1,400	13.1%	519	0.9%
EU4	747	7.0%	1	0.0%
EU5	1,664	15.6%	36,126	61.6%
EU6	565	5.3%	42	0.1%
EU7	617	5.8%	84	0.1%
EU8	902	8.5%	497	0.8%
EU9	1,936	18.2%	6,511	11.1%
EU10	357	3.3%	3	0.0%
EU11	256	2.4%	111	0.2%
Total	10,665		58,607	

Dating the Tobias Site Deposits

Documentary sources suggest that there was a house standing at the Tobias site in 1823 (and perhaps as early as 1797) and that this house was torn down around 1900. To add more detail to this chronology, we can also look at the dates of manufacture of the artifacts recovered. Analysis of ceramics from the site identified 678 diagnostic sherds, most of which derive from ceramic types common at nineteenth-century sites (Meta Janowitz, Historic Ceramics from the Silas Tobias Site and the Jacob and Hannah Hart Home Site, Setauket, New York, 2018, Department of Anthropology, Montclair State University). Ceramic types recovered include British Buff-bodied Slipware, Creamware, Pearlware, Castleford, Chinese Export Porcelain, Salt-glazed Brown-bodied Stoneware, Gray-bodied stoneware, Slip-glazed stoneware, Bone China, Whiteware, Ironstone, Yellowware, Rockingham, White Granite, and Hotel Ware. Of these, the majority of diagnostic ceramics were Creamware (1762–1825), Pearlware (1775–1840) Pearlware/Whiteware (1775–1900), Whiteware (1815–1900), and White Granite (1840–1900). The mean ceramic date for the entire collection is 1839.65, which is close to the mean date of occupation derived from the documentary record of 1845–50. As a result, the ceramic data align with the documentary data and suggest the Silas Tobias site was occupied over the course of the nineteenth century. Chapter 5 provides further discussion of the recovered materials from the Silas Tobias site.

Documenting the Jacob and Hannah Hart Site and Family

There is a possible family connection between the Tobiases in Old Field and the Harts who lived on the corner of Lake and Main Streets in Setauket. Jacob Hart was born in Setauket in the 1850s.[6] His parents were William H. Hart and Rachel Lucretia Hart. According to the Hart family tree, Rachel Lucretia Hart was born Rachel L. Tobias around 1830. From the census we know that an 18-year-old woman named Lucretia Tobias was living as a servant in Stephen S. Roe's household in the nearby village of Patchogue in 1850. This woman was still working for Roe in 1860. While she is listed then as 24 years of age, these records overlap enough to suggest these are the same Lucretia Tobias as the one listed in the Hart family genealogy. By 1865 Lucretia Tobias appears to have married William H. Hart, who was born in New York City between 1820 and 1825, since she is listed in the New York State census that year as Rachel L. Hart, the mother of Jacob Hart and other children (New York State Archives 1865).

We do not know the ancestry of Rachel L. Tobias, so her connection to the

Tobiases who lived at the Old Field site is hard to determine. However, the Hart family tree suggests that her brothers were Charles Tobias, born in 1827, and Abraham Tobias, born in 1833.[7] There are census records for men of these names born approximately in these years. A 23-year-old Abraham Tobias was the head of his household in 1850, and 22-year-old Charles Tobias was living in Jacob Tobias's household in 1850. This is same Charles Tobias who served in the Civil War. If Rachel L. Tobias was Charles's and Abraham's and sister, she would have been a daughter of Jacob and Rachel Tobias. She is not listed in this household in 1850, since by then she was already working the Roe household; however, there is a listing of a young woman between 10 and 24 years old in the Jacob Tobias household in 1840 that may refer to her. If this genealogy is accurate, then Rachel L. Tobias most likely did not live at the Silas Tobias site in Old Field. Nevertheless, she represents a bridge between the two families whose homes have been excavated by A Long Time Coming. I turn next to review the primary documents and archaeological fieldwork associated with the Jacob and Hannah Hart site to give a better picture of what we know about that site and its occupants.

Deed History

The Jacob and Hannah Hart site is located on the southwest corner of the intersection of Lake and Main Streets in Setauket. The home was part of a small cluster of households of color along Lake Street in the late nineteenth century discussed in chapter 2. The lot is recorded by the Town of Brookhaven as 109-6-1-A, a subsection of a larger lot owned since 1965 by the Three Village School District. The chain of title for this subsection indicates Jacob and Hannah Hart (under Hannah's name alone) purchased the lot in 1888 from Elliot and Lizzie Smith of Islip, New York, for $225 (Liber 412:234–235, Suffolk County Deeds). The property consisted of two parcels amounting to about one-quarter acre in size. While the deed notes that the parcel was sold "with the building and improvements thereon," it does not describe these in any detail. We can surmise then that the home the Harts lived in was built before they moved to the site.

There is no record of how and when the Smiths acquired the lot, but it was owned by several others in earlier years reaching back to 1829. It is not clear whether the Harts' specific lot was part of a larger parcel in earlier years. The best guess is that the lot was created in 1851, when a one-quarter-acre parcel was subdivided and sold to Joseph N. Howell (Liber 58:286, Suffolk County Deeds). The lot then passed to Mary Howell in 1854 (Liber 92:612, Suffolk County Deeds). It may be that Mary Howell later deeded the lot to the Smiths, though there is no known record. This story is complicated further by the 1870 census, which suggests Mary Howell was then living in Old Field with her husband, Stephen (coincidentally across the street from the Silas Tobias site). This, along with the fact that the Smiths lived in Islip at the time they sold the lot to the Harts, suggests the property was probably rented to tenants or used by extended family. The Y. Howell identified as the occupant of the home on the 1873 Beers atlas may have been such a tenant or a relative. This opens up the possibility that the Harts were also tenants before purchasing the property, a consideration that may have ramifications for interpreting their tenure at the site. For now, according to the property history, we can say only that they were living there as of 1888.

The subsequent deed to the property was filed in 1948 after both Hannah and Jacob Hart passed away and after the last known resident, their son Ernest Hart, moved out. This deed between Anna Hart and heirs and Mt. Gray Realty released any claim to the property the Hart family might still have. As the lot was purchased by a real estate company, it is likely that the plan was to develop the lot, though this did not happen. Rather, the lot was sold along with several other undeveloped parcels to another developer, Stony Brook Estates, in 1955. Stony Brook Estates then sold the property in 1965 to the Three Village School District, which used the bulk of the property for a new junior high school. The subsection of property that was the Harts' home site was forgotten about until A Long Time Coming proposed an excavation on the site in 2010.

Historic Maps and Photographs

Several historic maps help to document the Jacob and Hannah Hart site through time. The earliest map showing the area in detail is the 1858 "Map of Suffolk County, L.I., N.Y. from Actual Surveys by J. Chace." This map shows that Lake Street on the west side of the mill pond did not extend south of Christian Avenue; however, comparing the Chace map with the 1873 Beers atlas (figure 4.9) presents the possibility that a house stood on the Harts' lot by 1858 since there is a series of homes along Main Street on both maps. The 1873 Beers atlas shows a house identified as the home of Y. Howell at the corner of Lake and Main Streets that matches up with known location of the Hart site. The house immediately to the south is identified as the home of the Nevens family, which coincides with the 1909 Belcher Hyde map's depiction of the site (figure 4.9). On the 1873 map, the house is represented as one room deep and two rooms wide with an ell off the back. This layout mirrors what we see in a historic photograph, so this is likely the home the family moved into in later years.

The 1909 E. Belcher Hyde atlas identifies the site as the home of J. Hart, confirming the family lived there at the time. This map does not provide any detail regarding the shape of the structure. Like all other houses on this map, the house is represented by a small rectangle. The house appears again in the next edition of the Hyde atlas published in 1917, where it is still identified as the home of J. Hart (figure 2.9). This map again shows the house as a very small square shape, which contrasts with the other homes around it that are larger and have multiple features. This unexpected finding suggests the house was altered, but there is no other evidence that this is the case.

We are extremely fortunate that a historic photograph of the Hart house also survives (figure 4.10). This shows that the house was a frame-built, one-and-a-half story structure with a shingled roof. It had a centrally located front door with windows on each side, indicating two main rooms. The room on the right appears to be larger and was likely the parlor. The door and windows look over a small front yard that sits slightly below the curb, which is lined with a row of neatly trimmed hedges. A rear ell with a separate entrance is also visible. A handful of utilitarian tools and storage containers along with a spare window frame are alongside the home. A slightly off-center brick chimney rises through the peak of the roof. The foundation for the house is not visible. Behind the house is a dense stand of trees and brush, which confirms that the property was located near the mill pond creek. Without doubt this image provides a clear and compelling sense of the Hart house as it used to be. Of course, it is only a picture of the house and by itself cannot tell much about the people who lived there.

We are also lucky to have a series of family photographs that give a direct sense of the Harts themselves (figure 4.11). These photos were kept by the Harts' youngest daughter, Lucy Hart Keyes, and made available to A Long Time Coming by her grandson Ron Keyes. Included in the set are photographs of Jacob and Hannah Hart as well as four of their children, Daniel, Minnie, Lucy, and Ernest. These photographs give rare insight into the subjects of an archaeological study. Jacob is shown outdoors holding a long-handled tool and wearing a white shirt and woolen pants. The backdrop looks like a wooded area, which may be his home lot, or perhaps he is working or gardening away from home. Lucy Keyes (Transcript of oral history interview, 9 May 1987:15, Three Village Historical Society, Setauket, New York) described her father this way: "He's an Indian. . . . Hair was just as white and straight, tall, beautiful featured man." The portrait of Hannah is formal; she sits in a photographer's studio in fine clothes. The images of the children are clearer and likely from a later date. Daniel is dressed in a fine woolen suit holding his violin. We know from documentary records that he was one of the Harts' oldest children and lived at least part of his life in Philadelphia.

It is possible he was a professional musician. The photograph of Lucy and Minnie shows them as young children posing in nice dresses in a photographer's studio. The photograph of Ernest Hart shows him as a young man, perhaps a teenager. He is dressed quite nicely and, like his siblings, sitting for a posed photograph as we can see the fold in the drop cloth behind him.

These images reflect repeated trips to professional photographers suggesting the family wanted to and likely enjoyed having photographs of themselves. Posed portraits like these are intended to make the family members look their best, an effort made perhaps to counteract the lives they led as people of color in a small home in early 1900s Setauket. The image of relative success implied by the nice clothes and the capacity to afford a photographer makes a case for belonging in modern America and of course for counteracting the negative stereotypes people of color like themselves faced every day.

Oral History

Jacob and Hannah Hart's youngest daughter, Lucy Keyes, lived her entire life in Setauket. She was born in the family home on Lake Street and moved in 1920 to a home on Christian Avenue that still stands. Keyes was interviewed at her home as part of Dr. Glenda Dickerson's research project *Eel Spearing at Setauket* in 1987, and the tape and transcript of this interview are housed at the Three Village Historical Society. Keyes spoke about her father and mother and her childhood home. In one passage Keyes (transcript of oral history interview, 9 May 1987:9–10, Three Village Historical Society, Setauket, New York) recalled that

> My father always said "Save some and" . . . now how did he say that? Let me get that straight, "and eat well. Have, but always save some." I can't get it just like he used to say it, but . . . that's the way we came up. And those old folks had their own home there when a lot of people in Setauket didn't even have a home to live in . . . ain't got no place—them old folks had a lovely home down . . . that street. . . . My father kept it up beautiful. . . . A lot of *these* flowers come from down home. There used to be an old house there. They tore it down because it was right at the pond in the spring and the beams rotted out.

The values of homeownership and frugality passed from father to daughter. We also learn that the house was torn down after years of dealing with groundwater that rotted its base. A story told by elders Caroline Moore, Carlton Edwards, and Pearl Hart, who each had been in the house when they were children, is that the family could lift the floorboards of the house and see water underneath.

Hart Family History

The earliest record of the Hart family in Setauket is the 1865 New York State Census identifying the household of William H. Hart. The household consisted of William (44 years), Rachel L. Hart (29 years), William H. Hart Jr. (12 years), Jacob L. Hart (8 years), Anna A. Hart (6 years), and Selah B. S. Hart (3 years).[8] William is listed as a farmer, and based on the 1873 Beers map, it is thought that the family lived on Lake Street. In 1870 the Hart household consisted of William (45 years), Lucretia (40 years), William H. (19 years), Jacob B. (14 years), Selah (8 years), and Isaiah (1 year). William is listed as a farm laborer and a US citizen, while Jacob and Selah are listed as having attended school, though Jacob was unable to write. The family did not own real estate, suggesting they were tenants on the property where they lived, which again was most likely the home Lake Street identified on the 1873 Beers atlas. The absence of Anna Hart, who would have been 11 years old in 1870 is curious, though she could have been working in the home of another family by that age. Anna Hart does not appear in the census again. The Hart family history does not mention her, though it does indicate that there was another child named David T. Hart who was born in 1854 and died as an infant.

Neither William H. Hart, Rachel L. Hart, nor William H. Hart Jr. appear in the census again. The next mention of members of the Hart family is in the 1900 census. One reason for their absence, at least Jacob Hart's, is that he is known to have worked as a cook at sea before getting married. The date of his marriage to Hannah Taylor is likely in or before 1877, the year when their first child, Rebecca, was born. Hannah Taylor was born free in Powhatan, Virginia, in 1856. According to her obituary, Hannah was sent north by her family to work as a household servant for the Woodhull Wheeler family in Port Jefferson. She and Jacob likely met while she was living nearby in these years. Jacob and Hannah spent the rest of their lives in Setauket, living until at least 1888 in the small house on Lake Street. They had 12 children, 7 daughters and 5 sons (see table 4.7). In 1900 Jacob and Hannah Hart's household consisted of themselves (both 43 years), Rebecca (22 years), Hannah (20 years), Julia (12 years, in school), Selah (8 years), Minnie (3 years), and Lucy (1 year). Their older sons (Daniel, Jacob, and James) are not listed, suggesting that by 15 years of age the young men in the home had moved out, found work, or perhaps passed away. Jacob is listed as a day laborer and Hannah a laundress. By 1900 they also owned their home free of any mortgage.

In 1910 the household consisted of Jacob and Hannah along with their three youngest children, Minnie (12 years), Lucy (10 years), and Ernest (6 years). Jacob is listed as a mason's helper and Hannah a washerwoman. In 1920 the household consisted of Jacob, Hannah, and Ernest (18 years). Hannah was no longer employed, and both Jacob and Ernest worked at a shipyard, Jacob a bolter and Ernest a laborer. In 1930 only Jacob and Ernest (24 years) are listed as residents. Jacob was working then as a mason and Ernest as a laborer for a trucking business. The latest census record is from 1940, which shows only 36-year-old Ernest Hart living in the home, working as a handyman in an institution, such as a school or hospital.

Jacob's brother Selah Hart also had a large family. Along with his wife, Martha Sells, Selah had 10 children, many of whom later lived in Chicken Hill and on Christian Avenue. Selah Hart's family was much like Jacob's. For example, in 1910 the household consisted of nine children plus Selah and Martha. Selah was a farm laborer and Martha a washerwoman. Unlike his brother, however, Selah never owned his home. Selah died in 1913, after which Martha married Cassious Burton. Overall, the two families led similar lives and represent the typical sort of households in the community of color in Setauket in the early 1900s.

By the time Hannah Hart died in 1922, she had not only raised 12 children but according to her obituary also had 12 grandchildren living in Setauket. She was survived at the time by 8 children, including Daniel (living in Philadelphia),

Table 4.7. Jacob and Hannah Hart Family

Name	Relationship	Birth and Death Years (Spouse)
Jacob Hart	Father	1857–1931
Hannah Eliza Taylor Hart	Mother	1856–1922
Rebecca E. Hart	Daughter	1877–1955 (m. James Lewis)
Daniel Hart	Son	ca. 1880–post-1940 (m. Leona ?, moved to Philadelphia)
Hannah E. Hart	Daughter	1880–1959 (m. William Smith Sells)
Jacob Hart Jr.	Son	1882– ?
James Hart	Son	1885– ?
Julia May Hart	Daughter	1888–1952 (m. William H. Smith; m. Clifford Weir)
Martha Hart	Daughter	1890– ?
Selah B. Hart	Son	1891–1936 (moved to White Plains, NY)
Anna Hart	Daughter	1894– ?
Minnie E. Hart	Daughter	1897–1979 (m. Harrison Sanford)
Lucy Agnes Hart	Daughter	1899–1994 (m. William Keyes)
Ernest L. Hart	Son	1904–1978

Source: Hart-Sells family history.

Selah (living in White Plains), Rebecca Lewis, Hannah Sells, Julia Smith, Minnie Sanford, Lucy Keyes, and Ernest Hart who still lived in Setauket. Her other children (Jacob Jr., James, Martha, and Anna) appear to have predeceased her. Jacob Hart passed away in 1931. His obituary in the *Port Jefferson Echo* (31 May 1931) describes him as a

> much respected colored citizen . . . which we shall miss, as he passed daily along our streets as long as he was about, to be at his various employments. In past years he was accounted one of the best workmen at the rubber factory and when that enterprise failed, he took up the work of gardening and was always busy and ready to do all for friends and neighbors, and always had a ready smile and word of greeting for all who knew him.

Jacob Hart was clearly a recognized part of Setauket's local community, having lived there his whole life, worked at multiple jobs for multiple employers, and, perhaps like some of his ancestors who are depicted in William Sidney Mount's paintings, quick with a smile to keep the troubles that came with being a person of color at bay.

Archaeology at the Jacob and Hannah Hart Site

Archaeological fieldwork at the Jacob and Hannah Hart home site in 2011 and 2015 uncovered several features related to the house and the surrounding landscape as well as a clear stratigraphic record associated with a series of historic events. Twenty-three 1 m units and seven shovel tests pits were excavated at the Hart site (figure 4.12). With knowledge collected from historical maps and the photograph of the house, the site was initially approached with the goal of identifying the location of the house within the site. After the family left the site in the 1940s, the lot appears to have been untouched until the excavation began. In the intervening decades the site became inundated with abundant new plant growth that covered the remaining features of the house completely, though in places this ground cover was quite thin, especially where tree roots pushed foundation stones upward. Several foundation stones were exposed close to the ground surface in the initial units excavated. Additional excavations exposed the intact foundation of the chimney and hearth as well as surrounding wall supports (figure 4.13). Using the historic photograph of the house as a guide, the chimney base is thought to have been located just off center of the former house. Figure 4.12 shows a projection of the house's footprint based on architectural features exposed in the excavation. Due to limited time in the field, some relatively difficult excavation conditions, and the displacement of stones over time, the whole footprint of the house could not be exposed, so this projection is an approximation.[9]

Excavations in areas around the concentration of foundation stones identified additional architectural features that help to reconstruct other aspects of the site's landscape. These include a brick pathway running between the house and the street across the former front yard of the property (figure 4.14). The path is six bricks wide, with the bricks laid end to end. The path is not visible in the historic photo since the ground surface drops down in elevation to below the street level and behind the hedgerow. Other landscape features were exposed in the west yard of the house. One consisted of several flat-laying stones close to the surface and a line of more deeply buried bricks and cobbles. This feature seems to be the remnants of a foundation for an outbuilding not previously documented at the site, though not enough of the site was excavated to confirm this theory. Associated with this foundation is another brick pathway that ran northwest before turning 90 degrees to reach to the street front. This path suggests that the buried foundation supported a structure with a separate access path. A third landscape feature, exposed on the north end of the site, was a densely packed layer of cobbles and brick that provided a flat paved surface (figure 4.15). This surface was both stone and brick, which may indicate it served a different purpose than just a pathway; however, nothing was recovered in the area to suggest what this other activity might have been. It appears instead that the brick identified in this feature was part of another pathway, probably providing access to the well discovered still further to the north. It is possible the stones were used to create and demarcate a prepared working area close to the well, perhaps used by Hannah Hart for doing laundry.

Even though the site was covered with a variety of paved pathways and surfaces, none of the landscape features are visible in the historic photograph of the site. Rather, the most visible pathway, running along the side of the house, in the photograph appears unpaved. This finding suggests the finished surfaces were a later addition. A likely reason for this effort reflects back to Lucy Hart Keyes's memory that "they tore [the house] down because it was right at the pond in the spring and the beams rotted out." Dealing with ground wet enough to rot the beams of the house would have made the yard spaces a problem if they were regularly wet or muddy. There would have been bad footing on the lot and, considering Hannah Hart was a laundress, difficulty in keeping things like her clients' clothing clean. The Harts appear to have laid in walking paths and perhaps even a paved work area to create spaces that could have been kept relatively dry and clean. The Harts' spring-fed well toward the north end of their lot would have provided water for drinking, washing, and laundry. The paved stone surface would have been on a direct path between the house and the well.

The Harts' struggle with groundwater is also evident in the site's stratigraphy. The units excavated in the west yard exhibit a relatively uniform stratigraphic profile. The uppermost layer was a thick jumble of roots and soil with very few artifacts. A whole 1960s Pepsi bottle recovered from this deposit confirms this layer was created after the Harts' house was demolished. Below this root mat was a thick layer of gray sand that also had few artifacts, followed by a layer of dark soil that contained a wide range of historic domestic artifacts. The dark soil and abundant artifacts suggest the third layer was the ground surface when the Harts lived at the site. At or below this dark layer are the brick and stone surfaces just discussed. In some cases the sand layer rested on these paved surfaces, but in others there had been some accumulation of dark surface soils over the brick and stones. Below the brick and stones and the dark soil layer, the soils eventually became lighter in color and filled with small pebbles, a feature of the subsoil at this site (figure 4.16).

This stratigraphic sequence indicates the site went through four stages of development. The lowest and earliest stratum reflect an initial historic occupation over the natural subsoil. At a later date, in some areas this surface was covered with a brick or stone surface to provide dry and clean pathways and work areas in the yard areas adjacent to the house. In some places, these paths became buried by organic soils, evidence that for the latter part of Harts' tenure these yard areas were not used enough to keep the pathway clear of sediment. As the pathways and prepared surfaces might have been part of Hannah Hart's laundry work, it is likely that the accumulation of sediments over the brick paths occurred after she passed away in 1922. The yard itself was then buried almost completely by the gray sand layer.

Based on the dates of the Harts' occupation, the gray sand is thought to have been introduced by a flood caused by the Long Island Express, a category 3 hurricane that passed only a few miles to the east of Setauket in 1938. The Hart home site was located near the mill pond creek as well as the feeder stream they used for their well. These features, along with the fact that the home was in a low-lying and swampy area, made it very vulnerable to flooding. A storm of the intensity of the Long Island Express more than likely flooded the site and introduced the several centimeters of mostly sterile gray sand sediment found over the buried living surface in the side yard. This flood deposit is not found over the foundation stones associated with house, which means the home still stood when the flood came through. The last recorded resident of the home was Ernest Hart, who was still living there in 1940 (US Census, Town of Brookhaven, Suffolk County, New York, 1940), though he had moved by the time his siblings sold the lot in 1948. By then it is thought the home was either torn down or found derelict and removed soon after.

Dating the Archaeological Deposits

Based on documentary evidence we know that two generations of the Hart family lived at their home site between the 1880s and the 1940s. Archaeological deposits strongly suggest the site was flooded and buried by the sediments associated with the 1938 Long Island Express hurricane, which may mark the end of the family's tenure at the site. Ceramics recovered during the excavation add more information to our understanding of the site's chronology. The excavation recovered 217 ceramic sherds with attributes that allow us to assign dates of manufacture (Janowitz 2018). These sherds derived from a variety of ceramic types, including Tin-glazed Earthenware, Black Basalt, Bone China, CC Ware, Pearlware, Whiteware, Ironstone, Yellowware, Rockingham, Chinese Export Porcelain, Hard-paste Porcelain, Salt-glazed Gray and Buff-bodied Stoneware, Victorian Majolica, and White Granite. The majority of ceramics in the collection were Pearlware, Whiteware, and White Granite, a range of types common from the mid-nineteenth and early twentieth centuries. The mean ceramic date for the diagnostic sherds is 1864.7, which is earlier than the Harts are thought to have lived in the home. The early date may reflect the presence of materials from households who lived at the site before the Harts. The date is certainly also skewed by the early start dates and long manufacturing date ranges for types such as Bone China (1794–1900), Pearlware (1795–1840) and Whiteware (1815–1930). Bone China, Whitewares, and White Granite (1840–1930) ceramics remained in production up to and after 1900, so the mean date may not align with the actual cultural context that produced these materials. Another possibility is that the Harts obtained many of their ceramics as secondhand purchases or hand-me-downs when they first moved into the home. Skewing toward an earlier mean date also makes sense given that the household was quite small after 1920; the last residents were two adult men, Jacob and Ernest Hart, who may not have had a strong inclination to upgrade the household's ceramic wares.

Two glass artifacts add additional chronological information. One is a fragment of a bottle embossed with the words "Sperm Sewing Machine Oil" (figure 5.8). The oil of sperm whales was a prized resource in the 1800s used largely for lamps. Even though this use declined after the 1870s, sperm oil remained a common lubricant for small household tools like sewing machines well into the twentieth century. Most documented sperm whale oil bottles like this example date to the end of the 1800s, exactly when the Harts were living at the site. A second bottle, embossed with the name "L. S. Squires Propr.," was used for Green Mountain Oil (or Magic Pain Destroyer). While this product was guaranteed by the Food and Drug Act in 1906, its manufacturer, the Crittenden Company, was fined for misbranding the product in 1915, giving this bottle a fairly tight production timeframe that again falls within the period the Harts lived on Lake Street (United States Department of Agriculture 1915:355).

Conclusion

This chapter has introduced the Silas Tobias and the Jacob and Hannah Hart home sites that were the focus of archaeological study by A Long Time Coming. Both sites were the homes of families connected to Setauket's historic Native and African American community. The Tobiases were one of the leading families in the community in the nineteenth century, and the Harts were a leading family in the twentieth century. Descendants of both families still live in and near Setauket, and others from further away have found connections to Setauket and A Long Time Coming by learning about their ancestors who lived at these sites. These descendants have been vital to learning about the two families whose households have been excavated. It is thanks to their dedication to family and community, in fact, that we are able to discover these lost homes and can now begin to retell their stories.

This chapter also compiled a wide range of sources of historical information about the people who lived at these two sites. From historic maps and photographs, census records, genealogies, deeds, tax records, oral history and archaeology, the rich history of each site can now be engaged. Thanks to these records we know the names, kinship relations, occupations, histories of property ownership, and community roles played by many of those who also left behind material records of their lives in the ground. Both sites also have good archaeological integrity. Neither has been disturbed by such things as construction or bottle hunting that can so easily upend the stratigraphy or displace features and artifacts. Instead, both the Tobias and Hart home sites suffered mostly from neglect, having been essentially untouched since they were abandoned.

Finally, this chapter has shown how the Tobias and Hart sites present an important source for comparison. From the documents and archaeology, we know the Tobias site was occupied no later than 1823 and as early as 1797 through the end of the nineteenth century. The site was home to three generations of the Tobias family, and while we are not able to identify with certainty who lived at the site, I propose the most likely residents in table 4.3. The Hart site was occupied from the 1880s until the 1940s, and, with better documentation available from these years, we know the names of almost all its occupants. Taken together, the two sites provide a long-term view of the domestic life of people of color in Setauket between the 1790s and the 1940s. Since the sites were occupied sequentially, we can also compare the data from each to show how practices related to domestic and community life changed through time for Setauket's Native and African Americans. Comparing the two sites also reveals the historical dynamics of race involved in the shift from creole synthesis to racial modernity outlined in chapter 3. Understanding how the Tobiases and Harts negotiated the cultures of racism they experienced is the focus of chapter 5, where I discuss the meanings of the excavated materials recovered from the two sites.

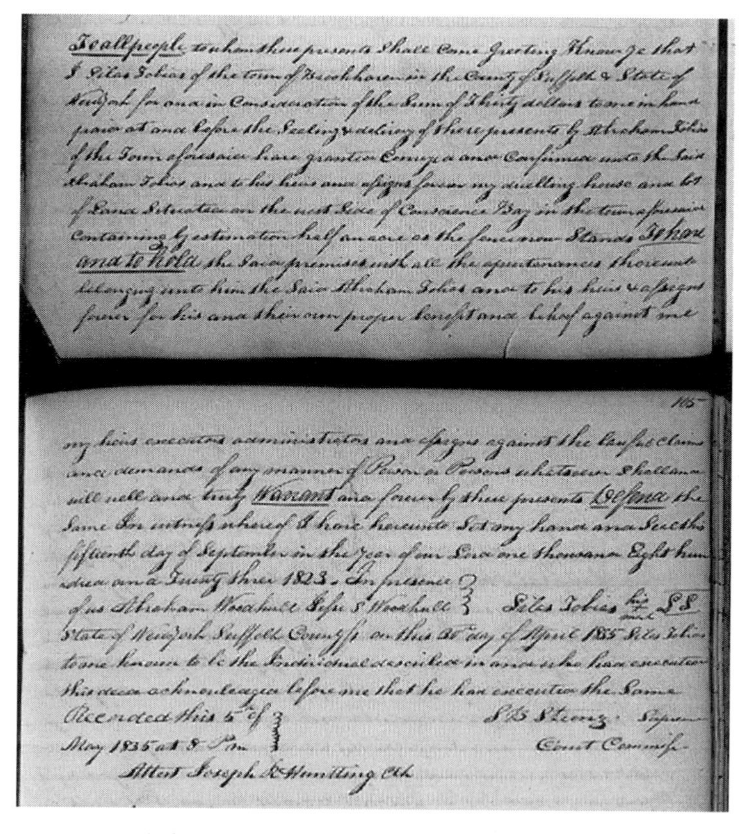

To all people to whom these presents shall come Greeting Know ye that
I Silas Tobias of the town of Brookhaven in the County of Suffolk & State of
New York for and in Consideration of the Sum of Thirty dollars to me in hand
paid at and before the Sealing & delivery of these presents by Abraham Tobias
of the Town aforesaid have granted Conveyed and Confirmed unto the Said
Abraham Tobias and to his heirs and assigns forever my dwelling house and lot
of Land Situated on the west Side of Conscience Bay in the town aforesaid
Containing by estimation half an acre as the fence now Stands To have
and to hold the Said premises with all the appurtenances thereunto
belonging unto him the Said Abraham Tobias and to his heirs & assigns
forever for his and their own proper benefit and behoof against me

105

my heirs executors administrators and assigns against the lawful claims
and demands of any manner of Person or Persons whatsoever I shall and
will well and truly Warrant and forever by these presents Defend the
Same In witness whereof I have hereunto Set my hand and Seal this
fifteenth day of September in the year of our Lord one thousand Eight hun
dred and Twenty three 1823. In presence
of us Abraham Woodhull Jesse S Woodhull } Silas Tobias his mark L.S.
State of New York Suffolk County ss on this 30th day of April 1835 Silas Tobias
to me known to be the Individual described in and who has executed
this deed acknowledged before me that he had executed the Same
Recorded this 5th of May 1835 at 8 P.m. } S.B. Strong Supreme Court Commissioner
Attest Joseph R Huntting Clk

Figure 4.1. Deed of sale of the Silas Tobias site from Silas Tobias to Abraham Tobias, 1823. Liber V:104–105, Suffolk County Deeds.

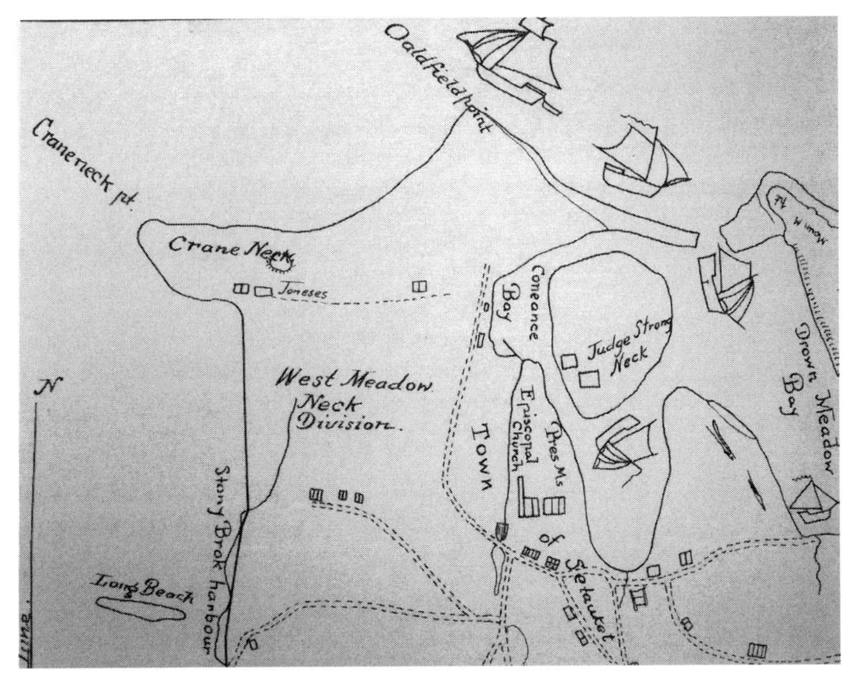

Figure 4.2. A 1797 map of the Town of Brookhaven by Isaac Hulse, detail of West Meadow Section. The small structure on the west shore of Coneance (Conscience) Bay is in the same location as the Silas Tobias archaeological site. (Collection of the Suffolk County Historical Society, Map Case IV.)

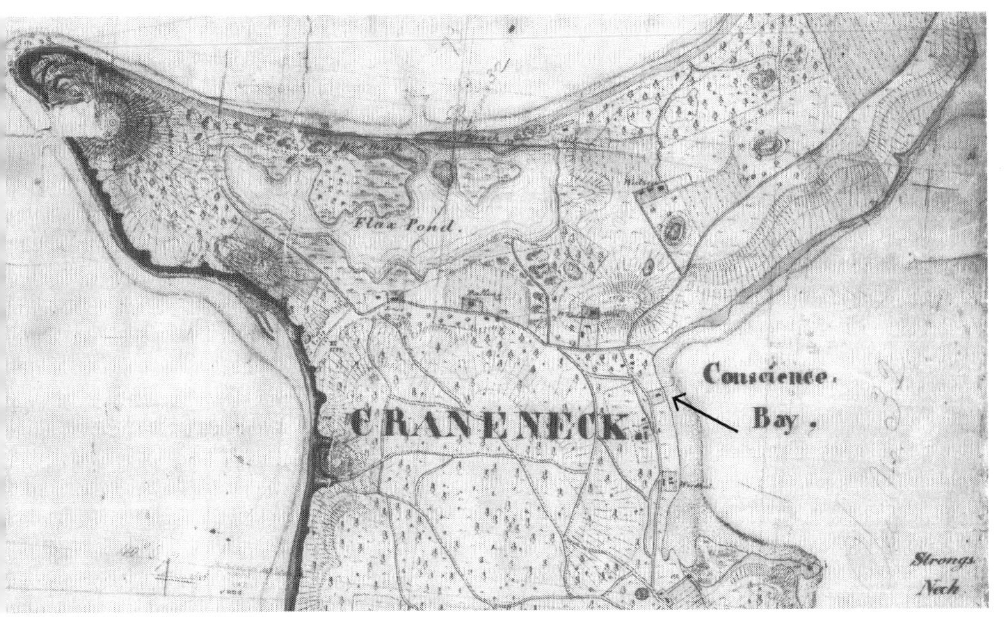

Figure 4.3. An 1837 coastal map. The Silas Tobias site is the unnamed house site on the west shore of Conscience Bay (see arrow) north of the "Woodhul" house. (Long Island Coastal Maps Collection, T-31-North, with detail. Stony Brook University Libraries.)

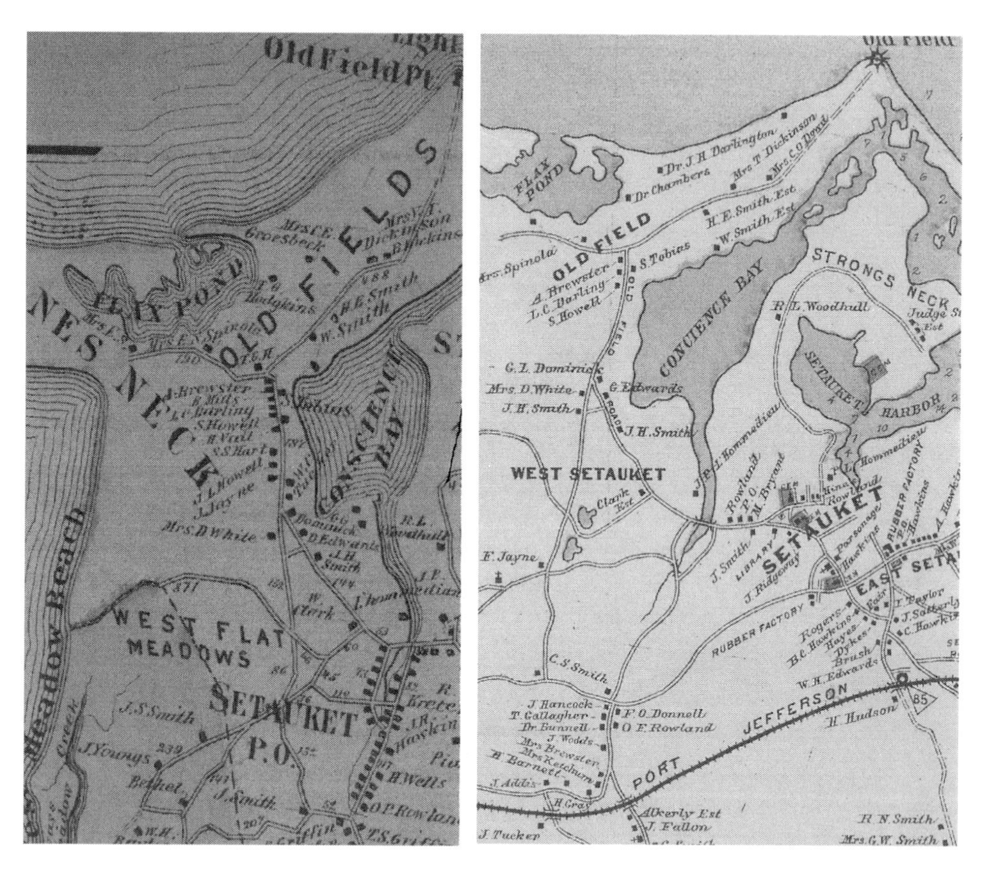

Figure 4.4. *Left*, detail from *Atlas of Long Island, New York from Recent and Actual Surveys and Records*, Beers, Comstock & Cline, 1873. (Lionel Pincus and Princess Firyal Map Division, New York Public Library.) *Right*, detail from *Map of Long Island: Based upon Recent US Coast Surveys, Together with Local Maps on file, Supplemented by Careful Territorial Observations*, Hyde and Company, 1896. (Lionel Pincus and Princess Firyal Map Division, New York Public Library.)

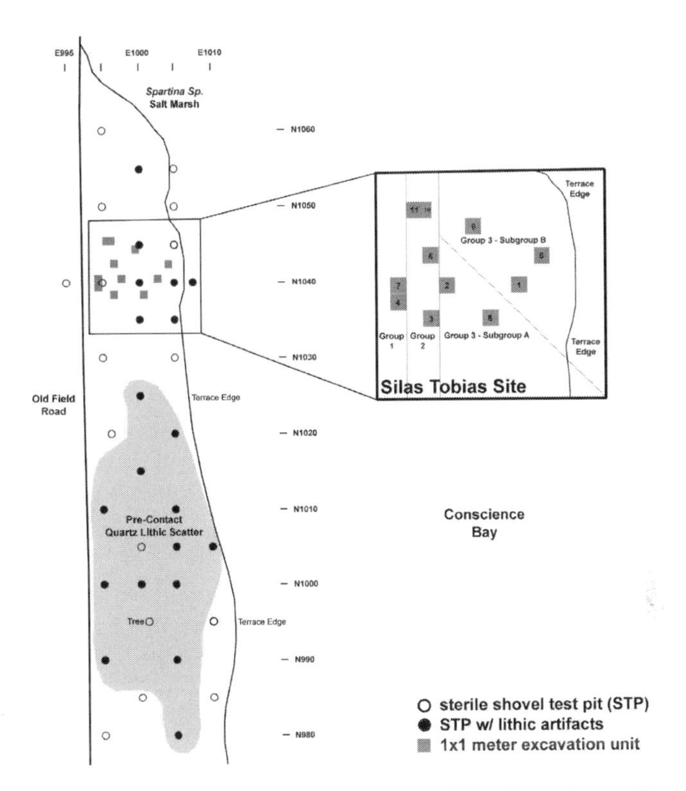

Figure 4.5. Plan of the Silas Tobias site showing location of shovel test pits as well as detail of the section tested with 1 m excavation units. (Courtesy of Mark Tweedie.)

Figure 4.6. Jamie Ancheta and Mark Tweedie at the Silas Tobias site, summer 2015.

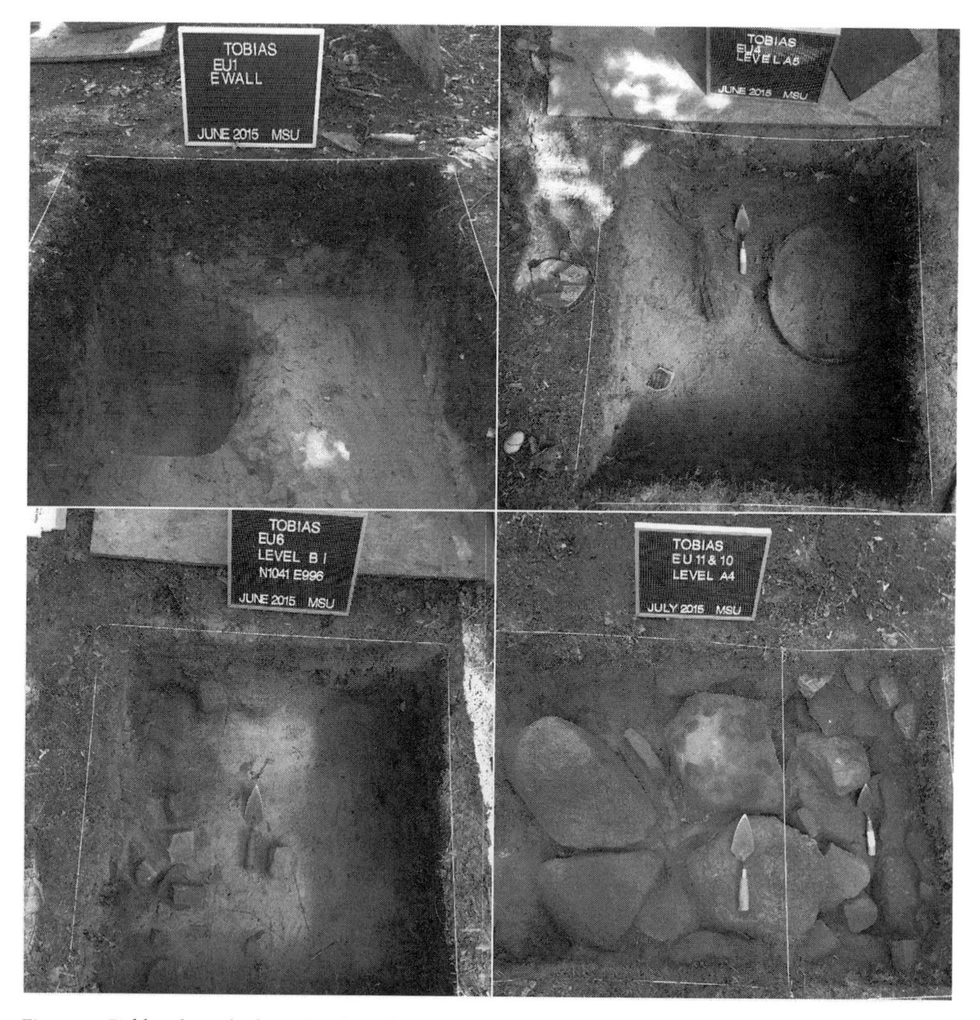

Figure 4.7. Fieldwork results from the Silas Tobias site. *Clockwise from upper left:* basic soil profile, large artifacts in situ under the central part of the former house, chimney foundation remains, pier support remains.

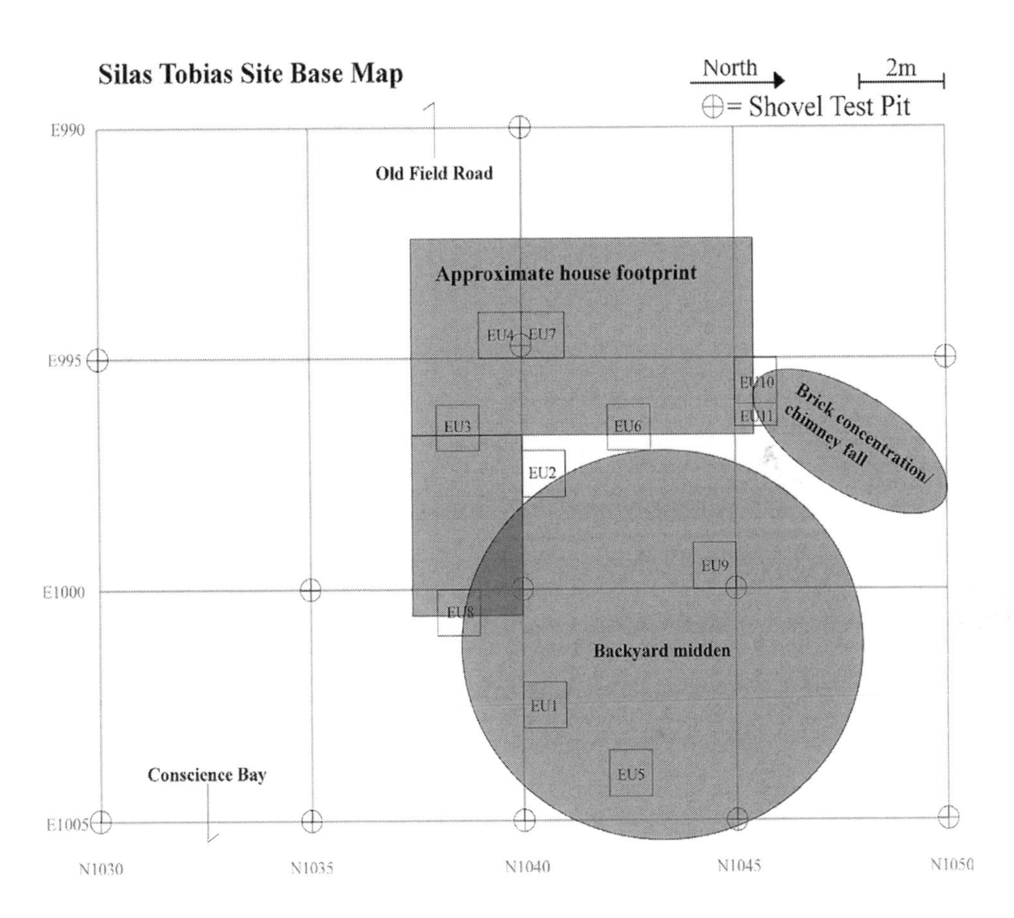

Figure 4.8. Plan of the Silas Tobias site showing the relationship between excavation units and major features at the site.

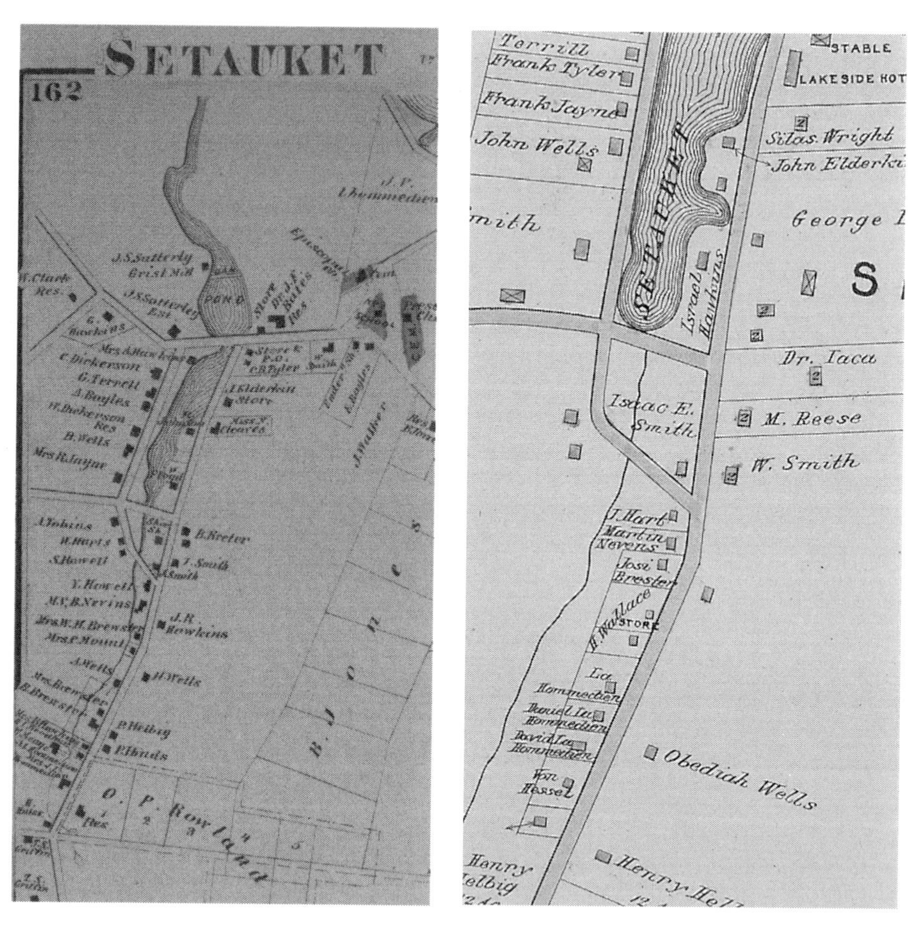

Figure 4.9. *Left*, detail from *Setauket, East Setauket, Tn. of Brookhaven, Suffolk Co.—Mount Sinai, Town of Brookhaven, Suffolk Co.—Lakeland, Town of Islip, Suffolk Co.*, Beers, Comstock & Cline, 1873. The Hart site is identified as occupied by Y. Howell in this rendering. (Lionel Pincus and Princess Firyal Map Division, New York Public Library.) *Right*, detail from *Atlas of Suffolk County, Long Island, New York: Based upon Maps on file at the County Seat in Riverhead and upon Private Plans and Surveys Furnished by Surveyors and Individual Owners; Suffolk County*, E. Belcher Hyde, 1909. (Lionel Pincus and Princess Firyal Map Division, New York Public Library.)

Figure 4.10. Undated photograph of the Jacob and Hannah Hart home. (Courtesy of the Three Village Historical Society, Long Island.)

Figure 4.11. Undated photographs of Hart family members. *Clockwise from upper left:* Hannah Hart, Jacob Hart, Ernest Hart, Lucy and Minnie Hart, and Daniel Hart. (Courtesy of Helen Sells, Ron Keyes, and Higher Ground Intercultural and Heritage Association.)

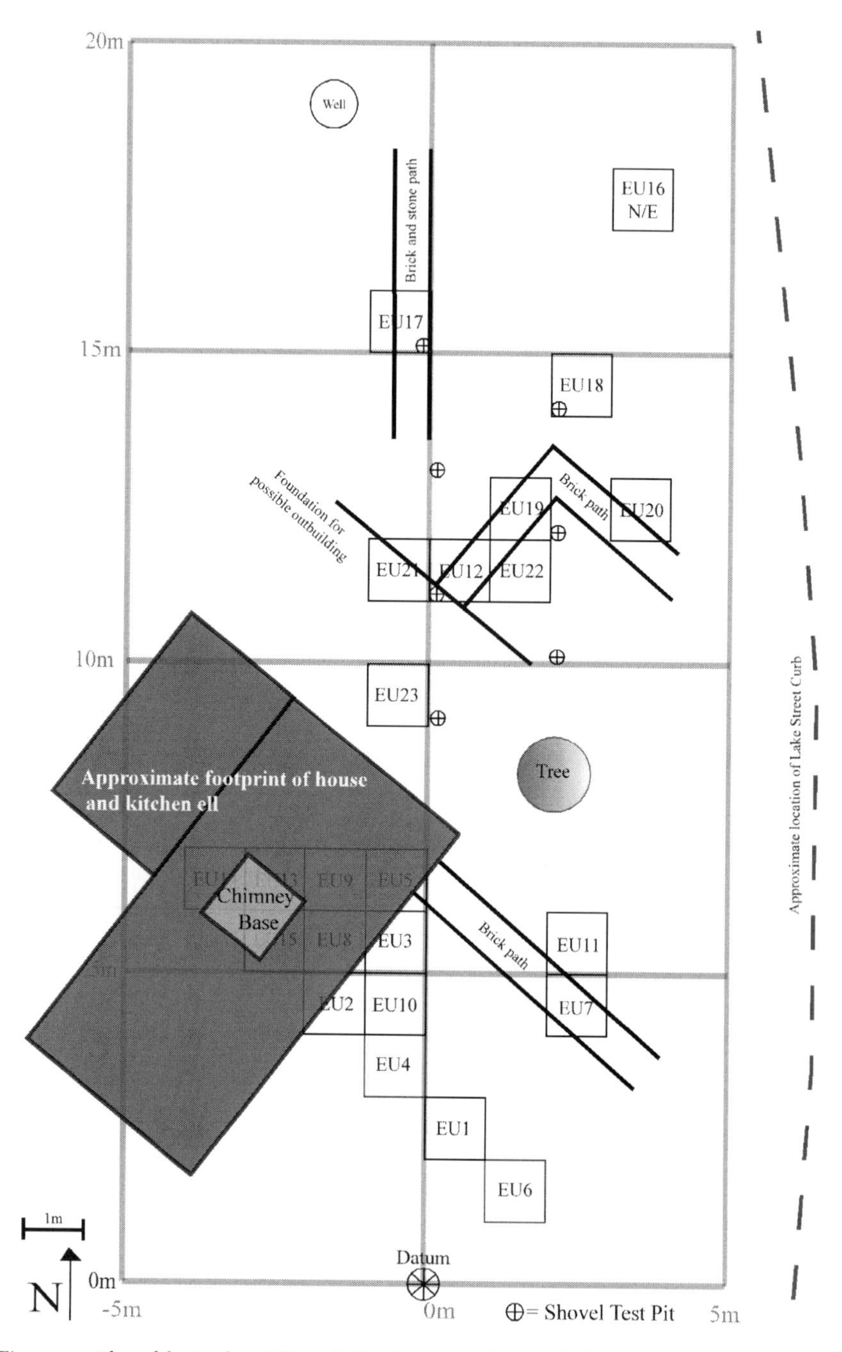

Figure 4.12. Plan of the Jacob and Hannah Hart home site showing the location of excavation units, site features, and a projection of the house footprint.

Figure 4.13. Exposed foundation of the chimney and hearth at the Jacob and Hannah Hart home site.

Figure 4.14. Buried brick walkway that connected the home to the street front at the Jacob and Hannah Hart home site.

Figure 4.15. Buried brick and cobble work surface or pathway exposed in the west yard at the Jacob and Hannah Hart home site.

Figure 4.16. Profile showing the generalized stratigraphy in the west yard of the Jacob and Hannah Hart home site.

Notes

1. Tax records for the Town of Brookhaven from 1810 and 1819 do show that other people of color owned small parcels of land, but their last names (Moore, Hamer, Miller, Ellsworth, and Cuffee) are not common for those who lived in or near Setauket. Arthur Ailsworth/Ellsworth was noted as living in Belleport in 1819 on Long Island's south shore. Tax records are on file the Town of Brookhaven Historian's Office, Farmingville, New York.

2. A home occupied by A. Brewster is located across the street. This refers to Adam Brewster, who was a founding member of the Native and African American Calvin lineage, some of whom still live in Setauket.

3. Records of the Caroline Church and First Presbyterian Church in Setauket are housed at the Town of Brookhaven Historian's Office, Farmingville, NY. Included in these records are the drowning death of 15- to 20-year-old Charles Tobias in 1803 as well as the marriage of Abram Tobias and Laura Groshing in 1847.

4. An STP is a hole dug about the width of a shovel and, in this case, at a depth of at least 50 cm below surface level. The contents of each STP were sifted through a ¼" mesh screen and artifacts were collected in labeled bags. Data on the STPs themselves were then recorded including STP depth, soil color (using the Munsell Soil Color Chart) texture of distinct soil strata, and a summary of all artifacts found. Each STP was then backfilled with the sifted soil. The STP survey was completed by students from Montclair State University enrolled in my Archaeology of African Diaspora seminar in Spring 2015. The collected artifacts were brought to the Montclair State University Center for Heritage and Archaeological Studies lab for processing. Artifacts were washed and catalogued based on material and use, and then stored in their respective labeled bags. Distribution maps of artifact concentrations produce using SURFER were produced to interpret the findings. Shovel test pits were excavated at the Tobias site in an offset a five-meter grid along four north-south transects. Additional STPs were excavated at intervening grid points in areas productive of historic artifacts and deposits at the site.

5. Excavation units were placed in the areas between already excavated STP locations to investigate intervening sediments and recover additional artifacts. All units, expect Excavation Unit 10, were excavated to sterile (non-artifact-bearing) soil. All excavations were completed by hand using small tools such as shovels and trowels. Excavations followed the natural soil stratigraphy, with each layer in each unit treated as a distinct sedimentary deposit, or provenience. All cultural material recovered was sorted and bagged by the unit and level they were found in. Excavated sediments were passed through ¼" mesh screens to recover artifacts. Where possible, the first two liters of excavated sediments in each provenience was reserved for later flotation processing. In addition, the first full bucket of sediments was passed through a ⅛" mesh screen to collect a sample of smaller artifacts than may have been recovered in the ¼" screen. All features encountered, such as stone or brick walls or floors, soil stains, or high artifact densities were recorded and photographed. All units were backfilled at the end of the excavation. Standardized recording forms were completed for all proveniences to document soil characteristics (color, texture, and inclusions), opening and closing elevations, recovered artifacts, and drawings of features and soil profiles. Digital photographs and scale draw-

ings of all features and select other deposits were collected prior to their excavation. All artifacts collected in the excavation were washed, labeled, and identified in the laboratory of the Center for Heritage and Archaeological Studies at Montclair State University. A fuller description of artifact analysis methods employed in this study is provided in the next section of this report.

6. The Hart family tree (housed at http://home.earthlink.net/~kds2/sitebuildercontent/sitebuilderfiles/william-and-rachel-tobias-hart-family-tree-Book.pdf) indicates that Jacob Hart was born in 1852, but the 1865 and 1870 census records suggest a slightly later birth date of 1856 or 1857.

7. As no independent documentation is provided for why these men are considered her brothers, this understanding is based on the family's memory.

8. Selah's full name is Selah Brewster Strong Hart, making a nominal connection between the Harts and the Brewsters as well as the powerful family headed by Selah Strong, who could very have been his father William's employer.

9. The excavation of the Jacob and Hannah Hart site was hampered by a high water table that flooded excavation units after they passed more than 20 cm below the ground surface. In some cases, units were flooded at shallower depths. The 2011 excavations were also impeded by the presence of virulent poison ivy growing over much of the site.

5

MATERIAL HISTORIES AND THE DYNAMICS OF RACISM IN SETAUKET

> Racism is a much more clandestine, much more hidden kind of phenomenon, but at the same time it's perhaps far more terrible than it's ever been.
>
> *Angela Davis*

The struggle against racism by people of color in the United States has been profound. Strategies of resistance have found many expressions as each person and community faced forms of oppression sometimes unique to their circumstances. Included among these has been the history of racism itself. Over time the way racism has worked and been deployed to damage marginal people has changed. Experiences of racism, that is, have been sometimes worse than others as the contexts of racialization change. Historian Gunja SenGupta (2009:55) assesses the world African Americans in nineteenth-century New York faced after emancipation in this light:

> The resilience of family and communal impulses among African Americans appears to have survived the ravages of slavery. Overall, the 1855 [New York State] census yields a collective portrait of black family support structures robust and flexible enough to adapt to the vicissitudes of working poor fortunes. The vulnerability of the community to poverty lay not in the disorganization of its family life, but rather in the progressive constriction of its economic, political, and civic freedoms.

Rather than the sources of their struggles being located within their homes and families, SenGupta explains people of color faced increasing constrictions due to the external pressures created by the dynamics of a constricting racism. She points out that African Americans were well placed to succeed as families and communities by virtue of a long history of self-reliance, a strategy used to survive and resist enslavement, racism, and poverty for generations. Yet she also notes that their struggles increased during the nineteenth century as the world around them changed. This chapter considers this assessment by tracing the impacts of intensifying racism in nineteenth-century Setauket on people and communities of color. I present evidence for how people of color faced these challenges as the racial dynamics around them changed. The central focus is an analysis of materials recovered from the Tobias and Hart archaeological sites and how these present evidence for the way people of color negotiated racism in Setauket.

The analysis is framed by the notions of creole synthesis and racial modernity. The concept of creole synthesis suggests that during the emancipation era (1799–1827) and thereafter, people of color occupied a liminal state defined by being neither enslaved by nor politically equal to the majority white community. This period of cultural change and racial ambiguity was for some a time of experimentation in which a creole mixture of African, white, and Native American communities developed. I look at the Tobias household as people who experienced and embodied this synthesis in Setauket. To date most research on this topic has focused on the creolization of whites who, as artists and progressive literate people, produced works reflecting a new racially ambiguous sensibility. The narrative of the creole synthesis we have so far thus moves in one direction: from people of color to whites as the grantors and receptors of new cultural inputs and ideas. Since the Tobiases were not white, we can examine how and in what ways people of color also experienced the creolization of American life. To be sure, their experience should be understood not only as a counterpoint to that documented for whites but also as the experience of a racialized minority community. So while the creole synthesis was certainly processed differently by the Tobiases and the Mounts, both families would have had relationships with and across the color line that were characteristic of the era.

After the end of slavery in New York, people of color and whites transitioned to a new culture of racial modernity. Racial modernity refers to a worldview in which racial groups were considered culturally and biologically distinct and hierarchically ranked. Separation of white and black experience grew as people of different backgrounds ceased living in the same households. Working-class whites also grew to see people of color as competitors in the labor market and with some frequency engaged in anti-black actions to establish their racial superiority and legitimate citizenship. The 1863 Draft Riot in New York City, for example, was a bloody retaliation by working-class whites against a Civil War draft policy that allowed draftees to avoid service if they paid a fee. Rioters destroyed the property of some wealthy whites but focused their blame and rage on African American bodies, homes, and institutions. This included the Colored Orphans Asylum, where children escaped from the back building while rioters chanted "kill the monkeys" (Bernstein 2005:295). Twelve black men were brutally killed by rioters who lynched, burned, stabbed, and drowned their victims (SenGupta 2009:128). For these white rioters, the presence of people of color in the United States was the reason they were being asked to put their lives at risk in the war. Eliminating people of color through murder or by other means that denied they were legitimate citizens with a right to belong is a basic feature of racial modernity.

African Americans were thus denigrated symbolically and politically. Blackface minstrelsy and other caricatures entertained whites by making African Americans seem primitive, savage, gullible, and ludicrous (Lott 1995; Roediger 1991). Racial restrictions on voting rights, housing, work, and welfare relief confined people of color to separate and inferior circumstances (SenGupta 2009). The criminalization of blackness in the second half of the nineteenth century further confirmed a sense not only of black inferiority but also of people of color as inherently dangerous people (Muhammed 2010; Sacks 2005). Altogether these cultural and material forces supported the institutionalization of formal and informal systems of Jim Crow segregation, which of course was legalized by the *Plessy v. Ferguson* decision in 1896, around the same time the Tobiases moved out of Old Field and just a few years after the Harts moved into their home on Lake Street.

While these far-reaching social and cultural forces reflect the intensification of racism in the United States, there have been relatively few studies that draw from material culture and archaeology to address racial modernity, especially in the North. Multiple studies have analyzed postbellum African American archaeology in the South (e.g., Barnes 2011; Brandon and Davidson 2005; Brown 2004; Cabak et al. 1995; Orser 1989; Weik 1997; Wilkie 1997), including Charles Orser's (1988b, 1991) documentation of racial oppression evident in depressed land values, poor housing, and bleak material culture on tenant plantations in South Carolina. Paul Mullins (1999a, 1999b; Mullins and Jones 2011a) demonstrates that African Americans strategically evaded white shopkeepers' racism by purchasing mass consumer goods. This decision not only served them locally but provided symbolic access to widely shared materials and ideologies connected to cultural belonging and American citizenship in the industrial era. Many other archaeological studies of African Americans in the nineteenth and early twentieth century focus on the preservation of African cultural traditions or other positive expressions of black alterity and community (Agbe-Davies 2011; Arjona 2017; Barnes ed. 2011; Battle-Baptiste 2011; Davidson 2014; Fennell 2007; Ferguson 1992; Franklin and McKee 2004; Leone et al. 2005; Matthews and McGovern 2015; Morris 2017; Ruppel et al. 2003; White 2017).

For the most part, archaeological studies of African Americans situate racist oppression and violence as a stable foundation over which cultural practices evident in archaeological data were performed. In contrast, I consider racism as a dynamic force that, because it changed in meaning and impact through time, required people to consistently negotiate their positions in society as they debated and contested the meanings of race. I illustrate this in a comparison of archaeological assemblages and historical data from the Tobias and Hart sites in Setauket to show how the community of color in Setauket experienced the impacts of this changing racial discourse and how these people developed historically specific ways to survive and resist their marginalization.

The Tobias and Hart Collections

The first step of the analysis is to consider the overall archaeological collections from the Tobias and Hart sites (tables 5.1 and 5.2). Artifacts are divided into functional categories following the system developed by Orser (1988a), which categorizes artifacts by their association with clothing, such as buttons or clasps; food-related activities, including food remains (e.g., bone and shell) as well as food preparation, serving, and storage artifacts; household and structural artifacts, including brick, stone, mortar, window glass, nails, other hardware, coal, charcoal, and slag; activities related to wage or craft

Table 5.1. Artifacts from the Silas Tobias Site Sorted by Functional Category

Category	Count	%	Weight (g)	%
Clothing	60	0.4%	54.9	0.2%
Food	4,970	32.2%	5,919.2	17.0%
Household/Structural	10,168	65.8%	28,603.7	82.3%
Labor	5	0.0%	59.0	0.2%
Personal	71	0.5%	91.8	0.3%
Unidentified	171	1.1%	33.6	0.1%
Total	15,445		34,762.3	

Table 5.2. Artifacts from the Jacob and Hannah Hart Site Sorted by Functional Category

Category	Count	%	Weight (g)	%
Clothing	34	0.2%	35.3	0.1%
Food	1,176	7.7%	5,479.7	8.7%
Household/Structural	13,906	91.4%	56,514.5	89.5%
Labor	7	0.0%	281.2	0.4%
Personal	46	0.3%	244.0	0.4%
Unidentified	42	0.3%	589.6	0.9%
Total	15,211		63,144.3	

labor, such as hand tools or sewing equipment; and personal items, such as small toys, tobacco pipes, and clothing accessories.

Overall, the Tobias and Hart collections are quite similar. Both consist of slightly more than 15,000 artifacts and contain small numbers of clothing, labor, and personal artifacts. The differences between the two collections are nevertheless quite interesting. The artifact assemblage from the Hart site weighs almost twice as much as the assemblage from the Tobias site. This is because household and structural artifacts are the majority artifact type in the Hart site collection in both count and weight and building materials are much heavier than other artifacts. There is indeed a pronounced difference in the number of household and structural artifacts in the two collections such that only 65% of the Tobias collection and more than 91% of the Hart collection is household and structural artifacts. This ratio is reversed in the percentages of each collection that are food-related artifacts. The Tobias collection has almost five times the number of food-related artifacts as does the Hart collection.

From this broad view, it is clear that the artifacts at the two sites reflect the practice of different sorts of activities. Both collections are predominantly household and structural artifacts, which is expected since the homes at both sites were demolished before the excavations and demolition produces a great deal of architectural debris such as nails, brick fragments, and larger objects related to foundations and house supports. These are dense and heavy objects, as is evident in the high percentage of the total weight attributed to household and structural artifacts. As foundation stones and bricks were not collected and weighed, these figures do not reflect the fact that the Hart house stood on a more substantial foundation than the Tobias home. Rather, the difference between the two collections reflects the influence of food-related artifacts at each site. The Tobias collection has almost five times the number of food-related artifacts as the Hart collection, which suggests the Tobias household more frequently and typically used its property for food-related activities. Notably, while the Hart site has many fewer food-related artifacts than the Tobias site, the weight of food-related artifacts at both sites is about the same. This means that the typical food-related artifact at the Hart site is heavier than at the Tobias site, a reflection of an underlying difference in both the type and character of the food-related artifacts at the two sites.

Examining the food-related artifacts at each site explains this difference (see tables 5.3 and 5.4). Most food-related artifacts from the Tobias site consist of food remains such as shells, bones, nuts, and the remains of other consumables and food service artifacts such as ceramic and glass tableware. At the Hart site, food-related artifacts include very few actual food remains (36 items, accounting for just 3% of the total collection). The majority of food-related artifacts at the Hart site are instead either food service artifacts (59%) or food storage artifacts such as bottles and jars (33%). This distinction means that while the Tobiases processed and disposed of food remains on their property, the Harts appear to have brought food to their property that was processed such that the bones or shells would have already been removed. This may reflect a sampling bias, if for example the Harts disposed of food remains in sections of the site that could not be excavated. The presence of some food bone and shell in the Hart collection suggests we did not simply miss all of the food disposal at the site. Plus, to address this possibility, I conducted a pedestrian survey of the site and a close analysis of the banks of the stream running along its western edge for any traces of food remains disposal. None were found, but the recovery of historic bottle glass and ceramics in this survey, especially along the creek bed, suggests the Harts did not bring shell and bone to their home in any great quantity that could be identified archaeologically.

The disparity in the number of food storage artifacts, which consist predominantly of glass bottles and jars, suggests a greater reliance on finished goods packaged for consumer purchase at the Hart site than at the Tobias site. Narrowing the focus to look at just the food-related ceramic artifacts (tables 5.5 and 5.6), similar differences are evident. Both the Tobias and Hart ceramic assemblages are dominated (>70%) by food-related service artifacts (such as tablewares), but the Tobias collection has significantly more food preparation

Table 5.3. Food-Related Artifacts from the Silas Tobias Site Sorted by Functional Subcategory

Subcategory	Count	%	Weight (g)	%
Food Remains	1,852	37.4%	1,273.1	21.6%
Food Preparation	536	10.8%	1,096.6	18.6%
Food Procurement	444	9.0%	841.5	14.3%
Food Service	1,538	31.0%	1,493.5	25.3%
Food Storage	584	11.8%	1,199.4	20.3%
Other	14	0.3%	13.7	0.2%
Total	4,954		5,904.1	

Table 5.4. Food-Related Artifacts from the Jacob and Hannah Hart Site Sorted by Functional Subcategory

Subcategory	Count	%	Weight (g)	%
Food Remains	36	3.1%	188.0	3.4%
Food Preparation	17	1.4%	162.7	3.0%
Food Procurement	38	3.2%	79.8	1.5%
Food Service	693	58.9%	1,965.7	35.9%
Food Storage	392	33.3%	3,083.5	56.3%
Other	0	0.0%	0.0	0.0%
Total	1,176		5,479.7	

ceramics (e.g., coarse earthenware bowls) than the Hart site. In contrast, the Hart collection has many more food storage artifacts (e.g., stoneware bottles) than the Tobias collection. This pattern, mirroring the evidence of food remains, shows a greater emphasis on home-prepared versus purchased food-related items at the Tobias site and the opposite at the Hart site.

Important, this analysis of recovered materials does not include the several thousand shell fragments collected at the Tobias site. To maximize process-

Table 5.5. Food-Related Ceramics from the Silas Tobias Site Sorted by Functional Subcategory

Subcategory	Count	%	Weight (g)	%
Food Preparation	536	25.4%	1,096.6	36.9%
Food Service	1,521	72.2%	1,435.7	48.3%
Food Storage	51	2.4%	438.6	14.8%
Other	14	0.7%	13.7	0.5%
Total	2,108		2,971	

Table 5.6. Food-Related Ceramics from the Jacob and Hannah Hart Site Sorted by Functional Subcategory

Subcategory	Count	%	Weight (g)	%
Food Preparation	14	1.9%	58.3	2.5%
Food Service	580	78.9%	1,143.5	49.3%
Food Storage	141	19.2%	1,116.5	48.2%
Other	0	0.0%	0.0	0.0%
Total	735		2,318.3	

Table 5.7. Shells from the Silas Tobias Site Sorted by Species

Species	Weight (g)	%
Soft-shell Clam	42,456.7	71.2%
Hard-shell Clam	6,268.6	10.5%
Scallop	10,248.5	17.2%
Mussel	38.5	0.1%
Whelk	112.2	0.2%
Oyster	367.7	0.6%
Other	41.1	0.1%
Total	59,604.7	

ing time, individual shell specimens from the Tobias site were not counted but sorted by species and weighed (table 5.7). If the shells are rearticulated with the other as food remains in the Tobias collection, food-related materials make up almost 70% of the total artifact weight and more than 92% of the weight of all food-related artifacts. With shell included, that is, the Tobias site's collection exhibits even more evidence of activities related to processing and disposing of food-related materials at home.

Defining the Contexts and Questions

There is clear evidence of two different ways of life in the material results of household activities, especially those related to food, in the Tobias and Hart site collections. Yet, the two sites were occupied at different times and the contexts that influenced how people lived changed. Given the premise that anti-black racism intensified over time, the question is whether the excavated data from the Tobias and Hart sites reflect this changing racial dynamic or if other factors were also in play that need to be considered. The clearest distinction between the two sites is evidence for a greater reliance on self-provisioning and processing food remains at the Tobias site, which dates to the early and mid-1800s. This evidence contrasts with a greater reliance on food-related goods obtained in the market evidenced at the Hart site, which dates to the late 1800s and early 1900s. A transition from self-provisioned to market-acquired goods over the course of the nineteenth century, however, is not necessarily evidence of an intensification of racism and nothing else. This was also the era of America's industrial and consumer revolutions, when more and more Americans gave up self-provisioning, rural ways of life and moved to cities for waged work (Hounshell 1984; Rees 2013). While it is important to consider the dynamics of industrialization, consumerism, and wage labor, I advise we consider these alongside rather than instead of the dynamics of race and racism. Two reasons for this are tied to the place and the community in this study. First, Setauket was a rural village that changed little during the 1800s (Edward P. Buffet, William Sidney Mount: A Biography, 1924, Three Village Historical Society, Setauket, New York). In fact, one of the attributes of Setauket that residents enjoy today is that so much of its historic landscape and character remain intact (Klein 1986). The preservation of Setauket is a benefit for those who appreciate history, but it also reflects that Setauket and its residents experienced little change over time. Few moved to Setauket for work, so even as much about life changed dramatically across the United States, Setauket remained much the same. This is not say that Setauket never modernized. We already know that the Setauket Rubber Company factory opened in the 1880s and that Jacob Hart worked there. As such, there is a need to understand how issues related to economic modernization played a role in the Harts' lives. Yet the Tobiases and Harts were people of color, so their experience of modernizing Setauket was also informed and made distinct by the dynamic relationships and communities created by race and racism. How did their being people of color affect the way the Harts lived as Setauket modernized? What challenges did they face as a result of the legacies and intensification of racism within the larger community? Given the evident differences between the material records of the Harts and the Tobiases, how much of the Harts' way of life was influenced not only by sweeping changes in society but also by the way the community of color lived through these changes in their hometown?

A similar set of questions can be asked about the Tobiases while they lived in Old Field. Yet I have proposed a different frame—creole synthesis—for this analysis that prompts other questions as well. In particular, how did free people of color establish themselves and their communities in the emancipation era? What challenges did they, as the first generation of free people of color, have to manage in order to survive? What opportunities were available to them, specifically in the liminal years between the eras of slavery and the emergence of racial modernity? Of course, for both households and historical eras, I also need to ask how answers to these questions can be found in the materials recovered from the two sites.

Creole Synthesis at the Tobias Site

Although Silas Tobias was named in the 1823 deed, there is virtually nothing else known about him. The deed history does suggest he built a home on Conscience Bay in Old Field and that he was its first resident. The same is true for the other Tobiases who lived at the site during the nineteenth century, though we know more about the later residents from census records, as discussed in chapter 4. The archaeology of the Tobias site thus allows us to add significantly more to our understanding of the Tobias family, including how they lived at the site and what this implies about people of color during the era of creole synthesis.

To set the stage for discussing the archaeology at the Tobias site, I want to briefly consider what an archaeology of the creole synthesis might look like. The creole synthesis was defined by two forces. The first was emancipation, which changed the legal and social statuses of people of color and challenged the older order that associated blackness with slavery. The second was independence, or the strategies that people and communities of color developed as they shifted from living with whites to creating their own households, communities, and institutions. While emancipation is mostly political and independence mostly economic, these are nevertheless overlapping and integrated forces. They will be explored here through a single hypothesis that people of color during the creole synthesis sought to maintain control over essential aspects of their lives and that they did so in a way that made their freedom intentionally visible to the larger community.

Perhaps the most visible material statement associated with the Tobiases was founding the Bethel AME Church in 1848. As mentioned, three of the original trustees of the church were part of the extended Tobias family, and one of these, Abraham Tobias, was likely a resident and head of household at the Tobias site in Old Field. Establishing a new church solely for their use and purchasing a small lot for a house of worship and a cemetery made a statement to the surrounding community in both word and deed that people of color were not only free but building an independent community within Setauket. Clearly, the church was a powerful and visible social and cultural statement. Founded in 1848, around the time racial modernity was being established, the new church might also be understood as a sign of separation, both as an achievement and as a necessity as racism intensified. It is actually quite likely that founding a new and separate place of worship was a way for people of color to find refuge as the world around them changed for the worse.

Statements related to the community of color that more clearly reflects the creole synthesis are the headstones of Cane (1804) and Anthony Hannibal Clapp (1816), the latter of which I briefly discussed in chapters 1 and 3 (figure 1.8). On his headstone, Cane is described as

> an honest man
> Tho nature ting'd his skin and custom mark'd
> Him "Slave"! his mind
> Was fair, free and independent.
> His life all through was such as did command
> Esteem from those who knew him, and
> In death he shew'd examples of
> Religion full / Convincing of his christian faith,
> That his Redeemer liv'd
> And he should see his face.

Thought to have been written by Micah Hawkins, these verses focus on the humanity and capacities of Cane. He is described as someone who, though marked a slave, did not fit common expectations for the enslaved. In fact, he commanded esteem for his independent mind. At the end, so Hawkins implies, Cane knew well what was going to happen to his soul; perhaps he also knew what would happen to the souls of those who underestimated him or claimed him as their property.

Anthony Clapp's grave marker is a testament to his contributions to the Hawkins family and the larger Setauket and Stony Brook communities. We learn from the headstone that Clapp was both a servant to the Hawkins family and "of a race despis'd" but also a master who "deserv'd . . . much respect," because of his skilled fiddle playing, which the whole community witnessed, enjoyed, and benefited from. The Hawkins family acknowledged as much by paying for an elaborate and beautiful headstone visible to family members, their guests, and passersby along a local main road (figure 5.1). The lasting power of this monument was later recorded in a letter William Sidney Mount wrote in 1853: "[I] was so much struck with the sublimity and originality of one of the monuments to a distinguished fiddler, and as my late uncle Micah Hawkins wrote the epitaph and placed the stone to the old Negro's memory" (Tyler 2018). For Mount, Clapp was an example of what he sought from his work and his society—"sublimity and originality"—characteristics which also describe the ethos of the creole synthesis.

These headstones and the AME church provide a physical and temporal framework for understanding the materiality of the creole synthesis. Each is a

Figure 5.1. *The Slaves Grave*, n.d., by Shepard Alonzo Mount. (Courtesy of the Long Island Museum of American Art, History, & Carriages. Gift of the Estate of Dorothy deBevoise Mount, 1959.)

monument to the way race was expressed on the landscape in Setauket as well as a touchstone for how race relations developed during the first half of the nineteenth century. Moving from an early nineteenth-century monument erected by whites to their former slaves for embodying the spirit of the new nation to the establishment of a separate space by and for people of color to worship in 1848, we see the way people of color changed as they gained their freedom and sought to express and experience independence. We also see here how independence fostered separation in order to provide people of color a refuge from the troubles that came with having "ting'd" skin and being "a race despis'd." While it is hard to excavate the musical talent supporting Clapp's limited personal autonomy or the feelings of refuge that derived from the religious community at the AME, the Tobias site provides a way to see something similar in the way this household maintained and expressed their cultural and economic autonomy in the emancipation era.

To start, look again at the 1823 deed, which notes there was "a dwelling house and lot of Land Situated on the west Side of Conscience Bay in the town aforesaid containing by estimation half an acre as the fence now stands." With a house, property, and fence, Silas Tobias owned and occupied a home that anyone could see from both the road and the water. How he acquired the property is not known, but his presence there certainly was understood and accepted. In chapter 4 I noted that the household was recorded in the 1800 Federal Census in a listing for "Silas, a Negro," the head of five-person family (figure 3.7). This household is found on the same census page as five other free households of color comprising 27 individuals. That the households were recorded together like this suggests they formed a substantial enclave in the neighborhood of free people of color who were certainly visible to the rest of the community.

There is no record explaining why Silas Tobias sold his property in 1823 to Abraham Tobias. This decision may have been for a simple reason such as a need for money or a desire to move away. Yet the sale came just two years after New York State installed a new constitution that required men of color, and only men of color, possess $250 worth of real property "over and above all debts and encumbrances" in order to vote (New York State Archives 2018). While the Tobias property sold for $30, the decision to sell and to create a deed of the sale established the property was legally owned by a man of color. In a very material way, therefore, the deed and the property announced that Silas and Abraham Tobias were property-owning free men of color at a time when their status as citizens was growing more contested.

From the archaeology, the Tobias house appears to have been about 24 ft

Figure 5.2. The Brewster-Calvin home in Old Field, New York, as it appears today.

wide and 12 or 15 ft deep (figure 4.8). A house this size was probably two rooms, and there may have been a one-room ell off the back of the house. The projection of the ell is based on the recovery of an isolated stone in EU8 that could have been part of a pier support. The house also had a brick chimney on its north side that stood on a substantial stone foundation (figure 4.7). A house of roughly the same dimensions still stands on the opposite side of Old Field Road about 400 ft north of the Tobias lot (figure 5.2). This home is on a lot historically owned by Adam Brewster, the founding patriarch of the Calvin lineage in Setauket's Native and African American community. According to the deed history, Brewster purchased this quarter-acre lot in 1868. The property was worth $700 according to the 1870 census. A Civil War veteran, Brewster may have acquired the funds used to purchase the lot from his military discharge. Based on its appearance, I think the Brewster-Calvin home is a model for what the Tobias home looked like.

The Brewster-Calvin house is extremely small compared to other houses in Old Field. The home is five rooms today, but it has a modern extension off the back and a renovated front that account for some of the space. The original section is a small, three-bay end-gable frame house with a chimney on its north side likely built in the nineteenth century. Many of the characteristics of the Brewster-Calvin house are similar to the Tobias house, as it has been reconstructed from the archaeology. Both houses were small frame buildings with brick chimneys on their north sides, and both are Anglo-American in style and construction methods. The Tobias and Brewster-Calvin households, despite being people of color, both lived in inconspicuous homes that did not distinguish them from their neighbors and others in the region.

Distinctions between the Tobias household and their white neighbors, however, do appear when we look at the materials recovered in the excavations. The first to stand out is the large amount of shell found in the backyard midden (table 5.7). While not as dense as precontact shell middens on Long Island (Bernstein 1990, 1993, 2002, 2006; Ceci 1984; Cerrato et al. 1993; Lightfoot and Cerrato 1993; Salwen 1962), the midden deposit was unusually dense with shells for a historic site. Even acknowledging the fact that site is located on the shore, the density of shell is not typical for historic sites in the region, especially those dating to the nineteenth century. The vast majority of shells were softshell clam (*Mya arenaria*), a local species found in sandy or muddy bottoms of waters and estuaries like Conscience Bay. Most other species in the shell collection are also common in estuary waters. The shells thus indicate the bay was a source of food for the Tobias family, and the consistency of species diversity and ratio throughout the vertical extent of the midden (table 5.8) suggests the Tobiases exploited the shoreline throughout their tenure at the site. The use of shellfish for food may also have been only one part of the economic utility of this resource. The 1823 day book of merchant William Wickham Mills in nearby Smithtown records that people of color acquired credit at his store in exchange for pots of butter, dressed flax, and bushels of clams.[1] The Tobiases may have benefited from clams not only as a primary food source but also as a medium of exchange with local merchants.

Other faunal specimens from the Tobias site are quite diverse. Varieties of animals present are from various mammal, turtle, bird, and fish species (figure 5.3, table 5.9). Domesticated mammals include cattle, sheep, and pig. There is no evidence of standardized butchery traces, such as saw marks, and there is a quite a bit of the non-meaty parts of the animals, such as phalanges, skull and mandible fragments, in the collection. This suggests the Tobias family raised and butchered the animals themselves, a fact consistent with the fence mentioned in the 1823 deed. There are also bones from snapping turtle and small mammals, including rabbit and opossum, that suggest they trapped and hunted to supplement their diet. Bird species are both domestic and wild,

Table 5.8. Distribution of Marine Shell Species within the Midden Layers at the Silas Tobias Site

Level	Species	Weight (g)	%
A1	Hard-shell Clam	1,174.8	13.3%
	Mussel	21.1	0.2%
	Oyster	13.3	0.2%
	Scallop	1,243.2	14.1%
	Soft-shell Clam	6,311.0	71.5%
	Whelk	39.9	0.5%
A2	Hard-shell Clam	1,576.0	11.4%
	Mussel	8.7	0.1%
	Oyster	123.1	0.9%
	Scallop	2,224.3	16.1%
	Soft-shell Clam	9,841.7	71.1%
	Whelk	32.1	0.2%
A3	Hard-shell Clam	2,129.7	9.4%
	Mussel	3.6	0.0%
	Oyster	25.3	0.1%
	Scallop	4,348.0	19.2%
	Soft-shell Clam	16,086.8	71.0%
	Whelk	32.8	0.1%
A4/A5*	Hard-shell Clam	821.3	6.7%
	Mussel	1.6	0.0%
	Oyster	102.0	0.8%
	Scallop	2,298.4	18.8%
	Soft-shell Clam	8,998.9	73.5%
	Whelk	4.1	0.0%
B1/B2*	Hard-shell Clam	27.4	5.1%
	Mussel	1.0	0.2%
	Oyster	0.1	0.0%
	Scallop	59.0	11.0%
	Soft-shell Clam	449.4	83.7%
	Whelk	0.0	0.0%

Note: Data derived from unit excavations in the backyard midden (EU1, EU2, EU5, EU8, and EU9). Terrestrial snails and unidentified shells are not included. All excavated levels were 10 cm in depth.

Levels A4 and A5 and Level B1 and B2 are combined because they were not designated in all excavation units.

Table 5.9. Animal Taxa in the Silas Tobias Collection

Taxon	NISP
Cattle (*Bos taurus*)	28
Sheep (*Ovis aries*)	6
Sheep/Goat (*Ovis/Capra*)	23
Pig (*Sus scrofa*)	29
Cat (*Felis cattus*)	1
Rabbit (*Sylvilagus*)	1
Opossum (*Didelphis*)	1
"Sheep-Sized"	17
"Cattle-Sized"	5
Rodent	2
Small Mammal	4
Unidentified Mammal	850
Chicken (*Gallus gallus*)	3
Goose (*Anser*)	1
Duck (*Anas platyrhynchos*)	17
"Chicken-Sized"	2
"Goose-Sized"	2
Unidentified Bird	55
Turtle	6
Fish	134
Unidentified	383

and specimens include chicken, goose, and several duck bones. The collection also includes a large number of fish vertebrae. Along with the water birds and shells, these indicate the use of the nearby shoreline for wild food resources (Crabtree 2018).

Analysis of botanical remains indicate that the Tobiases made use of wild plants with edible, household, and medicinal uses. Species identified include amaranth or pigweed, a leafy vegetable used as a dye, medicinal, and ornamental plant; *Galium* used as bedding material or mattress stuffing as well as a potherb, coffee substitute, medicine, and dye; huckleberry and cherry, wild edible fruits; and sumac, which is used as a tea, jelly, dye, and medicine (McKnight 2017:9–10).

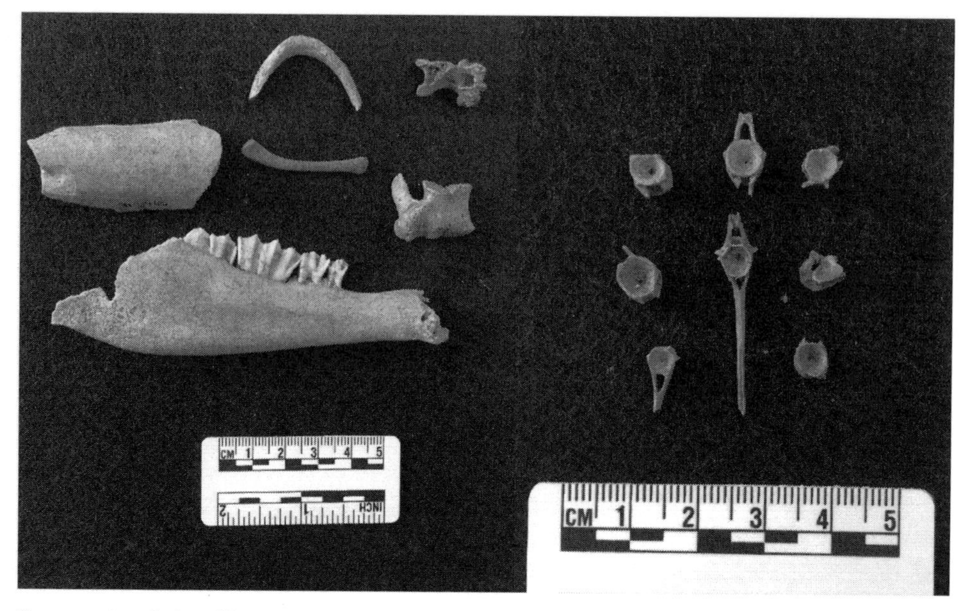

Figure 5.3. Sample faunal bone recovered at the Tobias site.

An unexpected component of the Tobias assemblage is 440 lithic tool and debitage fragments (figure 5.4). In an extensive analysis, Mark Tweedie (2017) makes a strong case that these artifacts are contemporaneous with the historic Tobias household and that they represent the use of lithic technology by the occupants in the nineteenth century. The artifacts are almost all quartz (98%), a stone readily available along the shore of the Long Island Sound. The majority (97%) of the tools were produced using centripetal, or free-hand, reduction of quartz cobbles, the most common technique used to produce lithic tools in the precontact period on Long Island (Bernstein and Lenardi 2008). The lithic collection includes evidence of primary debitage, retouching scars, and tertiary flakes, indicating the tools were likely made and maintained on-site. The chert point in figure 5.5 was more likely collected than made by the Tobiases, yet retouching scars may be the result of the family's sharpening of the tool to improve its usefulness. The collection of lithics indicates a wide range of possible functions including projectiles, knives, and a spectrum of generalized scraping, cutting, and engraving tools. These artifacts thus indicate the use of freely available materials for varied tasks that built on knowledge of traditional local technology and, as such, mirror the evidence of shoreline food exploitation.

A final set of artifacts rounds out this discussion of the Tobias site collec-

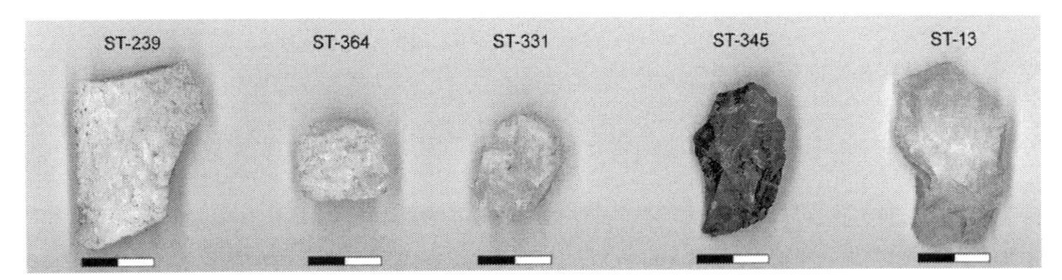

Figure 5.4. Selected modified flake tools from the Silas Tobias site. ST-239 (EU-9) modified thinning flake tool with lateral retouch. ST-364 (EU-11) thumbnail scraper with lateral retouch and beveled flaking wear. ST-331 (EU-9) modified flake tool with serrated flake scars. ST-345 (EU-10) chert flake tool with lateral wear. ST-13 (EU-1) modified flake of high quality quartz with beveled edge retouch. Scale: 1 cm. (Courtesy of Mark Tweedie.)

Figure 5.5. Chert projectile (ST-107) recovered at the Silas Tobias site. The white line shown on both faces of the artifact below delineates between the areas of retouch along the distal blade and the weathered cortex that formed at the proximal end. Scale: 1 cm. (Courtesy of Mark Tweedie.)

tion: the remains of two eel spearheads discovered in excavation adjacent to the house footprint (figure 5.6). Eel spears are long-handled wooden shafts with wrought iron heads used to capture and hold slippery eels by pinching their thick skin. The style of eel spears at the Tobias house would have had a central spoon that would have impaled the eel while the tines on each side would have aligned the eel's body and held it in place. The tool was designed to be able to capture the eel and keep it alive so that it could sold fresh (*New York Times*, 4 February 1985; Salive 2019). As eels live in Conscience Bay and other local waters, eel spearing demonstrates still more evidence that the Tobiases exploited their immediate local environment for food resources.

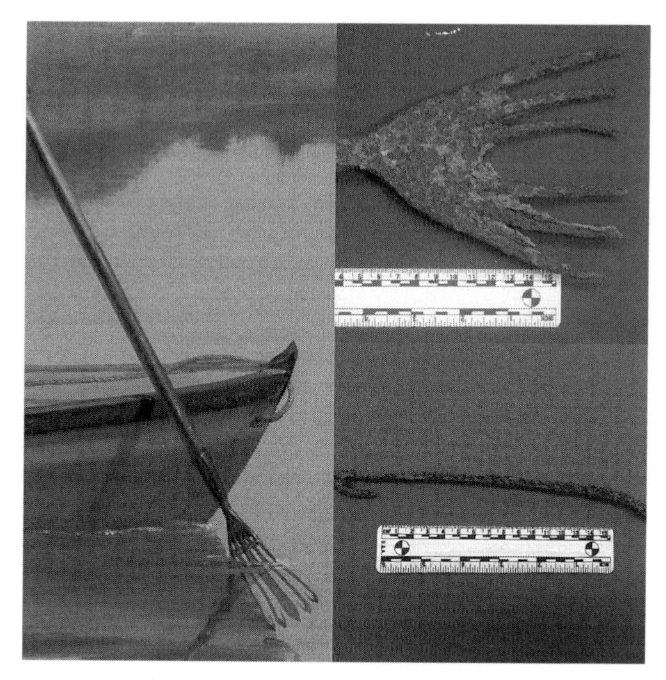

Figure 5.6. *Left*, detail showing the eel spearhead in William Sidney Mount's *Eel Spearing at Setauket*. *Upper right*, eel spearhead recovered in EU11 at the Silas Tobias Site. *Lower right*, eel spearhead tine recovered in EU3 at the Silas Tobias site.

Eel spearing also has a deep resonance in Setauket because of William Sidney Mount's master work *Eel Spearing at Setauket* (figure 1.6). As discussed in chapter 1, this painting was commissioned by a member of the wealthy Strong family as a reminder of the simpler days of his youth. Important here is that the spearhead in the painting is the essentially the same type as those recovered at the Tobias site. Historical documents indicate the setting of the painting is Conscience Bay, looking east across the water toward Strong's Neck. This vantage point would have been close to the Tobias property. As a local resident, Mount likely knew the Tobias family. He was known to employ local people of color as models, so some think that the model in *Eel Spearing* was named Rachel Holland Hart, who was born Rachel Tobias (Green 1999). There is an argument, therefore, that the woman in the painting and the eel spear she is holding were both from the Tobias household and that the eel spear she is holding may be the same one recovered in the archaeological excavation at the site.

In sum, the material evidence from the Silas Tobias archaeological site provides clear evidence that the family made regular use of locally available natural resources to support their livelihood. The evidence also suggests they knew and used traditional Native American cultural knowledge, including both lithic technology and the choice to live near access to essential shoreline resources such as fish, shellfish, and water bird species long used by indigenous Long Islanders. While there is no documentation indicating the Tobiases identified as Native Americans, in many ways they lived lives quite similar to local indigenous people.

The question now is whether these archaeological findings support the hypothesis that the archaeological record from the Silas Tobias site embody aspects of the creole synthesis. I proposed that people and households like those associated with the Tobias site would have maintained as much control as they could over essential aspects of lives and would have done so in a ways visible to others. I described how the 1823 deed identifies a small property with a house situated in clear view of the community from both the road and the water. In this way, members of the Tobias household would have been in regular view of the community as they lived and worked on their property. The location and building methods of a small home were identified archaeologically, confirming data found in the deed. The house was built in an Anglo-American style, standing on stone and brick piers with a brick chimney set on a stone foundation. Faunal remains show the family kept and butchered their own animals. Given that the deed says lot was fenced in, it is likely the property functioned as a small rural household typical of the region in the early nineteenth century. While the backyard was a rich trash midden, the site was easily demarcated archaeologically into different sections, showing it was well organized, a feature that would reflect well on a household trying to minimize the visible distinctions that others would have looked for because of their race. The archaeological record also shows the Tobiases made regular and extensive use of the shoreline and waters of Conscience Bay for subsistence. Evidence that they collected fish, eels, turtles, water birds, and shellfish is abundant in the assemblage. Again, these would have been typical activities for other households in Setauket with shore access to supplement their food resources. In this way, the Tobiases minimized the distinctions between themselves and others and did so through activities that would have been clearly visible to neighbors.

At the same time, the archaeological collection provides evidence for activities the Tobiases practiced that others in Setauket likely did not perform. Hunting and trapping animals and collecting practical, medicinal, and food resources from wild plants was in decline in Setauket as the market came to be the source for these sorts of items as the nineteenth century progressed.[2] Most of all, the manufacture and use of stone tools would have been unfamiliar to white neighbors who did not have any tradition or experience using this technology. Collecting forest resources and cobbles for stone tools would not have been as visible as collecting resources along the shore or on the water, so perhaps these practices were less of a concern for the Tobiases in their attempt to minimize visible differences between themselves and other free people. However, these practices are based in traditions originating with the indigenous people who lived in Setauket before colonization. Perhaps these activities were embraced by the Tobiases as core parts of their ancestral culture, even if they made family members seem different from their neighbors.

It is also true that making use of ancient subsistence and technology would have helped the Tobiases maintain autonomy from white merchants and neighbors, which would have offered its own set of strategic benefits. For one, access to and use of freely available local resources gave the Tobiases the economic autonomy and control to pursue work and other relationships with whites approximating equity between the races. Second, being able to provide for themselves through natural resources would have allowed the Tobiases to show other people of color the benefits of working for economic autonomy, which may have included and been expanded by land ownership and, after 1821, citizenship rights. Finally, the preservation of indigenous knowledge and technological skill would have symbolized the diverse heritage of people of color in Setauket giving descendants multiple lines of memory and identity to celebrate and share.

The effects of living autonomously may also underlie the meaning of other historical materials that reflect the creole synthesis. First, the authentic and carefully crafted image of the eel spearer painted by Mount—a woman who dominates and controls the scene by towering over the boat and her young white charge—aligns with an understanding that the daily life at the Tobias household was organized, successful, and framed by the family's autonomy. It is arguable that Mount was trying to express this message by making a woman of color the central subject of the work. Given the tendency of genre painting to depict life as it was, Mount may have chosen his subject exactly because of how impressive this woman, who may have been a member of the Tobias family, was in real life. Second, the autonomy of the Tobias family is likely also why the community of color at large selected three Tobias men as founding trustees of the Bethel AME Church in 1848. While the trustees themselves deserve credit for organizing and leading the congregation and purchasing the property for a church and cemetery, these men certainly enjoyed the support of their community to be selected as its representatives. It is likely their leadership rested on an ability to live autonomously from whites as free people of color, evidenced by their maintaining their own property, enjoying the benefits of freely available natural resources, and gaining the respect of peers and such white allies as Mount. Notably, in this case, it was not the preservation of their Native American or African ancestry that was at stake but the capacity to successfully lead a household of color in the context of an increasingly racist culture.

Racial Modernity at the Jacob and Hannah Hart Site

On September 21, 1938, the category 3 Long Island Express hurricane swept across Long Island, the eye of the storm passing just a few miles east of Setauket. The storm caused considerable damage and resulted in as many as 100 deaths. It remained an intense storm as it traveled into New England, where winds and flooding killed another 700 people in five states (*Washington Post*, 21 September 2018). In and around Setauket, the effects of the storm were clearly powerful. In Northport, 13 miles west of Setauket, "trees fell like match sticks," substantial property damage was caused by "uprooted trees, washouts, and flooded cellars," and boats were "piled up at the head of the harbor" and "private docks destroyed" (*Northport Journal*, 23 September 1938). The hurricane's specific impact in Setauket is not known, but there is evidence of the storm in the archaeological record at the Hart home site, where Jacob and Hannah Hart moved in 1888. Both Harts lived at the site until their deaths; Hannah passed away in 1922 and Jacob passed away in 1931. In the 1930 census only Jacob and his youngest son, Ernest Hart, were living at the home. Listed as the sole resident in the 1940 census, Ernest Hart is thought to have been living in the home when the 1938 hurricane struck but left soon after. The Harts' property included a frame house with an attached kitchen ell that stood on a stone foundation. The home also had a series of brick pathways and stone-covered surfaces as well as a spring-fed well that provided easy access to fresh water 10 m west of the house. Another 10 m west, the property abutted a creek that feeds the mill pond downstream. The creek would have provided cool air, occasional food and medicinal resources, and certainly a lovely and safe place for children to play. In all, it seems to have been a small yet tidy and well-apportioned household and property.

Further research suggests a different interpretation. Archaeological evidence suggests that the site was a difficult place to live because of a constant battle with ground water. The sense of the site as waterlogged was obvious to the archaeological team who quickly encountered ground water during excavation, sometimes just a few inches below the ground surface. Though the water created difficult conditions for the excavation, we thought that the high water table was the result of the silting in of the mill pond downstream over time after the mill closed. Furthermore, it was assumed this silting occurred after the Harts left the site; who would live in such a wet place?

Carlton "Hubble" Edwards, Pearl Lewis Hart, and Caroline Moore, elders in the descendant community, each remember visiting the home when the Harts lived there and recall that there was a well under the home that the Harts accessed by lifting the floorboards. There is no archaeological evidence for a feature like this under the house, so I think these elders remember instead that the family could lift the floorboards to reveal standing groundwater. In fact, community historian Theodore Green (1999:66) recalled the Harts "maintained a boat to clear the millpond of weeds." Green's implication is that Jacob Hart should be praised for his contribution to the beautification of the village. Based on the trouble with water at his home, however, it is as likely he was clearing weeds from the pond so that the water would flow better away from his property. The struggle with groundwater is also a good reason why the family laid in multiple brick pathways and stone surfaces (see chapter 4). These landscape features connect the front and side doors of the home to the street front and provide a paved path to the well west of the house. Stone, especially, is not easily accessible on Long Island, which consists mostly of a sandy subsoil, so the use of stone for a pathway suggests a strong desire to create solid ground, perhaps to mitigate the way water created a slippery and muddy surface across the site.

The Harts' struggle with groundwater ended in 1938 because of the Long Island Express. By then Ernest Hart was the last person living in the house, so he likely experienced the storm alone, hoping the house would withstand the assault. A 1948 document signed by three of his sisters noted that the home was abandoned and torn down in earlier years. Those who knew Ernest recall that he moved to Bridgeport, Connecticut, where he lived for several years before returning to Setauket and moving to a small house on his sister Lucy's property on Christian Avenue (see chapter 2). It seems most likely that the house was damaged badly enough by the storm that Ernest and his siblings found no reason to try to save it.

Archaeological evidence in fact suggests the site was seriously affected by the hurricane. As discussed in chapter 4, the excavated western yard section of the site contained two stratigraphic layers that tell the recent landscape history of the site (figure 4.16). The uppermost layer is a thick jumble of roots and soil that was virtually impenetrable, and below this matte was a gritty gray sand that was up to 16 cm thick. These layers contained few artifacts overall, suggesting the site was mostly unused when they were created. Below the sand is a buried former ground surface, the brick and stone landscape features, and an abundance of domestic artifacts. This stratigraphic sequence indicates that the ground surface at the time the Harts lived there was buried by the gray sand deposit. This deposit is thought to have been introduced by flooding associated with the Long Island Express, which effectively ended any further use of the site by Ernest Hart or anyone else.

Notably, the Harts' home was the only house in the area damaged enough by the storm to be torn down. Every other structure depicted on the 1917 Belcher Hyde map not only survived the hurricane but still stands in Setauket today (figure 2.9). These homes survived because they were built on higher and more stable ground than the low-lying swampy land the Harts contended with. That the Harts lived on a poorly drained lot likely reflects the limitations they faced as people of color in Setauket. In addition, homes nearby that survived the storm now contribute to the Old Setauket Historic District, which recognizes their historic architectural significance and the past and present white homeowners who lived in the neighborhood. The loss of the Hart home to storm and water damage is one way Setauket's community of color has been left out of the dominant heritage narrative, and in this case the community also lost out on the benefits of owning a property with an inflated value due to its historical associations.[3]

Recent home values, though, have historical roots. Census data from 1930 included an assessment of the value of properties in the neighborhood surrounding the Harts. Thirty of the 40 homes on Main Street were owner occupied in 1930 and had an average value of $8,540. Twenty-eight of these 30 homes were white-owned, with an average value of $9,064. Only two homes were owned by people of color. Jacob and Hannah Hart's home was valued at $2,000, while Charles and Roselene Scott's home was valued at just $400. The average value of homes on Main Street owned by whites in 1930 was thus more than seven times greater than homes owned by people of color. Expanding this comparison, 25 households of color in Brookhaven Township owned their own homes, with an average property value of $2,297, a figure comparable to the value of the Harts' home. Yet the nine people of color who owned homes in Setauket had an average property value of $3,756, much higher than the Harts. The low value of the Harts' home suggests census takers were aware of the poor situation the house was in. Notably, many of the highly valued properties owned by people of color in 1930 were on Christian Avenue, including the home owned by Lucy Keyes, Jacob and Hannah's youngest daughter. This racialized settlement pattern was felt across the village. By 1940 almost 80% of all people of color in Setauket lived on Christian Avenue, and no people of color have lived on Main Street since 1950. This displacement was followed soon after by the designation of the properties along Main Street as a historic district. It is hardly a surprise that the historic district fails to note the people of color who lived in and in some cases owned the homes now celebrated for their history, but it is interesting to see that the movement for historic designation occurred after people of color lost or gave up their homes there.

The Harts' home is documented in both a historical photograph and in the archaeological record (figures 4.10 and 4.12). A projected footprint based on a combination of features identified in the excavation and the historic image indicate the house was about 24 ft wide and 12 ft deep with a 12 ft by 6 ft kitchen ell attached to the back. In the photograph the home had a central front door with one room on each side. The room on the right was slightly larger and had the hearth, which suggests this was the parlor, while the smaller room on the left was likely a bedroom. A window in the peak of the gable end suggests a loft probably used as a bedroom for children. A side door provided direct access into the kitchen ell from the side yard.

The Hart and Tobias houses were actually very similar. Both homes were frame construction, though the Hart home was built at least in part on a more substantial stone foundation. This may have been an accommodation so the home would better withstand the impacts of the high water table. It may also be a feature that was original to the house, which, assuming the home was built by owners who preceded the Harts, reflects a greater investment in the property by the Smiths or other previous white owners. Other than the differences in their foundations, the two homes are both small having only about 360 square ft of living space. Given such limited interior space, the Tobiases clearly made extensive use of their yard area as a work space and household refuse disposal area. Having a similarly small home, the Harts certainly also used their yard for various activities. A 1902 certificate of marriage for William Smith Sells and Hannah Hart (who grew up in the home) in fact states that they were married at "the house of Jacob Hart, Setauket, Long Island." This ceremony and perhaps a reception after likely took place both inside and around the Harts' home.

Both Lucy Hart Keyes and Theodore Green remember the yard having animal pens and gardens. Green (1999:66) recalled that the "Harts had a house . . . where they kept pigs, chickens, and ducks." Keyes noted that "those old folks [her parents] had a lovely home down there. . . . My father kept it up beautiful. . . . A lot of these flowers come from down home" (Lucy Hart Keyes,

This Certifies
Marriage
Witnesses

Figure 5.7. Marriage certificate for William Smith Sells and Hannah Hart, 1902. The ceremony was held at the "House of Jacob Harts." (Courtesy of Helen Sells.)

Transcript of oral history interview, 9 May 1987:2–3, 10, Three Village Historical Society, Setauket, New York). Keyes also recalled that her parents kept an orderly yard, noting that "everybody here had a garden." The Harts also had a neatly trimmed hedgerow along the street front that can be seen in the photograph (figure 4.10). These hedges are still growing at the site, reaching now to more than 10 ft in height.

While the Tobias site likely also had a garden, there is no direct evidence for one in the documentary or archaeological record. However, the meaning of gardening may have shifted over time as conditions for people of color changed. The Tobiases likely enjoyed having a garden as it provided both fresh food as well as independence from the market, like the shoreline food sources they collected. By the time the Harts lived on Lake Street, a garden likely played a different role. For one, Jacob Hart's obituary notes that "in past years he was accounted one of the best workmen at the rubber factory, and when that enterprise failed, he took up the work of gardening." Archaeologically, there is material culture connected to gardening at the Hart site in the form of fragments of ceramic flower pots, an artifact type not found in the Tobias collection.

Based on the obituary, gardening appears to have been a marketable skill in the early 1900s, though gardening may have been a euphemism for a more generalized domestic labor on the area's large estates. Gardeners were, after all, one of the groups exempted from racial covenants in Old Field South. Lucy Keyes experienced a reversal of this process. She noted that she had to give up gardening when she was younger because she had to leave home for work: "So when I decided to go to work, you see, somebody had to be around to look after the pigs and chickens so I got rid of all of them. Well, I needed the money! (Big laugh) Need the money, dearie! Hoo-hoo, I'm telling you when you have two children—I only had the two—but when you have to dress 'em and you know well years ago wages was cheap here! my god!" (Lucy Hart Keyes, Transcript of oral history interview, 9 May 1987:2–3, Three Village Historical Society, Setauket, New York). At the same time, she described her gardening as a necessity: "lawd knows, have to have everything to make a living here. . . . You didn't have those pigs and chickens and things to help you along during the winter. . . . Yea I tell you . . . you's in a bad fix."

The physical characteristics of the Hart site show the family faced more difficult conditions there than did the Tobiases at their home in Old Field. The Harts dealt with high groundwater and flooding that not only made living at the site a challenge but also devalued their property and ultimately eliminated their home from the landscape. The site itself also reflects aspects of challenges shared with the Tobiases, as both families occupied very small homes. Yet the space surrounding the Tobias home afforded the family opportunities to gather from the shore and their property essential resources that sustained their autonomy from the market and white-dominated laboring activities. The Harts' home site likely afforded some similar opportunities, including even hosting a family wedding there. Yet the clearest evidence is of a consistent effort to manage the landscape against the impact of flooding. While oral history tells us that the family enjoyed gardening, the landscape of the site as well as the flower pot fragments suggest even this was a struggle. One result is that gardening became a waged job for Jacob Hart to do for others. That Jacob Hart had to sell his gardening labor on the market while the Tobiases gardened for their own benefit provides a sense of how racial modernity took hold in the lives of people of color in Setauket.

The Harts and Tobiases at Work

Stories of gardening follow a steady progression in the work experience of people of color in Setauket. Early families like the Tobiases enjoyed access to land and shoreline where they collected and produced essential resources. Those like the Harts who lived in later years lost access to these private resources, which had helped to sustain social and economic stability. They relied instead on the labor market to earn the income required for the goods they needed. Census and other documents indicate Jacob Hart worked in the Setauket rubber factory, as a mason, and for a shipbuilder. We also already know that at some point he "took up the work gardening," presumably meaning that he sought to work as a gardener for pay. Lucy Hart Keyes's experience reflects a next step in this trajectory in which she had to give up gardening in order to do other work, which for her was domestic labor in white households. Records show that both Jacob Hart and Lucy Hart Keyes kept gardens and even animal pens at their homes, but this work was done in addition to other labor performed elsewhere and for other people. Doubling the workload required for survival certainly reflects more difficult circumstances experienced by the Harts and their children than the sort of routines that we have evidence for at the Tobias site.

Another example of the increasingly difficult experiences for the Harts derives from work performed by Hannah Hart, Jacob's wife. We get a sense of her work in an entry made on October 23, 1907, in the Tyler Brothers Store account book.[4] In addition to two pounds of sugar and a piece of candy, Hannah Hart purchased four collars and a spool of thread. She had already purchased two other collars that year and would buy eight more over the following months as well as a length of silk fabric. These items confirm census data that documents that Hart was a laundress and seamstress, both common and important ways women of color in Setauket made a living. Notably, Hannah Hart's store account was credited $2.75 on November 16 and again on December 3 in 1908 for unspecified work. One wonders if this was for doing laundry or seamstress work for the Tyler family?

Census records show that women of color in the Town of Brookhaven experienced substantial change in the sorts of work they did during the Harts' tenure in their Setauket home. A summary of occupational records for women of color between the 1860 and 1930 is presented in table 5.10. In 1860 women of color with occupations mostly lived in independent households and made a living doing laundry for others in the community as well as working as domestics in white-headed households. By 1900 the number of women of color living in-

Table 5.10. Occupations of Women of Color in the Town of Brookhaven, 1860–1930

Type of Labor	1860	1900	1930
Resident Domestics	41	63	20
Nonresident Domestics	17	8	32
Laborers	3	24*	2
Laundresses	38	29	15
Wage Workers	0	8	14
Self-Employed	0	0	3
TOTAL	99	132	86
Living in White-headed Household	36	68	30
Living in Independent Households of Color	63	64	55

Note: *Many of the laborers in 1900 were probably nonresident domestics.

dependently declined, and more than half of those with recorded occupations lived in white-headed households working as resident domestics. While most of those living in independent households in 1900 still did laundry and domestic work, eight women were part of the waged workforce as waitresses and nurses. By 1930 the number of working women of color living in independent households rebounded. Most of these women continued to work as domestics and washerwomen, though the number of waged workers rose to 14. Wage work recorded for women of color included mostly laboring jobs in hospitals, institutions, and private laundry companies, though three women ran businesses of their own: dressmaker Jessica Osborn, farmer Mary Cuffee, and fish dealer Mary Jones.

These occupational data show working women of color in the Town of Brookhaven shifted from living in independent households with their families in 1860 to having to give up their separate homes and live with their employers in 1900 to again mostly living independently in 1930. This trend suggests that in 1860 the local economy and standing of people of color was strong enough that most could support themselves through a variety of work, which gave them residential autonomy from whites even though most still earned their living by working for whites. Many women who made a living doing laundry for whites likely used their homes as workplaces, providing an additional sense of autonomy. A decline in the economic standing of people of color between the end of the Civil War and the start of the twentieth century forced almost half of employed women of color to give up residential autonomy and move to live with their white employers. In addition, we also see a significant decline in the percentage of employed women of color taking in laundry (38% in 1860 versus 22% in 1900). This decline meant more women of color worked outside the home to earn an income, including those working for wages in 1900.

In 1930 the number of women of color earning a wage from nondomestic employers almost doubled and indeed does double if we include those who operated their own businesses. Certainly these entrepreneurs should be recognized for the talent and bravery required to operate businesses of their own, but in two of the three cases (Osborn and Jones) this work contributed incomes that supplemented those earned by men in their homes. The data from 1930 also show a decline in the number of women of color taking in laundry as well as a decline in the number of women working as resident domestics in white-headed households. The shift in preference among white-headed households for nonresident domestic servants is likely connected to other issues related to economic and race relations in the 1920s and 1930s. These include the establishment of new home developments such as Old Field South that came with racial covenants. This was also an era on Long Island that saw marches and meetings of the Ku Klux Klan and the American Nazi Party in Nassau and Suffolk Counties (*New York Times*, 6 July 1926; *New York Post*, 20 May 2017). The point is that by the 1920s many whites were becoming increasingly uncomfortable sharing a home with nonwhite employees and even preferred not to hire women of color to do their laundry. The fact that four of the women performing waged work were employed by private laundry companies provides evidence of an alternative to hiring women of color directly to do laundry. Of course, women of color who had previously earned a living taking in laundry not only lost clients, but some likely had to start to work for white managers to do the same job. The women of color employed by hospitals and social institutions probably also did laundry for a living while working for white employers. These data thus show a sharp reduction in the independence and autonomy of women of color, a factor that clearly made life more difficult for them in the early decades of the twentieth century.

Hannah Hart's obituary noted that she was born in Virginia in 1856 and came to Port Jefferson as a young woman to work as a domestic servant for the Woodhull Wheeler family (*County Review*, 27 October 1922). It is also reported that she received an education in exchange for this indenture. During these years, she met Jacob Hart, and the two were married in 1874 and their first child, Rebecca, was born in 1877. The 1900 census record for the Hart family indicates Hannah was a laundress, and in 1910 she is listed as a washerwoman (US Census, Town of Brookhaven, Suffolk County, New York, 1900, 1910). As discussed, laundry work was a common occupation for women of color in the region, and this work provided a way to maintain autonomy since women did this work in their own homes and were thus self-employed. Yet the number of women of color doing laundry after 1900 declined, and many entered the waged work force as a result.

Hart's laundry work is evident in the archaeological record at her home site. Excavations recovered sewing- and laundry-related artifacts such as a thimble, a scissor blade, 27 buttons of a wide variety, a straight pin, and a fragment of a sewing machine oil bottle (figure 5.8). It is certainly possible that some of these materials derived from members of the Hart household, but the fact that Hannah Hart was documented as a laundress suggests that some or all are results of her work. Each button recovered was a different type, which suggests the buttons were from laundry work rather than lost from clothing owned by the family. These materials can be better understood if they are compared to similar artifacts found at the Tobias site. Tobias clothing and sewing artifacts include two buckles, 34 buttons, six clasps, a shoe heel, shoe nails, a rivet, two straight pins, a thimble, a hair clip, glass bead, a pierced brass ornament, and a decorative pin (figure 5.8). While the Tobias collection is more diverse in terms of the different types of artifacts present, this reflects the better preservation and excavation conditions at the Tobias site compared to the Hart site as well as the fact that the Tobias site was home to three generations instead of just one. Still, a very large number of women of color reportedly worked in the laundry business in 1860 including Emeline Tobias, who is among those thought to have lived at the Tobias site. These materials are thus likely also a result of her work at the home. It is notable nonetheless that there is an absence of certain artifacts directly related to sewing and laundry labor rather than the family's clothing at the Tobias Site. Specifically, unique to the Hart site is a scissor blade and a sewing machine oil bottle.

The scissor blade recovered from the Hart site shows that making and repairing clothing was part of the work that Hannah Hart did to earn an income at her home. I mentioned that Jessica Osborn, another woman of color in the community, was a dressmaker in 1930. It is thus likely that other women of color made clothing to sell, though perhaps they did not see it as a business separate from working in laundry. The collars Hannah Hart purchased could be a sign of clothing manufacture or repair. Given that Emeline Tobias was a washerwoman in 1860, the absence of scissors may reflect a different set of expectations of what would be involved in laundry work than for Hannah Hart.

The sewing machine oil bottle tells a complementary story of how laundry

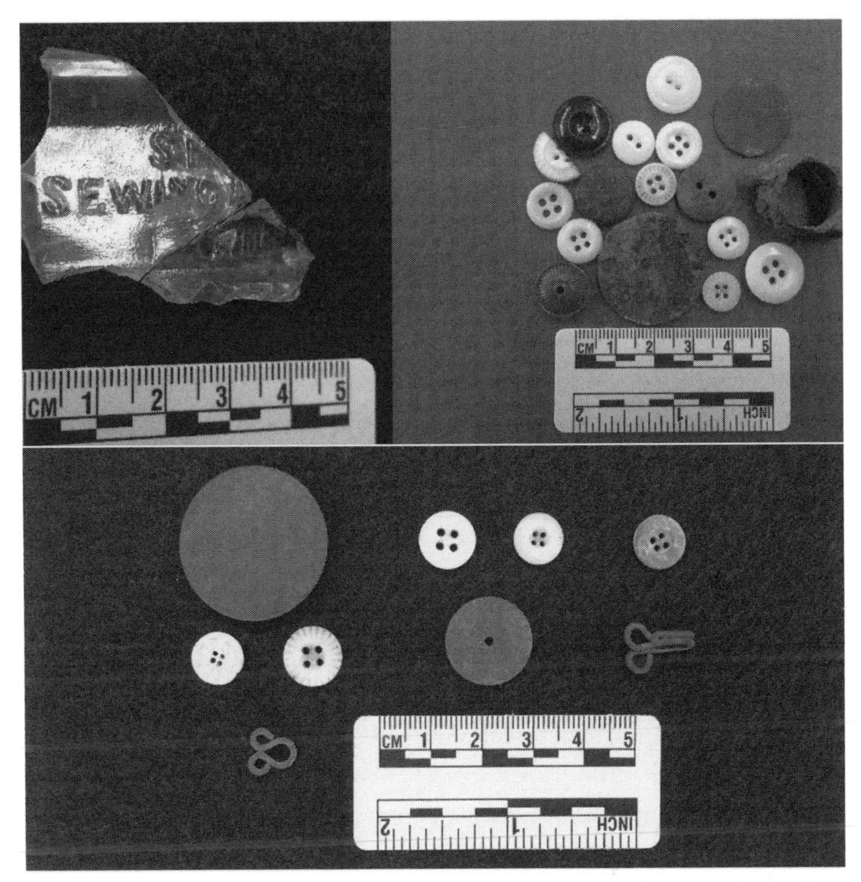

Figure 5.8. Sewing and laundry-related artifacts from the Jacob and Hannah Hart site (*top*) and the Tobias site (*bottom*).

work changed for women of color in the late nineteenth century. The small glass fragments of the machine oil bottle are embossed with the word "sewing" as well as fragments of two other words. The full phrase was "sperm sewing machine oil," indicating the bottle contained a lubricating oil derived from sperm whales (Devantier-Thomas 2017). Sperm oil, more properly a wax, was a prized resource in the 1800s used especially in lamps because it burned brighter and cleaner than other fuels. Even though its use as lamp oil declined after the introduction of kerosene in the 1870s, sperm oil continued to be used as a lubricant for household tools such as sewing machines and watches well into the twentieth century. The excavated sewing oil bottle fragments from the Hart site dates to the late nineteenth century, suggesting the Harts had a sewing machine early on in their home on Lake Street. A sewing machine would have been a good investment, since it would have allowed Hannah Hart to be more productive and efficient as a laundress. Yet it was a tool that certainly cost the family the price of the machine and of course other materials, like the sperm oil, to keep it maintained. The extra costs of a sewing machine and its maintenance, scissors, thimbles, and the many other items laundresses used indicate that laundry work developed into a professional sort of employment with higher expectations for the levels of effort and skill required. The extra cost of this work perhaps explains why fewer women of color did this work in 1900 than in 1860. It may also reflect advantages that Hannah Hart acquired, such as sewing skills learned as an indentured teenaged servant at the Wheeler Woodhull home, that allowed her to stay in the laundry business even as many of her peers had to give up their independence and work as live-in domestics for white families or do waged work for white employers.

It is also possible that the sperm whale industry may have had special meaning for Jacob Hart. We know from his obituary he "followed the sea for a time." Native American and African American men from Long Island and New England often found well-paying jobs on whaling ships and other maritime trade vessels in the nineteenth century (Barsh 2002; Bolster 1997; Handsman 2011; Linenebagh and Rediker 2001; McGovern 2015b). With no record of Jacob living in Setauket between the 1870 census, when he was 14 years old, and 1888, when he and Hannah purchased their home, it is likely he worked at sea during those years. So while the oil bottle may have had a basic functional and economic purpose supporting Hannah's laundry labor, it could also have been part of the story the Harts told themselves about how working on the water helped them survive as people of color on the margins of their home community.

If Hannah Hart's laundry work contributed to the family's income while they lived on Lake Street, we should then think of the Hart home site as a place of work. Elders in the community today remember that it was common for women of color to take in laundry as late as the 1950s (interview with Carlton Edwards, 12 June 2014; interview with Barbara Russell, 11 July 2013). These elders remember that laundry work consumed households both inside and out. Inside, clothing was washed and rung out in tin tubs and then ironed, and outside, laundry was dried on clotheslines before it was folded to make it ready for its owner to pick up. Thus, the landscape of a site used for laundry would have had to be tidy and vast, and, with laundry drying on the lines, clearly visible. At the Hart site I think we see evidence of this in the multiple paved surfaces uncovered in the excavation (figures 4.14, 4.15). Two buried brick pathways exposed in the excavation led from the house to the street front. One that led to the front of the house may have been a formal walkway for visitors, but the other led out from side door of the kitchen ell before turning at a right angle toward the street. It is likely this pathway provided a paved accessway for customers to Hannah's laundry space. A second paved surface further west of the house formed a path that led from the side of the house to the well, providing a paved walkway for Hannah and her helpers to reach the water source they would have relied on to do their work. The stones are flat and large and level with the brick path, suggesting they were selected for these qualities to produce a flat and stable ground surface. Set apart from the house, this surface seems to have been prepared as a space for work. This surface was likely prepared so Hannah had a stable and clean space for washing and drying the clothes of her customers. Given that the site itself is low lying and wet, these prepared surfaces would have been especially important for a successful laundry business.

Evidence of laundry and sewing at the Hart site is more pronounced than what we see at the Tobias site. The differences reflect a greater investment in laundry work by the Harts, including both the tools and materials they obtained to be successful and the way they developed their property to create a suitable workspace. The lack of similar evidence at the Tobias site suggests they were less pressed by the world around them to produce a stable income through laundry work. The evidence that they, particularly Emeline Tobias, did laundry is clear, but the impact of this labor on the site is less intense. Laundry work was part of an overall economic strategy for each household but this work was practiced differently by these two families. For the Tobiases, doing laundry would have provided a useful extra income to supplement their capacity to provide for themselves with the resources of the forest and the shore, as well as what they produced on their property, where they kept domesticated animals and likely had a garden. For the Harts, laundry work was a necessity; the income it produced was needed to support the household, especially given that they did not have access to the freely available natural resources that the Tobiases did. Certainly, these contrasting household economic strategies reflect aspects particular to the location of each site, but they also suggest that for people of color access to vital resources and the autonomy this provides grew more restricted. Moreover, the preservation of their autonomy required the Harts to produce a sustainable income, even if this meant investing more in tools and developing suitable spaces to overcome their limitations and meet the demands of their clients. Ultimately, evidence of laundry work at the Tobias and Hart sites shows the increasing level of effort required of people of color in Setauket to make a living that came with racial modernity.

At the Store

Despite increasing restraints, we know the Harts earned incomes from their work, and they would have used this income to provide for their family. Information about the Harts' consumer life can be gleaned from the Tyler Brothers Store account books. The Tyler store was located close to the Hart home at the intersection of Main Street and Old Field Road. Account records for Jacob Hart were found in the books for 1896, 1898, and 1899. There is also a record for Hannah Hart in 1899 as well as an H. Hartt in 1907 and 1908. These records show the Harts frequented the Tyler store to obtain a variety of staples including meat, milk, flour, baking powder, salt, pepper, butter, lard, eggs, produce, sugar, molasses, kerosene, canned corn, canned salmon, crackers, coffee, tea, matches, tobacco, and soap. The family also purchased medicines such as camphor, Castorina, pain balm, and the narcotic Paregoric, as well as household items such as nails, tacks, mason jars, and stamps. Occasional purchases included collars, spools of thread, pins, laces, and starch by the pound, likely related to Hannah Hart's laundry work. Rounding out their purchased items were candies, cakes, cookies, and pies as well as pencils and paper likely purchased for the Hart children.

A school attendance book for the 1898–1899 academic year documents that both Julia Hart (age 10) and Selah Hart (age 6) attended the Setauket school (Register of School Attendance for School District No. 2 [Setauket School], 1898–1899, Town of Brookhaven Historian's Office, Farmingville, New York). They were two among nine children of color among 80 5-year-old to 13-year-old students at the school. Children of color attended school as or more often than their white peers. For example, Henry Bristol (61 days) and Wesley Marshall (70 days) went to school more often than the average 8-year-old (58 days) in the first term (the record only recorded attendance in the first term for 8-year-olds). Similarly, Julia Hart (147 days) and Eddie Calvin (136 days) came to school much more often than the average 10-year-old, who showed up 95 days during the school year. Among older students (8- to 13-year-olds) there were at least two children of color in each cohort, and four of the oldest nine students were from families of color. That children of color attended school more often and stayed in school for more years than their white peers suggests families of color valued education for children more than work, even though it is likely that families of color may have benefited more from additional income than their white neighbors. Rather, because their children were being raised in a racist society, their parents knew they would need every advantage they could find, and a free education was among the best opportunities available. It is possible as a result that the Harts' multiple entries in the Tyler Brothers Store account book for candy, cakes, and, pies were obtained as rewards for the children's successes in school.

A review of other families of color who kept accounts at the Tyler store shows very similar results. People of color identified in the account books include Albert Sells (1896–1898), Becky Hart (1908–1909), Charles Scott (1896), Daniel Hart (1896), E. Calvin (1911–1912), E. J. Seaman (1896), Grant Sells (1896), H. Bristol (1907, 1911), Hannah Bunce (1896), Isaac Bristol (1898), Isaiah Hart (1897), James Calvin (1896), James Lewis (1911), M. Sells (1907), Martha Sells Mitchell (1896), Rachel Hart (1898) Sam Calvin (1911), Selah Hart (1897–1898), Silas Seaman (1911), and Abraham Tobias (1896). None of these individuals had as many entries in the account books as Jacob and Hannah Hart, which likely reflects the Harts were more established than their most of their peers. For those with many entries, their purchases are, like the Harts, dominated by household staples. For example, Selah Hart, Jacob Hart's brother, also spent his store credit on basics such as flour, eggs, beans, pork, lard, Cottolene (shortening), and sugar. Selah also purchased candy, a possible reward for some of his six children. In contrast, Albert Sells, related to the Harts by marriage, did not purchase any candy from the Tyler store, perhaps because he did not send any children to the school.

Some unusual purchases were made by people of color at the Tyler store. For example, on January 16, 1896, Daniel Hart, Jacob and Hannah's oldest son, bought a pair of ice skates and skate straps, presumably to use on the mill pond across from the Tyler store and the Hart home. His only other recorded purchases were for unnamed merchandise and candy. Another unusual purchase by James Lewis on July 4, 1911, was for fireworks. At 23 cents, these were an expensive item, though he certainly picked them up for the holiday. In both of these instances we see men buying items that connected them to normal community activities in Setauket, though these might also have been special moments when people of color were able to join in as peers of their white neighbors in socially acceptable ways. In fact, the account records for Jacob Hart show he made a very large purchase on July 1, 1898, that included unusual items for him—eight mackerel, a pork shoulder, pickles—as well as a long list of regular staples. This seems to be items obtained in preparation for a holiday party for his family if not also for others in the community.

Another unusual set of items were several boxes of shotgun shells purchased by Sam Calvin between 1912 and 1914. These are the only munitions purchased by a person of color recorded in these account books. The shells were probably for hunting since he bought them in November, December, and January. It is notable that Sam Calvin over these two years purchased at least eight smoking pipes. No other person of color in the account books purchased more than one. Calvin did not purchase many staple goods, thus his use of the Tyler store was for special needs. The most expensive set of items was purchased by Becky Hart on December 18, 1908: $11.43 worth of building materials, identified in the account book as "wall" and "ceil," which were perhaps main timbers used for building a new home. Becky Hart was Jacob and Hannah Hart's oldest child. Being over 30 years old in 1908, these materials were likely purchased to build a new home for her and her husband, James Lewis, on Christian Avenue.

Like Hannah Hart, several other women of color were laundresses, and evidence for this work is present in the Tyler account records. For example, Emma J. Seaman (née Tobias), a washerwoman in the 1900 census, purchased lye, a "ww" brush, starch, and blacking in May 1896. Her neighbor Ulysses S. Grant Sells, whose wife, Mary Sells, was a laundress, purchased soap, lye, bluing, starch, spools of cotton thread, a brush, "safe" pins, and other pins several times between January and July in 1896. Mary Sells herself purchased 13 collars in January 1909. E. Calvin (probably Edward G. Calvin) paid to have his laundry done six times in 1911 and 1912. Calvin was in his early twenties at the time, though he was already married to his wife, Caroline, in 1910. It seems they preferred to send their laundry out, even though that broke a tradition of laundry work done by women of color in Setauket, including Edward's mother, Tabitha, who was identified as a washerwoman in 1910. That year Edward G. Calvin was a coachman and later a chauffeur, and he was likely expected to have clean and fine clothing for this job. In fact, the extra expense of paying for his laundry may reflect a necessary strategy tied to the way a young man of color could overcome racist attitudes regarding his person, appearance, and abilities.

There is only one record in the Tyler store account books for a member of the Tobias family. Abraham Tobias purchased a handful of items between January and September in 1896. This was most likely the Abraham Tobias who was known to many at the time as Uncle Vet because he had served in the Civil War (Edward P. Buffet, William Sidney Mount: A Biography, 1924, Three Village Historical Society, Setauket, New York). A son of Jacob Tobias and Rachel Young, he was a cousin to the family who lived at the site excavated in Old Field. The 1890 veterans schedule indicates that Abraham Tobias lived in Setauket, and a headstone for Abraham Tobias in the Old Bethel Cemetery indicates he died in 1898. It is also likely that this is the same A. Tobias shown as living on Lake Street in 1873 on the Beers atlas (figure 4.9). The purchases recorded in 1896 are thus for an elderly man who was perhaps a close relative of both the Tobiases and the Harts whose homes have been excavated.

Abraham Tobias purchased two locks (January 9, 1896); a half-dozen lemons (April 15); a bottle of beer (May 6); two bottles of "Ex" (alcohol?), two cakes, and two plugs of tobacco (May 27); five plugs of tobacco (September 9); one bottle of Ex and five candies (September 12); and a rifle stone (September 15). These items differ from those of the heads of families like Jacob Hart, Selah Hart, and Grant Sells. Abraham Tobias likely lived alone, spending his final years drinking, smoking, and protecting something (hence the locks and rifle stone). Abraham Tobias also differed from his peers in that he paid for his items either at the time of purchase or within the same month. Just as his Tobias relatives in Old Field had recently given up their property, these data suggest Abraham was also abandoning Setauket. As mentioned in chapter 4, the Tobias family name was no longer found in Setauket by 1900, as the last members of the family moved to Port Jefferson and other places further away.

Ceramics, Labor, and Culture Change in Setauket

To examine changes in the experience of people of color through time, I consider here ceramic artifacts recovered from the Tobias and Hart sites. The identification and preliminary analysis of these ceramics was completed by Meta Janowitz, an expert on historic ceramics in the northeast and mid-Atlantic (Janowitz 2018). There are 2,184 ceramic sherds in the Tobias Site collection and 713 sherds from the Hart site. Each sherd was identified by ware type, vessel form, decoration, vessel body part, function, and other attributes. The focus here is the distribution of ceramics vessel forms, so, since not all sherds could be assigned a vessel form, this analysis is based on 1,046 sherds from the Tobias site and 455 sherds from the Hart site. Ceramics from the Tobias and Hart sites were sorted into the following vessel-type groups: cosmetic, household, food preparation, storage, table service (flat), hollowware, tea and coffee wares, and toys (table 5.11). Results of this analysis are illustrated in figures 5.9 and 5.10.

The Tobias ceramic collection is dominated by sherds from hollowware vessels. The hollowware category consists of vessels that could be categorized as tablewares (such as small bowls or soup bowls) or food preparation and storage (such as large bowls), but the nature of these collections did not permit the separation of the hollowwares into discrete categories. Nevertheless, hollowwares make up more than half (52.9%) of the sherds in the analysis. Other prominent vessel groups in the collection are table service vessels (23.9%) and tea or coffee vessels (13.6%). These three types are also the largest groups in the Hart ceramic collection, though the distribution is different. At the Hart site sherds from table

Table 5.11. Assignment of Ceramic Vessel Forms to Vessel-Type Groups

Vessel-Type Groups	Contributing Vessel Forms
Cosmetic	Pot, Pharmaceutical
Household	Chamber Pot; Flower Pot; Pipe, Sewer/Water
Food Preparation	Pan; Pan/Dish
Storage	Bottle; Jar; Jar/Jug; Jug; Jug/Bottle; Lid; Pitcher
Table Service (flat)	Dish; Flatware; Plate; Tableware, General
Hollowware	Bowl; Nappie; Hollowware; Porringer
Tea/Coffee Wares	Coffee Cup; Saucer; Tea Cup; Tea Pot; Tea/Coffee Cup; Teaware, General
Toys	Toys

Source: Janowitz 2018.

service vessels make up almost half (43.7%), while tea and coffee vessels (24.6%) and hollowware vessels (24.2%) have roughly the same number of sherds.

These results show that the Tobias household used hollow vessels such as bowls more frequently than the Harts, who more often used flatwares like plates. A pattern in the preference for bowls or plates in collections like these has been observed in multiple instances. James Deetz (1996) identified an increase in the frequency of the use of plates as evidence of greater individualism associated with the Georgian era in eighteenth-century Anglo-American culture. Plates were seen as the centerpieces of increasingly elaborate individual place settings that separated diners from one another at the table. Deetz argues the use of bowls in earlier "medieval" contexts reflected cooking and serving communal dishes such as soups and stews rather than meals consisting of segregated cuts of meat, grains, and vegetables prepared for individuals. In an African American context, John Otto (1980) observed a distinction in the use of plates versus bowls at Cannon's Point Plantation in coastal Georgia. While the collection of artifacts associated with the plantation owners and overseers showed a preferences for plates in these households, collections associated with enslaved laborers reflected a greater reliance on bowls. Consistent with Deetz's thinking, Otto argues planters preferred plates to express their civility, formality, and individuality. That enslaved laborers used mostly bowls for their meals suggests they placed less value on individuality and etiquette, preferring instead to share meals and use those occasions to build solidarity. In addition to racial differences between planters and slaves there were also status differences. Ceramics from the overseers' household contained more plates than those associ-

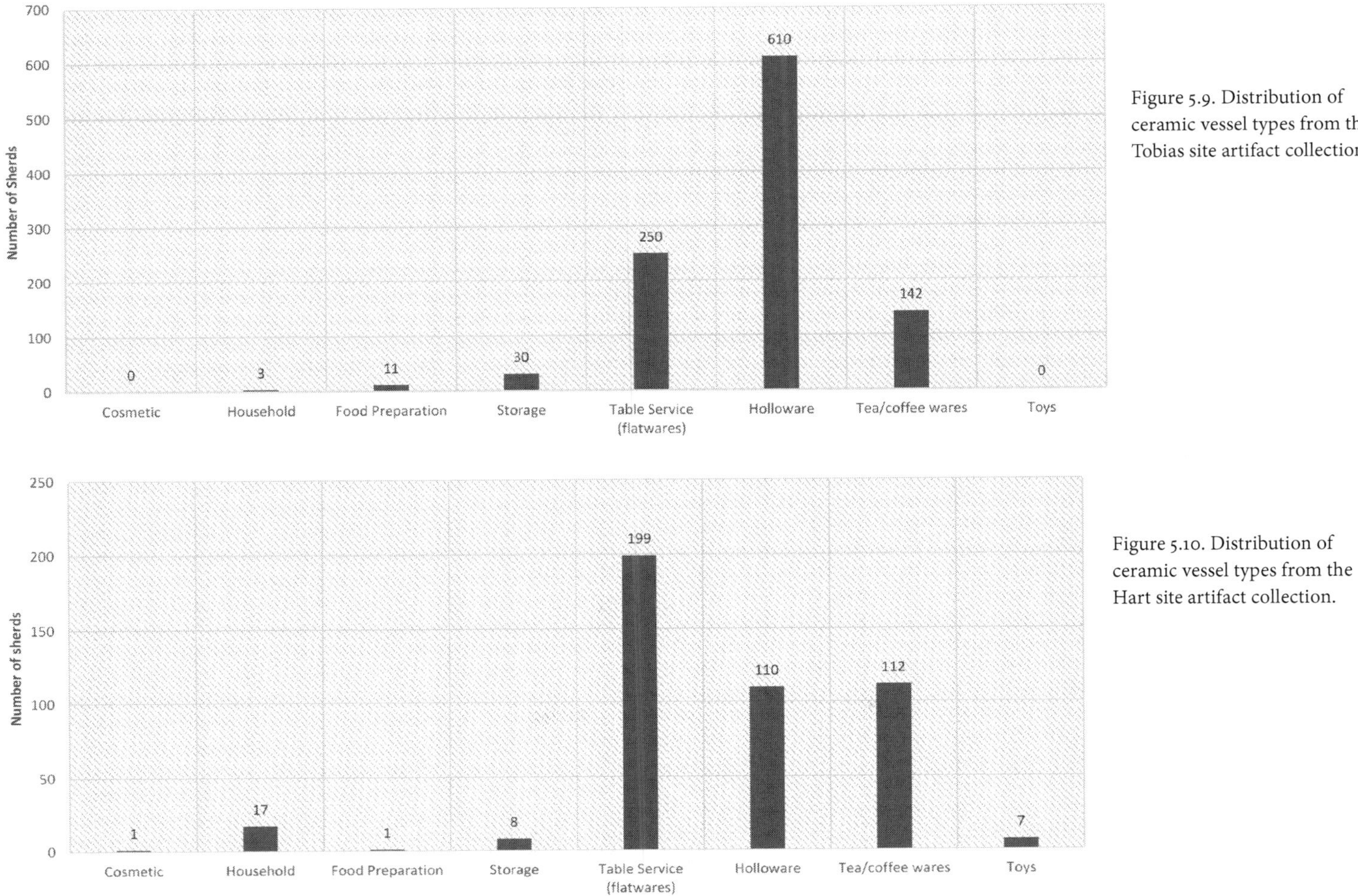

Figure 5.9. Distribution of ceramic vessel types from the Tobias site artifact collection.

Figure 5.10. Distribution of ceramic vessel types from the Hart site artifact collection.

ated with the enslaved laborers but many fewer than found at the planters' home site. Based on this and other data, Otto (1980:10) concluded,

> Not only did the slaves and overseers have limited time for food collecting, but they also had limited time for food preparation and a limited variety of cooking utensils. Given this situation, the slaves and overseers may have combined their grains, meats, and vegetables in "seemingly incongruous mixtures" in iron cooking pots, forming pottages, rice perlous, and stews. These one-pot meals could be left simmering for hours, while the slaves and overseers engaged in other work.

The ceramic vessel data from the Tobias site suggest they also relied on such one-pot meals, which likely reflected varied aspects associated with their cooking practices. Certainly, the Tobiases were relatively poor, so the use of less expensive if not freely available foods cooked together as stews, soups, or pottages would have been a useful strategy to stretch their limited resources. At the same time, a preference for bowls was also a way to preserve key cultural traditions related to food preparation. While we do not know exactly what they cooked, clams, oysters, pork, and other meats are commonly combined with rice, potatoes, corn, and other grains and vegetables in dishes such as gumbos, perlous, and, peculiar to the region, chowders. Such single-pot meals are commonly associated with African American and white working-class communities. Traditional Native American cooking on Long Island was also based in stews and porridges cooked in ceramic bowls (Bernstein et al. 1993). The seeming preference for bowls at the Tobias site and the mixed foods and one-pot meals they were used for were likely a key site of common experience for whites and all people of color during the time of the creole synthesis.

There is a regional variation of a one-pot meal known as Long Island clam chowder (*Long Island Press*, 4 September 2013), which may very well have been prepared at the Tobias home. Chowder was highlighted in a provocative way by Herman Melville in *Moby-Dick* (1851). In a chapter simply titled "Chowder," Melville describes the experience of characters Ishmael and Queequeg on Nantucket at a chowder house:

> Upon making known our desires for a supper and a bed, Mrs. Hussey, postponing further scolding for the present, ushered us into a little room, and seating us at a table spread with the relics of a recently concluded repast, turned round to us and said—"Clam or Cod?"
>
> "What's that about Cods, ma'am?" said I, with much politeness.

"Clam or Cod?" she repeated.

"A clam for supper? a cold clam; is *that* what you mean, Mrs. Hussey?" says I, "but that's a rather cold and clammy reception in the winter time, ain't it, Mrs. Hussey?"

But being in a great hurry . . . , and seeming to hear nothing but the word "clam," Mrs. Hussey hurried towards an open door leading to the kitchen, and bawling out "clam for two," disappeared.

"Queequeg," said I, "do you think that we can make out a supper for us both on one clam?"

However, a warm savory steam from the kitchen served to belie the apparently cheerless prospect before us. But when that smoking chowder came in, the mystery was delightfully explained. Oh, sweet friends! hearken to me. It was made of small juicy clams, scarcely bigger than hazel nuts, mixed with pounded ship biscuit, and salted pork cut up into little flakes; the whole enriched with butter, and plentifully seasoned with pepper and salt. Our appetites being sharpened by the frosty voyage, and in particular, Queequeg seeing his favourite fishing food before him, and the chowder being surpassingly excellent, we despatched it with great expedition: when leaning back a moment and bethinking me of Mrs. Hussey's clam and cod announcement, I thought I would try a little experiment. Stepping to the kitchen door, I uttered the word "cod" with great emphasis, and resumed my seat. In a few moments the savoury steam came forth again, but with a different flavor, and in good time a fine cod-chowder was placed before us.

We resumed business; and while plying our spoons in the bowl, thinks I to myself, I wonder now if this here has any effect on the head? What's that stultifying saying about chowder-headed people? "But look, Queequeg, ain't that a live eel in your bowl? Where's your harpoon?"

Fishiest of all fishy places was the Try Pots, which well-deserved its name; for the pots there were always boiling chowders. Chowder for breakfast, and chowder for dinner, and chowder for supper, till you began to look for fish-bones coming through your clothes. The area before the house was paved with clam-shells. Mrs. Hussey wore a polished necklace of codfish vertebra; and Hosea Hussey had his account books bound in superior old shark-skin. There was a fishy flavor to the milk, too, which I could not at all account for, till one morning happening to take a stroll along the beach among some fishermen's boats, I saw Hosea's brindled cow feeding on fish remnants, and marching along the sand with each foot in a cod's decapitated head, looking very slip-shod, I assure ye.

While Melville's point here is to emphasize the general fishiness of the chowder house and the people of Nantucket, he describes a way of life tied to clams, fish, and chowder such that a single word was all it took make the order. Even the milk and butter used in the chowder was fueled by cows eating (and apparently wearing) fish. Based on his description of the ingredients, it is likely that what was needed to make clam chowder was readily available at the Tobias house. It is also notable that the name of the hotel they patronized was the Try Pots, named for the pots of chowder that were always boiling, but which Melville also explained was a way to "try pot-luck," sampling different types of chowder.

It is also interesting as well that Queequeg, a native South Pacific islander—who is often understood to represent shipboard racial equality and to stand in for other sorts of people of color—is said to consider clams his favorite fishing food. At the same time, he is also the butt of a joke, perhaps suggesting that as a person of color he was a foolish chowder-head, though notably the joke mentioned Queequeg harpooning an eel, making a compelling connection to Setauket's famous eel story. In another passage, Queequeg was described by Melville as having "large, deep eyes, fiery black and bold" with "tokens of a spirit that would dare a thousand devils. And besides all this, there was a certain lofty bearing about the Pagan, which even his uncouthness could not altogether maim. He looked like a man who had never cringed and never had had a creditor." Melville equates here the supposed sophistication of white men with the stress of bearing debt and implies that the life of a "pagan," though uncouth, passed without cringes or creditors. The latter could be a way of describing the experience of the Tobias household in Old Field, at least to the degree they survived off the fruits of the land and their own labor instead of accumulated debt.

The greater frequency of plates at the Hart site may then reflect a loss of the sort of autonomy that the Tobiases enjoyed, especially as this autonomy was materialized in shared communal "bowl" foods like Long Island chowder. For archaeologists, a predominance of plates in a ceramic assemblage suggests that dining was based on the consumption of foods prepared for individuals rather than for communal eating. Deetz (1996) writes the adoption of individual place settings correlates with other changes such as an increase in the number of chairs, forks, mugs, napkins, and even chamber pots. Butchering patterns reflected a shift from bones split and splintered by an ax to be used for stews to bones precisely cut by saws to produce individual steaks and chops. Overall, Deetz describes a cultural shift in which people, even as they dined together, were segregated as individuals. Adding to this understanding, archaeologists Mark Leone and Paul Shackel (1987; also see Matthews 2010) argue that the adoption of individual place settings and segregated dining practices was part of a larger cultural shift tied to producing individuals who were prepared to compete against each other in the labor market. Leone and Shackel argue that segregation at dinner allowed workers to see themselves as individuals, unencumbered by social relations, even with family, that might distract them from what they needed to survive in the market. Leone and Shackel explain this shift was tied to the emergence of a culture of capitalism and the demand that workers place their individual relationship with their creditors at the front their minds. Following Melville, we see that Queequeg did not suffer these relations and thus lacked the wrinkles and lines of a face that cringed. This may also have been a good way to describe the Tobiases, though it less likely describes the Harts.

Jacob Hart made his living mostly through wage labor, as he worked in the local rubber factory, for shipbuilders, and as a gardener and mason. Hannah Hart also worked for wages as a laundress, though she likely fared better than her female peers in terms of maintaining her autonomy and being able to work from home. Still, the family did not have access to freely available shoreline resources as the Tobiases did. This difference in their ways of life reflects further-reaching changes tied to the local and regional economies. For one, in the late nineteenth century, shopping at stores like Tyler's was increasingly common for basic food and household items. Another way to document this change locally is by tracking the employment of people of color over time.

Data from the federal census detailing the occupations of people of color between 1850 and 1930 in the Town of Brookhaven (table 5.12) show a significant decrease in the percentage of people of color who made their living as farmers or working on the water. In both categories, we see a dramatic drop-off after 1870, after which the number working in these fields remained low. This decline indicates people of color lost access to occupations that would have supported household autonomy such as farming one's land or making a living with one's boat. These data may be directly related to the Tobiases and Harts in the fact that 6 of the 14 farmers recorded in 1850 were members of the extended Tobias family, and no member of the Hart family was ever recorded as a farmer. Notably, one farmer in 1850 was Richard Ackerly, who along with Jacob, David, and Abraham Tobias was a founding trustee of Bethel AME Church in 1848.

Why did people of color give up farming? One reason is likely related to changes in the way farming was practiced on Long Island in the late nineteenth century. While the average overall farm size in Suffolk County dropped from 154 acres in 1850 to 84 acres in 1900 (US Bureau of the Census 1902a), the num-

Table 5.12. Distribution of People of Color among Typical Occupations, 1850–1930, Town of Brookhaven, New York

Occupation	1850	1860	1870	1900	1910	1920	1930
Farmer	10.3%	0.4%	5.6%	0.9%	1.2%	3.3%	0.3%
Laborer	72.1%	38.6%	72.2%	43.6%	46.7%	49.2%	48.0%
Servant	0.7%	32.2%	2.8%	27.8%	29.7%	22.7%	37.2%
Service Business	0.0%	0.8%	0.0%	2.1%	0.0%	2.2%	2.6%
Maritime Trades	16.9%	10.6%	15.3%	2.1%	1.2%	0.6%	0.3%
Professional/Skilled Occupations	0.0%	0.0%	4.2%	3.3%	3.5%	7.7%	4.3%
Delivery and Transport	0.0%	0.0%	0.0%	7.8%	6.9%	2.8%	5.3%
Laundry	0.0%	17.4%	0.0%	12.5%	10.8%	11.6%	2.0%

Source: Decennial Federal Census.

Notes: Occupation type is as recorded in the census.

Farmer: farmer, duck farmer

Laborer: laborer, day laborer, farm laborer

Servant: servant, domestic, housekeeper, odd jobs, helper, chopper, chauffer, caretaker, housekeeper, cook, coachman, gardener, housework, house maid, maid, yarddresser, butler, mess boy, pantry man

Service Business: waiter, chef, kitchen worker, hotel worker, waitress, elevator man, dishwasher, fireman, janitor, piano player, watchman

Maritime Trades: fisherman, boatman, oysterman, seaman, sailor, mate

Professional/Skilled Occupations: teacher, minister, preacher, overseer of highways, bookkeeper, clerk, fish dealer, horse trainer, merchant, nurse, paper hanger, salesman, proprietor, mason, brickmaker, boarding house proprietor, shipyard work (bolting, crane leader, crane worker, electrician, foreman, helper, ship hitter, watchman) mechanic (coal yard), dialer, clergyman, engineer, superintendent

Delivery and Transport: driver, expressman, hostler, livery, porter, horseman, stableman, teamster, wagon driver, stage driver, groom, hod carrier, truckman, attendant, truck driver

Laundry: washerwoman, laundry, laundress, seamstress, laundry man

ber of larger farms outpaced smaller farms. For example, in 1860 62% of farms were smaller than 50 acres, but by 1880 farms larger than 50 acres accounted for 54% of all farms. It is likely that larger farmers were pushing out or purchasing smaller farms, a process that probably involved the elimination of most farmers of color. Richard Wines (1981) also notes that farming in eastern Long Island became much more labor and capital intensive as more farmers used fertilizers and machinery to increase their output and profits. Fertilizers including ground bone, hardwood ash, manure, guano, fish scrap, and poudrette were commonplace after 1860. Fertilizing itself was also labor intensive. Wines (1981:59) noted one farmer recorded "that he, his father, his brother, and two hired hands carted an incredible 240 loads of barnyard manure." One has to wonder about the color of the hired hands in this story, but we can certainly see the increased level of effort and cost of fertilizing the fields. Long Island farmers also quickly adopted the latest farm machinery, such as mechanical reapers, self-rakes, hay presses, seed drills, mechanical corn shellers, and plows with double moldboards (Wines 1981:60–61). Like fertilizer, this machinery was an extra capital cost; moreover, it worked together such that "without a self-rake or self-binder, a nonconvertible reaper would not have saved enough labor . . . to make purchase worthwhile" (Wines 1981:60). This increase in the level of investment as well as a decrease in the number of smaller farms are evidence that nonwhite farmers would have struggled to keep up with their white peers. As a result, only 15 farmers of color were still working in all of Suffolk County in 1900 (US Bureau of the Census 1902b).

With declining opportunities in farming and water-based work, the experiences of people of color increasingly shifted from working autonomously to working for an employer who was almost certainly white. While census data shows that more than 70% of people of color in the Town of Brookhaven worked as laborers or domestic servants throughout the period under study, after 1900 many also found work in newer fields such as delivery and transport; service jobs like waiters, chefs, and musicians; in professions as ministers, teachers, and nurses; or as skilled workers, such as masons, brickmakers, or electricians. These new occupations were waged work or work for hire, so it can be said that after 1900 virtually all people of color in the Town of Brookhaven were employees for white-owned employers and businesses. AME preachers on Long Island seem to have been the only people of color not employed by whites after 1900.

Useful additional details about employment can be gleaned from the 1920 census, which provides information in many cases about the type of industry people worked in. In particular, 20 men were listed as working in a shipyard likely in Setauket or Port Jefferson. Nine were listed with distinct occupations, including bolting, crane leader, crane worker, electrician, foreman, helper, ship hitter, watchman, and laborer, and 11 were shipyard laborers. The list shows a diverse set of skills and statuses among these workers. Clearly, shipyards were large employers who hired workers at multiple ranks, likely with increasing pay scales. Besides earning an income, therefore, workers would also have easily recognized the value and rewards of individual skill and accomplishment. Both Jacob Hart (ship bolting) and his adult son Ernest Hart (laborer) were employed at a shipyard in 1920, suggesting they would have been exposed to this labor hierarchy.

Looking back to the Harts' ceramic collection, the predominance of table service wares such as dishes, general flatwares, plates, and general tablewares seems to match with changing patterns in occupations and the local economy. Not having the resources the Tobiases enjoyed in terms of arable land and access to the waterfront, the Harts and most other people of color in Setauket turned to the white-controlled labor market as well as white-owned stores to find the work and resources they needed to survive. This transition was likely jarring for Jacob Hart, who was born in the era when many people of color were able to maintain their autonomy and avoid the worry associated with wage labor and debt. It is quite likely therefore that Jacob Hart and his family knew well the sources of cringing Melville wrote about. In this light, their preference for ceramic plates, objects that individualized dining within the household, would have been useful for the family as they engaged in the labor market. Such artifacts and associated etiquette would have taught them about the expectations employers had to be able to work as individuals who, in order to earn a wage, would need to show up on time and understand the rules of proper social interaction and deference to employers. All of these were the lessons reinforced at the dining table, and those who knew how to act properly at home were more likely to be rewarded with promotions and extra pay, a recognition as much of their skill as of their compliance and conformity to the market order.

Personal Artifacts and Small Finds

Some of the most interesting finds from archaeological excavations are personal items left behind by former residents, such as the lost buttons or clasps from clothing related to doing laundry as well as other artifacts that perhaps meant more to their owners. As is typical, only a few of these items are present in the collections from the Tobias and Hart sites. Tobacco pipe stems and bowl fragments were the most common personal artifact type at both sites, with 62 at the Tobias site and 30 at the Hart site. Given that the Tobias site had a more distinct midden deposit where broken tobacco pipes would have been discarded, these figures likely reflect comparable levels of smoking at both sites. We also know from the Tyler store account books that the Harts regularly purchased tobacco. The most notable difference between the assemblages is the greater uniformity of the pipes in the Tobias collection compared to the diversity of pipes at the Hart site. Pipes from the Tobias site are all white ball clay, and the majority are plain and unmolded. At the Hart site there are molded pipes as well as pipes made from gray and black clays in addition to white ball clay. This difference suggests the Harts thought more about their purchases and perhaps spent more to have a diversity of pipes, signifying a greater interest in owning objects reflecting their individual tastes.

Other personal artifacts from the Tobias site include two slate pencils, a hair clip, two ornamental or possible jewelry artifacts, possible watch parts, and a fragment of mouth harp (figure 5.11). These items indicate a variety of activities related to writing and education, personal presentation, and the enjoyment of "nice things," as well as playing music. Certainly, these artifacts reflect an engagement with the market, but the interests here are focused on personal improvement and social enjoyment. These finds contrast with the personal artifacts from the Hart site, which similarly include slate pencils but also a pocket knife, pharmaceutical vessels, marbles, and fragments of a toy porcelain tea set. The pocket knife is an interesting find, though the collection from the Hart site also includes a butter knife blade as well as fragments of five spoons. No such utensils were recovered at the Tobias site. These utensils confirm the Harts invested in materials used for dining, and the pocket knife suggests readiness for a variety of basic household tasks. It is possible the pocket knife can be considered alongside the eel spears

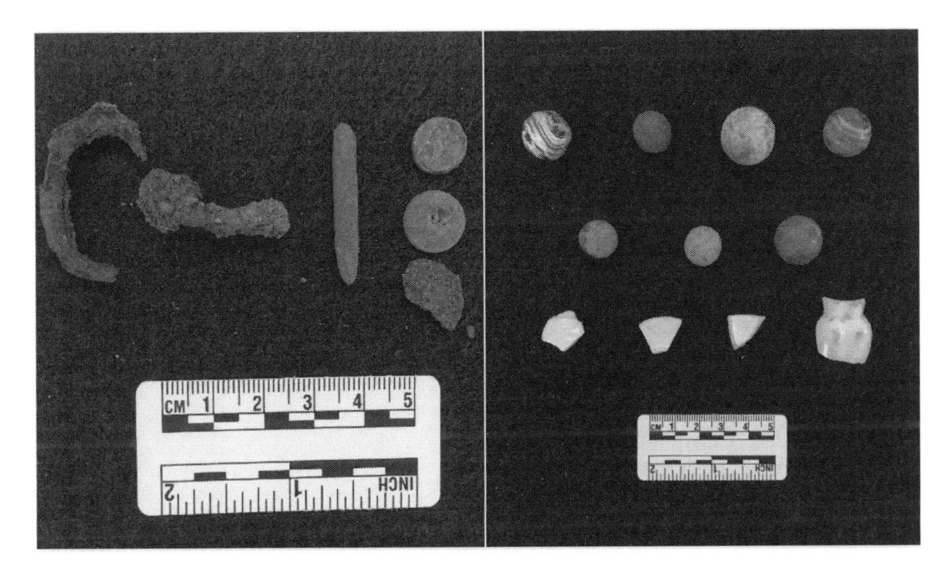

Figure 5.11. Personal artifacts from the Tobias and Hart sites. *Left*, Fragment of jew's harp, slate pencil and buttons from the Tobias site; *right*, toys from the Hart site including marbles and toy tea set fragments.

at the Tobias site in the sense that each family invested in metal tools useful for productive tasks, though the Tobiases were focused on a specific activity while the Harts were prepared for more general work. Jacob Hart's diverse work history suggest this was likely the case.

Pharmaceutical products excavated at the Hart site include a whiteware pot, found whole, that was the bottom half of a small jar. It was fitted for an out-sitting lid that would have been decorated. Another pharmaceutical artifact was a clear glass bottle embossed with the name "L. S. Squires Propr." (figure 5.12). This bottle was sold as Green Mountain Oil (or Magic Pain Destroyer), a cure-all for multiple ailments including "diptheria, croup, deafness and sore eyes," as well as "all nervous complaints" (US Department of Agriculture 1915). Similar health products, such as camphor, Castorina, Paregoric, pain balm, and Vaseline, were also purchased by the Harts at the Tyler store. While it is not unusual to find over-the-counter remedies for common ailments like minor pain, diarrhea, and head colds in the artifacts from households of this era, the lack of pharmaceuticals at the Tobias site illustrates again the changes that occurred for people of color by the late nineteenth century. While the archaeobotanical analysis showed the Tobiases counted on natural botanical remedies, the Harts purchased what they needed from Tyler's store. Another notable pharmaceutical artifact at the Hart site was a small porcelain pot likely used for toothpaste. As others (Shackel 1993)

Figure 5.12. Bottle from the Hart site artifact collection. The "L.S. Squires Propr." embossing indicates this was bottle contained as Green Mountain Oil (or Magic Pain Destroyer).

have discussed, cleaning one's teeth was an important part of modern forms of etiquette by the late nineteenth century. Clean teeth were not only hygienic but also exhibited a commitment to individuality, since having a healthy and attractive body was one way to distinguish oneself from others.

Other personal artifacts unique to the Hart site are children's toys (figure 5.11). These include eight marbles made of both clay and glass and a metal ball bearing about the size of a marble. Playing with marbles was a common childhood game, and a marble could have been a nice gift. Marbles have been made for millennia, though the mass production of marbles dates to the 1880s, so their presence at the Hart site is not a surprise (Lamme 2015). Other toy artifacts include five fragments of porcelain toy teacups and saucers, artifacts that were also common in the late nineteenth century. Still, even though these toys were common objects for their era, difference in the toy artifacts from the Hart and Tobias sites is worth consideration.

Toys from the Hart site were mass-produced goods that the Harts likely purchased from Tyler's or another store in the area. They thus contribute more evidence of additional expenditures the Harts chose to make to provide for their family. Yet toys like these were cheap, so their cost is not the basis of their significance. Rather, the gift of a toy or other things like candies, cakes, or pies provided happiness to children. Whether rewards for good work or behavior or presents for holidays or birthdays, these items expressed the bonds of love and family and brought joy to the family. That this effort to create happiness was aimed at children exposes one of the most powerful ways that the labor market changed everyday life for Americans like the Harts. Before the predominance of waged work, children worked as helpers in the shops and farms their families ran. Once family survival became tied to waged work, labor moved elsewhere, and children spent less time working and more time playing at and around their homes. We see evidence for this in a widespread increase in the number of small toys like those at the Hart site in the archaeology of later nineteenth-century sites associated with working-class and poor households (Yamin 2001, Brighton 2001). Children growing up in this time were also socially reconstructed as not just physically but also socially and emotionally immature (Baxter 2005). Small toys like marbles and toy tea sets thus symbolize the presence of children but also a new notion of childhood as that time in life before adulthood and the struggles adults face in the labor market (Matthews 2010:113–115). Put another way, the gift of toys confirmed the bonds of family love, but they also marked a time when the child was free from the worries that cringed their parents' brows.

Comparing the children's toys in the Hart collection to the mouth harp from the Tobias site, another object related to play, helps explain this cultural change. A musical instrument, the mouth harp was a way for everyone, no matter their age, to enjoy their time at home with the family. The lack of child-specific toys in the Tobias collection suggests the family did not segregate childhood as time apart from the rest of life, especially if happiness was shared more widely among all members of the family. In contrast, toys at the Hart site suggests a cultural separation of material culture as belonging to either adults or children, reflecting a presumed separation of experience between the generations. Segregation by age of course contributed even more to a sense of individual distinction within the home.

Discussion

This chapter has examined and compared multiple types and characteristics of archaeological data from the Silas Tobias site and Jacob and Hannah Hart home site in Setauket. Both sites were homes where families of color lived and engaged with their local communities. The historical archaeological record at both sites is rich and gives us details about how people of color lived in Setauket and how their experiences changed through time. I argued that that life was more difficult for the Harts than the Tobiases. The Tobias household was better positioned to act autonomously in many aspects of life, especially those activities related to foodways and sources of income. The Harts faced more restrictions in terms of acquiring food and other vital resources which by the time they settled in their home on Lake Street were available to them almost entirely through the market, which very much enforced an understanding that their labor was a marketable commodity.

Evidence of everyday experience at the Tobias household was defined by traditions of working, cooking, and living that stretched into the past. Collecting shoreline and forest resources, making and refinishing stone tools, and preparing stews, soups, and chowders employed a mode of production that would have been just as familiar to their Native American and African ancestors. These traditions were of course practiced alongside the family's engagement with the local market, which is evident in the ceramic, glass, and iron artifacts that that were buried alongside the seeds, lithic tools, shells, and bones in the site's midden. These purchased materials should not be seen as an accommodation to the dominance of the market but as a strategic use of the benefits it offered. If the local merchant would exchange glazed pottery for their clams, bartering clams was a way for the Tobiases to acquire new things without simultaneously giving up the resource base they had counted on for generations.

This typical experience for the Tobiases was not shared by the Harts. While the Harts' home was close to the center of the village, it was nevertheless ultimately located in a vulnerable place. Their property was also small and could not be used to produce resources that the family might use for their survival as had the Tobiases. Rather, its primary natural resource, a spring-fed well, was used to support Hannah Hart's laundry business, a principal source of income for the family. As the site became increasingly difficult to manage due to a high water table, the family had to invest the labor and expense of creating brick pathways and a cobblestone work surface so that her business could survive. These difficulties were mirrored in other aspects of their material lives. For one, the Harts, along with most of their peers in the local community of color, had to work for white employers to earn the wages they needed to obtain food, medicine, clothing, and other necessities. Their engagement with the market was therefore not as much on their own terms as was the Tobiases'. Comparing the ceramic collections from both sites shows furthermore that the Harts adopted dining practices that differed from the Tobiases but matched those of the majority of whites of the time. These would have included meals served on flat plates with accompanying utensils, likely served at specific times and in proper sequences. This shift in dining practice has been observed in many other instances and is understood to be a means of instituting individualism and an acceptance of the labor market as the norm. That we see this change in dining practice emerge at the same historical moment people of color lost access to the types of work that had previously allowed them to avoid the dominance of waged work is a compelling correlation.

Memory Objects

To conclude this chapter I consider two specific artifacts excavated from the Tobias and Hart sites (figure 5.13). These artifacts speak to how each household reflected on their conditions by selecting meaningful images and objects that connected them to previous times and allowed them understand how they were living their lives. The first of these memory artifacts is sherd of red transfer-printed whiteware discovered in the Tobias midden. The vessel broke in a fortuitous manner that framed the head, neck, and upper body of a quail-like bird that was part of its printed design. The larger design this bird was part of has not been found in any transfer print databases, but its meaning here may have been one identified by the Tobiases rather than the manufacturer. Specifically, a backward-facing bird like this one is one way of depicting the concept of Sankofa,

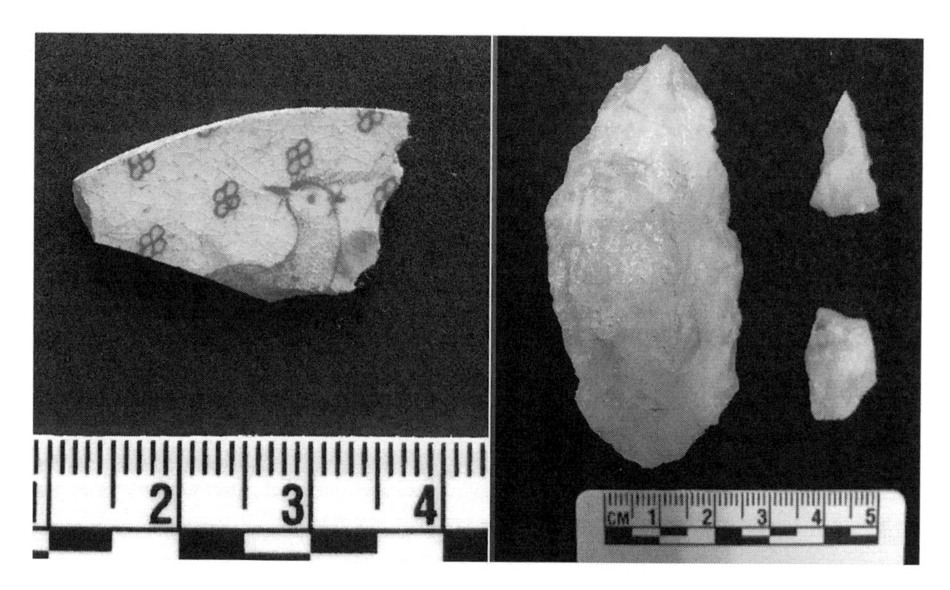

Figure 5.13. Memory objects from the Tobias and Hart sites. *Left*, transfer-printed whiteware sherd from the Tobias midden; *right*, quartzite tool from the Hart site.

originally associated with the Akan people of Ghana. Sankofa means “it is not taboo to fetch what is at risk of being left behind” (Carter G. Woodson Center 2019), though it is commonly understood to mean that as we move forward we must not forget our past. The image on this sherd characterizes this concept by showing the bird looking back over its body while its feet face forward. This simultaneous two-way perspective captures the sense that people live in their own time, but to move into the future they must recognize and reflect on the past. We cannot know what was in the minds of the Tobias family member who chose this ceramic vessel perhaps from the Tyler Brothers’ inventory, but the small bird in the design may have caught their attention as a reference to Sankofa, a concept they may have recognized and found meaningful to the way they lived on the shore of Conscience Bay in the nineteenth century.

The second memory artifact is a white quartz tool in the Hart collection. The tool was found with a core and two debitage flakes. Tweedie (2017) identified the tool as a “scraper-like biface with cortex on ventral face, multiple step fractures on both faces creates a beveled cross-section, multiple retouch scars along thinner lateral margins.” He also noted no evidence of use-wear. Rather, the artifact was likely collected by a member of the Hart family, who may have noticed it when a tree was uprooted or found it lying on the ground surface after erosion from a hillside. The flakes recovered with tools suggest it may have been made or altered at the Hart site. There is not enough evidence to determine which of these possibilities is correct. In either case, however, the meaning of the artifact can be related to cultural memory of the Hart family. Rather than invoking an ancient African symbol of remembrance, the quartz tool suggests the Harts were connecting to their immediate ancestors, who would have been contemporaries of the Tobiases and their forebearers, people that Jacob Hart likely knew while he growing up in Setauket. These people were the last to use lithic technology in Setauket and, as I have argued here, this would have been one of the ways they resisted being drawn into dependence on the labor market. Stone tools were a solution that required cultural knowledge rather than cash, and Jacob Hart may have learned this skill and shared in this knowledge. Yet he was unable to capitalize on its benefits while working in the rubber factory or the local shipyards. Rather, this tool was more likely a memento to a world he remembered but lost as the modern labor market encompassed his life. For the Harts, this artifact may very well be a record of where they came from, a story that would have been useful and important, though not one they could truly use. Instead, the tool would have served as a placeholder in case the world around them changed so they could find their way back. We know the world they lost did not return, but we can recognize that despite their difficulties they may have kept something on hand to guide their sense of self in ways that set them apart from what white society provided.

Notes

1. Entries related to people of color were compiled by researchers for Bruce Robertson, who shared his notes with me.

2. Store records for the region grow in number in the later 1800s. For example, the Tyler Brothers store in Setauket has records dating to as early as 1871.

3. According to Zillow, properties on Main Street in Setauket in 2018 had an average value of $511,000, which is roughly 10% higher than the median sale price ($471,000) of properties in all of Setauket.

4. Tyler Brothers was a general store that operated in Setauket from mid-1800s until 1931. Several of their account books are housed at the Three Village Historical Society; others remain with Beverly Tyler, a descendant. This entry is in the Tyler Brothers Store Account Book, 1907–1908:17, Three Village Historical Society, Setauket, New York.

6

CONCLUSION

Resistance, History, and Civil Rights

If someone went into your cemetery. Where your relatives are, and started to dig, you should go there and stop them. And that's what's going on here.

Ted Green

It's tragic. . . . It's like: "You can have three wishes if you agree to sell your soul."

Robert Lewis

In 1995 the Suffolk County district attorney learned of the possibility that the remains of a missing woman named Alice Parsons may have been buried in the Old Bethel Cemetery in the 1930s. Parsons was white and a former resident of Stony Brook who was kidnapped in 1937 and never heard from again. The informant in this case was Harry Hart, a member of the Native and African American community who took care of the cemetery and dug graves throughout the county. Even though Hart shared the information, no one else in the descendant community was consulted before investigators attempted to dig in the historic African and Native American graveyard. Ted Green was one of many community members horrified to learn of the police's intentions and the only one bold enough to act. The *Three Village Herald* captured the drama that unfolded next, as Green faced off against a cadre of powerful, predominantly white residents:

> There was quite a crowd at the cemetery on Thursday afternoon: the DA himself, the chief assistant district attorney, other assistant district attorneys, a representative of the Suffolk County Medical Examiners' office, four anthropologists from the University at Stony Brook, Dr. Sherman Mills,

> chairman of the Three Village Historical Society's cemetery committee, society director Michelle Morrison, and Tom Stanton, who, as a cop in the 1960s became interested in the Parsons case [as the subject of a true crime book]. They opened the reported grave and began the careful dig process.

This was clearly a well-financed and widely supported project, organized to gather evidence for the case. Representatives from various public agencies as well as the local university anthropology department, historical society, and media were all present. Missing were any representatives of the descendant Native and African American community, that is, until, as the article put it: "Enter Theodore Green" (figure 6.1).

> Mr. Green is a descendant of the black and Indian families who settled here centuries ago, a descendant of the Tobias and Hart families. He is commander of the Irving Hart Memorial Legion Post and member of the Suffolk County Native American Task Force. He is proud of his heritage and family—loyal to both. He is slight, wiry, sometimes limping as the result of an old war wound. He has tended this cemetery for Bethel church for decades. . . .
>
> Mr. Green was red hot with anger. "Stop this digging," he announced as he came through the fence. "*No more digging.*" The phalanx of astounded ADAs and professors stared at him. So, too, Mr. Stanton and Dr. Mills stepped back. Mr. Green went to the edge of the hole. "This is our cemetery. *Nothing more is going to happen here.* I know that *for sure.*" . . .
>
> ADA Karen Peterson, bright in a hot pink ski jacket, again told Mr. Green there was a court order to dig. He look at her incredulously. "If someone went into your cemetery. Where your relatives are, *and started to dig,* you should go there and stop them. *And that's what's going on here,*" he said. . . . When the hole was filled, the shovels still, the earth tamped down, Mr. Green put his papers down and stepped into the Indian mode of prayer, one arm across his chest, one arm raised to the sky. Those present stared, confounded, anxious, until Mr. Green stirred, picked up his papers, and faced those around him.

This dramatic and powerful act of resistance by Ted Green, working in this instance alone but with the benefit of his knowledge, history, and the power of ancestry, gives a real sense of how the preservation of their history has been essential to the survival of Setauket's Native and African American community. Green shut down the work of people with much more authority and status than him, including a cadre of apparently clueless anthropologists. In fact, he flipped the entire

Figure 6.1. Photograph of Ted Green printed with a news story about his successful injunction of unauthorized excavations at Old Bethel Cemetery. Clipping from the *Three Village Herald,* November 22, 1995. (Three Village Historical Society, Long Island.)

relationship: the assistant district attorney was heard saying to Green as he was leaving, "We'll meet with you anytime, at your convenience." We learn here that Green had been taking care of the cemetery for decades for Bethel AME Church, indicating his esteemed role in the community. Green also asserted both his family's honor and his Native American heritage, reminding those who thought they were in power of their own spurious heritage and essentially unfounded claims to the proprietorship of the site. This impressive action, in which one man upended the plans of many others, encapsulates three essential findings of this study that highlight how historical archaeology can change our understanding of the past and empower movements for social justice in the present.

Resistance

Green's audacious action in 1995 is just one example of the long history of effective resistance to marginalization and neglect by the Native and African American community in Setauket. People of color have been part of the community in Setauket since its beginning, but their membership has always been questioned and treated as provisional. As such, they do not have a central role in constructing the region's history and identity. To challenge this whitewashing of local history, people of color have banded together to articulate their significant contributions in Setauket through organizations such as Higher Ground, the Setalcott Nation, and Bethel AME Church. They have also crafted narratives to empower themselves, as is evident at Bethel AME Church and Laurel Hill and Old Bethel cemeteries, the Irving Hart Legion Hall, and the homes of families like the Tobiases, the Harts, and others on Christian Avenue.

This book emphasizes the importance of these alternative narratives by detailing the strategies Native and African Americans have used to thrive for generations in Setauket. We see this when Silas and Abraham Tobias secured a property and a built a home for their family so they could make a living with their own hands. The successes of the Tobiases at home empowered them to lead their community to establish a separate church for people of color, a church that has been an anchor institution for Native and African Americans in Setauket for more than 170 years. Later in the nineteenth century, as racism intensified and opportunities for autonomy disappeared, people of color adjusted and developed new strategies to care for themselves. Hannah Hart did this by taking in laundry and transforming her home and yard so that she could work despite dealing with flooding and wet ground. Women of color across Setauket also took in laundry, each contributing to the financial support of their families and sustaining their community. As watermen, many men in the community also earned incomes without having to be employed directly by white employers, securing for themselves and their families the benefits of financial independence.

In the early twentieth century, women of color such as Mary Eato, Lucy Keyes, and Rachel Midgett forged still new strategies; purchasing lots on Christian Avenue where they built homes, raising families, and passing their property as a legacy to their children. These women organized the community through active membership at Bethel AME Church and later the legion hall, which was built on land donated by Rachel Midgett. Bill and Irving Hart's clambakes, which drew from the community's historical connections with the local shoreline and its bounty, also provided people of color a collective means for earning incomes that did not rely directly on white employers.

Native and African Americans living on Christian Avenue since the early twentieth century have always fought for their community's survival. When Chicken Hill and Stony Brook Village were razed so the properties could be modernized, people on Christian Avenue welcomed these displaced people of color as new neighbors. Similarly, Ethel Lewis and Caroline Sells-Moore worked hard to convince Ward Melville to sell undeveloped lots in Kalmia Woods at a discount to people of color in the 1960s so that there would be more places in Setauket for people of color to live. We also see this in the way Lucy Keyes made space for her brother Ernest Hart to live in a small cabin on her property in the 1970s. Ethel Lewis's activist spirit passed to her son Robert, who worked to document the community's history in the 1990s and in 2004 established Higher Ground Intercultural and Heritage Association as a community-based historic preservation organization. These achievements are individually important and collectively transformative. They show how the community of color in Setauket exists as a direct result of the tenacity of community members who refused to give up on their heritage and their home.

Historical archaeology has been an essential part of the toolkit used to recover and interpret this history of resistance by people of color in Setauket. Excavations and artifact analyses of materials from the Tobias and Hart sites produced data not known before the fieldwork began. Questions about these discoveries led to new connections, for example, between the famous paintings of William Sidney Mount and the role of eel spearing as a tradition and vital source of food and income for people of color in the early 1800s. Similarly, artifacts such as flatware ceramics, straight pins and buttons, and children's toys reveal the everyday struggles of the Harts to adjust to wage labor and the need to engage with the white-dominated market to survive. Oral history and archival research complementing archaeological fieldwork brought to light the racist history that forced the community to open its own legion hall where "all races" are welcome and, since they were not permitted elsewhere, to go to a "colored beach" for rest and relaxation. These myriad details of everyday life related to labor, foodways, childrearing, social life, and leisure fill out the anemic historical record found in traditional archival sources and give us a clearer sense of how the Native and African American community in Setauket has survived for generations in a hostile political climate.

Refusing to Forget

When Ted Green showed up to protect Old Bethel Cemetery, he demonstrated the power of memory to effect meaningful change in the present. Green stopped a powerful group of government officials and scholars who had legal authority to exhume remains from the cemetery. He did so through his physical presence at the site, which forced others to acknowledge the long history of people of color in Setauket, a history that continues in the present day. When the gathered experts insisted they had legal and scholarly authority to dig around in the graveyard as they saw fit, Green asserted his more compelling moral authority to protect the hallowed remains of his ancestors and his community. In his final act of prayer, he made sure they understood his heritage was Native American as much as African American and that he laid claim to the cemetery and its residents as their direct descendant.

Green's protests were both remarkable and essential for the Native and African American community since he stood firmly against their erasure. His protest exposed what Michael Wilcox (2009a) describes as the terminal narrative that limits our understanding of Native Americans in the United States. Part of the apparatus of settler colonialism, terminal narratives reframe histories of conquest, dispossession, and replacement into stories that ignore violence in favor of triumph and patriotism. To exist and to be seen, people of color have always had to battle against this narrative. Green showed he was still there and that his community still cared about and for Old Bethel Cemetery. That he had to do so in the face of scholars, politicians, and journalists reveals how entrenched the terminal narrative is in Setauket, an assessment I explained in detail in chapter 1.

The chapters that followed amplified the presence of Setauket's historic community of color and the meaning of their legacy to the larger community. The counter-map and archaeological research in this book reconnect people of color to the spaces and places that framed their lives. To know the history of the houses owned by the Thompsons, Brewsters, and Strongs, we also need to know about Sharper, Killis, Abel, Dorcas, Unice, and the many other enslaved laborers of both African and Native American descent who lived at these historic homes. Stories of Main Street and Old Field are incomplete without mentioning that people of color lived there for generations before being displaced and, in the case of the closing of Mud Road, being formally cut off from where they used to live.

Despite enduring a history of dispossession, Native and African American people in Setauket have maintained their history, culture, and community. The preservation of stories has been one way they resisted their marginalization, since knowing their own history is how they remained connected to each other and knew they belonged in Setauket. This is visible in the use of indigenous knowledge and lithic technology by the Tobias family as well as in the curation of a lithic tool by the Harts. Lucy Keyes likewise curated plants from her childhood home that she transplanted to her own garden. We see their autonomous preservation in the many ways the community has maintained awareness of its Native American ancestry, such as when Lucy Keyes identified her father as an Indian or when Ted Green performed a blessing at Old Bethel Cemetery in 1995. Of course, the Hart-Sells reunions and the Setalcott Pow Wow are clear statements of memory, presence, and persistence that recur each year.

Setauket's coastal setting also looms large in the community's history and identity. Clamming, eel spearing, fishing, capturing water birds, and collecting quartz cobbles from the beach were everyday activities at the Tobias household. Their descendants made a living as a baymen and working in local shipyards. Some, including Jacob Hart, worked in maritime trades on whaling ships or coastal vessels.

There is another story about the coastal landscape that makes the connection between preservation and the community's way of life clear. It starts with a letter from 1905 found in the Three Village Historical Society archive. John Overton, the lawyer representing the Board of Trustees of the Town of Brookhaven, wrote to Frank Melville:

> At the last meeting of the Board, I presented your letter of the 5th inst. In which you state that you *do not* wish to renew [the] lease giving the public the privilege of trespassing on your land to catch clams. . . . Unless, I am mistaken, the town has not sold the shore adjoining your land on the bayside, below [the] high water mark. . . . If you hold title from high to low water, of course there can be no claim for reservation for clamming, and in that case I think there would be no trouble to get the lease granted; but if the ownership to high water is rested in the town, then, by your desire, and by the probable action of the Board, a grant of lease it, I think, doubtful.

Melville lived then at Red Roof, his home in Old Field across the road from the Silas Tobias archaeological site. Since he had also purchased the lot previously owned by Silas and Abraham Tobias, the "land on the bayside" is a direct reference to where the Tobias family lived. The letter indicates that Melville was breaking a local tradition that the public had the right to "trespass" on private property "to catch clams." This "public" would have included people of color who still used the shoreline to collect clams even though the Tobias home was no longer there. Remembering this spot was good for clamming and continuing to use it preserved an ancient way of life in the face of newcomers such as Melville who were attempting to change how things worked in Setauket.

Memory of the Old Field shoreline appears in another archival document found in materials collected by Glenda Dickerson for the *Eel Spearing at Setauket* project in 1989. On the back of a draft of the script Dickerson wrote, "*Clam Flats* . . . Rt hand near light house embankment on left is where Vi's father was born." "Vi" here referred to Violet Thompson, who lived in Setauket most of her life. She was born Violet Sells in 1917, daughter of Hannah Hart-Sells and William Smith Sells and granddaughter of Jacob and Hannah Hart. William Smith Sells was a leader in the community through Bethel AME Church, where he became a full church member at the age of 17 and served as associate pastor for most of his adult life. In 1910 Sells lived on Crane Neck Road in Old Field, where he worked as a coachman, groom, and gardener for Eversley Childs, a wealthy peer of Frank Melville. By 1930 Sells lived on Mud Road in Setauket having moved out of Old Field like most other people of color after its incorporation as a separate village. The note in the Dickerson files tell us he was born in Old Field by the lighthouse. Just like the Tobiases, who lived on the same shoreline further south, the Sells family had a home with easy access to clams in Conscience Bay. William Smith Sells's family had long lived in that spot. His father, Jeremiah Sells, was born in 1817 and is recorded in several censuses, including in 1860, when he was identified as a boatman and lived and owned property in Old Field.

This story shows that "Vi's father," William Smith Sells, came from an Old Field family, just as the Tobiases did. He was also born when people of color made a living connected to coastal resources freely available near to if not on their own property. The memory of this way of life survived through the generations so that both the activity and the place could be recorded by a researcher 100 years after William Smith Sells was born. This was the case despite the fact that Melville and his peers denied the community access to these shoreline resources and later displaced families to build the exclusive elite enclave Old Field has become. Maintaining knowledge of significant historic places, landscapes, ways of life, and family history is essential to how Setauket's community of color has survived. Refusing to forget their past has also been a way to resist the effects of being displaced from the homes, neighborhoods, and resources they knew and relied on. As they continued to face displacement, each generation of Setauket's community of color fought to remember what they lost each step of the way. This includes the community living on Christian Avenue today.

Historical archaeology is designed to address how histories are constructed and put to work in the effort to effect change. Identifying and excavating sites not previously known and hearing stories from people not consulted before produces new narratives that run counter to what we learn from establish sources and archives. The archaeology done as part of the A Long Time Coming project asked questions about the everyday experiences of people of color not posed before in Setauket. Memories of clamming, gardening, work, and community life recovered in this research transform the history of Setauket, which in turn alters contemporary social and political relations. The materialization of Pearl Lewis Hart's memory of sitting with friends on Indian Rock epitomizes how her presence in Setauket's history can be recovered and deployed in powerful new ways.

Civil Rights

Finally, it is important to recognize Green's protest at Old Bethel Cemetery as a defining feature of the larger Native American and African American civil rights struggle in the United States. To publicly stand against state power and demand equal rights, Green forced a recognition of the racism that permeates Setauket society. A long history of racial discrimination created a deliberate erasure of Native and African American people in Setauket from local history. This is typical of heritage work in the United States, which largely fails to accommodate diverse perspectives on the past, especially those that come to light through collaborative research with communities of color. The A Long Time Coming project has worked to lay bare the power of history to rationalize political decisions that affect the minority community of Setauket and at the same time how a retelling of history from the perspective of Native and American people is a political act calculated to protect and advance larger struggles for civil rights.

The best example of the Native and African American story that challenges the racial suppression in twentieth-century history of Setauket is the Irving Hart American Legion Hall. Founded in response to postwar racism, the legion hall is a monument to political resistance and cultural survival. In addition to memorializing its founders, the legion hall recognizes generations of military service to the United States by members of the Native and African American community. From the Civil War to the present, documentation of service by people of color from Setauket presents a counterpoint to claims they are not legitimate, patriotic citizens. Their service crafts a parallel narrative to the Revolutionary War focus of the authorized heritage discourse in Setauket. Instead of a connection to a mass-produced American story, the legion hall, from its recognition of Irving Hart's service in both world wars to its celebration of service by generations of the community, is a space for memorial reflection on Setauket's citizens of color, who are otherwise overlooked entirely in the village.

Ted Green was commander of the hall when he protested at the Old Bethel Cemetery, so his actions that day spoke for legion hall members. A photograph published in a local newspaper shows him standing next to the grave of Abraham Tobias, aka Uncle Vet, a Tobias family member and Civil War veteran. Green himself is part of an esteemed lineage of men and women such as Isaiah Hart, Rachel Midgett, Harry Hart, Carlton "Hubble" Edwards, and Idamae Glass who filled leadership roles in the hall. These trailblazers collected military portraits of legion hall members, which are now proudly displayed on a wall of honor. Other walls in the Hall are covered with dozens more photographs detailing the history of the community. Some of these show official legion hall activities, such as members marching in local parades (figure 6.2), as well as less formal events like parties honoring veterans' service or hall anniversaries. There are also photographs of special activities such as members playing for the Suffolk Giants, a team in the local Negro baseball league, and Hart-Sells family reunions. Entering the legion hall today is like visiting a museum dedicated to the Native and African American community. Unlike at the other museums and historic sites in Setauket, the focus is on people of color as active and contributing citizens over the town's long history. Recognizing that historical erasure is a dire threat to its survival, the Native and African American community built a monument to its own history, proving that the preservation of history can be a powerful act of resistance and a significant source of inspiration for contemporary civil rights struggles.

Archaeologists and other heritage professionals can certainly learn about the community at the museum in the legion hall, but the collection should prompt reflection on how historic sites related to communities of color should be approached as political acts. Writing the history of marginalized peoples challenges established wisdom about America's past. When a person or group aligns with dominant historical narratives in the United States, people and resources rally around them without question. If a person or group does not fit the narrative, attempts to assert their rightful place require more nuance, depth, and political voice. Adding the stories of people of color challenges existing narra-

Figure 6.2. Members of the Irving Hart Memorial Legion Hall marching in a Setauket parade, courtesy Carlton Edwards. (Collection of the Three Village Historical Society, Long Island.)

tives and threatens the way people interact with the past by creating discomfort among those who have neglected them. More than questions about why they are not already represented, the absence of people of color in local history emphasizes how heritage professionals control the past.

This is why A Long Time Coming is a civil rights project. If the dominant narrative in Setauket references the stories of colonial and Revolutionary America, then of equal importance is the narrative of people of color about their long struggle for civil rights. Our guiding purpose is to establish the historical experience of Native and African Americans in Setauket in the story of the village and the nation and to recognize why they have been excluded. This stance is a call for changing the praxis of history in the village and across Long Island to be more inclusive, self-critical, and open to engaging difficult but meaningful pasts. The problem we have faced in our project is that normal practice in heritage and historic preservation is not prepared to support changing narratives since an understanding of the politics of culture and history is not well-developed in these fields. It is not enough to contribute new stories if they are created with the same tools. We need new methods and more critical reflection on the history of exclusion if archaeology, heritage, and preservation are to serve communities of color effectively.

The limitations of the heritage industry became evident during the process of nominating the Bethel–Christian Avenue–Laurel Hill Historic District to the National Register of Historic Places. National Register listing is the gold standard and sets the guidelines for the determination of historical significance in the United States (National Register of Historic Places 2019). National Register listing enhances the status of a historic site or district and opens up opportunities to fund restorations and programs. Robert Lewis and preservationist Judith Wellman led a team of researchers who prepared a nomination of the BCALH historic district, and the BCALH historic district was added to the National Register of Historic Places in 2017.[1] Higher Ground has since been recognized for its leadership in Long Island preservation and celebrated for recognizing the history of communities on color on Long Island.[2] The nomination process was educational and enjoyable, and it provided ample opportunities to apply the research done by A Long Time Coming, but in the end it was not enough.

Little has changed on Christian Avenue since the historic district was added to the National Register. The feel of the place and the issues the community faces are the same. One problem is that the dominant heritage community and the authorized heritage discourse in Setauket have not changed focus, nor have people embraced the new status of the BCALH historic district. The lack of attention from local leaders in the heritage industry suggests that the presence of a historically significant community of color is not interesting to them. This may be the result of the path that Higher Ground took to pursue National Register listing. Because local historians and historical societies were not included in the nomination process, they perhaps feel no connection with the positive result. If this is the case, it adds more evidence to the history of racism in Setauket, since what should be recognized as an achievement of Native and African American self-determination is instead taken as an act of defiance and separation. This is a sign that the majority community in Setauket still fails to see that racism is their problem to overcome, rather than a problem contained in Christian Avenue.

The other problem we see is that the National Register listing is not set up to address Robert Lewis's primary concern that the community is being displaced by a combination of factors, including high costs of living and restricted access to good jobs. As one family after another leaves and are replaced by newcomers with little knowledge or care for Native and African American people and history, memory loss in the community grows every day. A Long Time Coming has tried to leverage support for the preservation of the community by joining the National Trust's This Place Matters program and seeking attention through the New York Preservation League's Seven to Save program and listing on the National Register of Historic Places. Results so far have been inconsequential. Community members are right to question the value of these official recognitions. What good has been done? How do scholarly research and National Register listing provide the sorts of support they need to survive as a community? What does externally awarded historical significance do to stem the exodus of community members that is creating refugees out of the indigenous community and archaeological sites out of their homes? Robert Lewis voiced his critique incisively:

> It's . . . true that leading historic preservation organizations have done many good things in the business of historic preservation. Obviously, people need to be able to "hear" and "see" where and how damage is occurring to the fabric of American history. [However,] . . . the "meeting of the minds" . . . of people . . . convinced that new, more equitable and legally protected approaches to the preservation of significant historical cultures is necessary . . . [but] will not happen until New York State and the National Parks Service have seen that we have fulfilled all the requirements for "*their registry*." . . . I hope that someday people might agree with me there needs to be, (or should have been) a different historical registry agency specifically dedicated to highlighting and preserving historically significant cultural communities, with just as much clout as . . . [the] National Register of Historic Places. However, I feel that just because certain aspects of historic preservation [i.e. the preservation and interpretation of historic places and sites rather than people and communities] are prioritized by New York State and the National Parks Service, they should not be allowed to act as a road block [against] small historic organizations not having the support of money and technical services. I have always felt that, due to their grossly bureaucratic structure, large, financially powerful, and influential preservation organizations could be accused of having "special interests" (a hidden agenda), other than what their business implies. . . . It's tragic. The fight for any minority community residents

> to exist—to survive in a certain place is always far greater in importance than the value of the land upon which they live. They know that if they get displaced from the land on/in which they live, they will die. It's like: "You can have three wishes if you agree to sell your soul." (personal correspondence, 29 October 2016)

As Lewis suggests, as those granting recognition set the terms of what is historically significant, the burden of proof and the acquisition of resources and labor rests entirely with the applicants. When those seeking recognition start from such different points in terms of experience, knowledge, access, and resources, the results will always be biased in favor of elites. This is why in Setauket and most historic places nationwide, we see the same historical narratives mechanically reproduced, since there is no need to justify significance if the story stays the same. As long as the politics of preservation and history are not based in questions of power and equity, why would we expect anything else? The point here is that parity is not a given in the heritage industry. While everyone has a past, not all pasts are treated, understood, or accepted equally. Minority communities require our additional professional and political support if they are to have a fair chance to preserve not only their history but also their future.

What we need is an affirmative action program in the heritage industry. Like strategies used by governments, universities, and businesses that allow for preferential treatment in admissions, hiring, and promotion of individuals from historically underrepresented groups, it would be reasonable to embrace a similar policy regarding the way funding and expertise is distributed in the heritage industry. State and local agencies as well as private preservation organizations and firms should not only be tasked with supporting applications from minority organizations like Higher Ground; they should be mandated to actively solicit them along with open-ended offers to provide their expert assistance as an accommodation for the needs of these usually poorly funded and lightly credentialed community-based organizations. Our heritage expertise is an asset to be deployed, and it can be used to support social justice and civil rights—or not. There is no neutral position. From a civil rights perspective, extensions of expertise should create a more inclusive historical narrative that both adds new and underrepresented stories and reflects on why some stories have been left out and how their inclusion changes existing narratives. This is no different than a university or company recognizing its own role in past discrimination and working to remedy the harm it has caused.

Such affirmative work puts the resources of the heritage industry behind the preservation and advocacy of historic communities and their way of life. This is very different from traditional preservation practice, which focuses on historic houses, objects, and artifacts from the past more than the people these things belong to. In cases where historic communities still exist, a focus on preserving historic structures and material culture suggests the people themselves are absent, which is exactly what surviving communities are fighting their hardest not to be! It is strange, actually, that the heritage industry works this way, but it does not have to. It is not "mission creep" to help a historic community survive by documenting its past and leveraging preservation resources to resist its displacement.

Justice for the Native and African American community in Setauket, New York, has been a long time coming, but as Sam Cooke's civil rights anthem promises, "change is gonna come, oh yes it will." This book has argued that recognizing the full history of Native and African American people in Setauket is essential to the larger struggle for racial, economic, social, and political justice. Documenting this history and memorializing it in public spaces is a potent act of resistance and a powerful source of community engagement. Archaeology, anthropology, and historic preservation can and should be marshaled to empower struggles for full equality. It is our hope that the result will be a more accurate and robust American history and a greater recognition of how scholarship on the past contributes to political struggles in the present.

Notes

1. Wellman is a professional preservationist and researcher with a series of successful nominations to her credit in New York State. The team consisted of Judith Wellman, Robert Lewis, Judith Burgess, myself, Karen Martin, Cynthia Shepard, Jim "Zak" Szakmary, Tanya Warren, and Scott Zukowski.

2. Higher Ground was honored in 2018 by Preservation Long Island with an award for Organizational Excellence (2018 Preservation Awards, Preservation Long Island, http://preservationlongisland.org/2018-preservation-awards/).

REFERENCES

Author's note: Digital audio files and interview summaries on file with Higher Ground Intercultural and Heritage Association, Setauket, New York and the Department of Anthropology, Montclair State University.

Adams, Karen M.

1975 The Black Image in the Paintings of William Sidney Mount. *American Art Journal* 7(2):42–59.

Adkins, Edwin P.

1980 *Setauket: The First Three Hundred Years, 1655–1955*. 2nd ed. Three Village Historical Society, Setauket, New York.

Agbe-Davies, Anna S.

2011 Reaching for Freedom, Seizing Responsibility: Archaeology of the Phyllis Wheatley Home for Girls, Chicago. In *The Materiality of Freedom: Archaeologies of Postemancipation Life,* edited by Jodi A. Barnes, pp. 69–88. University of South Carolina Press, Columbia.

Alemy, Alexis, Sophia Hudzik, and Christopher N. Matthews

2017 Creating a User-Friendly Interactive Interpretive Resource with ESRI's ArcGIS Story Map Program. *Historical Archaeology* 51(2):288–297.

Ancestry.com

2010 US, Selected Federal Census Non-Population Schedules, 1850–1880. Ancestry.com Operations, Provo, Utah.

Archer, John, Paul Sandul, and Katherine Solomonson (editors)

2015 *Making Suburbia: New Histories of Everyday America.* University of Minnesota Press, Minneapolis.

Arjona, Jamie M.

2017 Homesick Blues: Excavating Crooked Intimacies in Late Nineteenth- and Early Twentieth-Century Jook Joints. *Historical Archaeology* 51(1):43–59.

Atalay, Sonya

2006 Indigenous Archaeology as Decolonizing Practice. *American Indian Quarterly* 30(3):280–310.

2012 *Community-Based Archaeology: Research with, by and for Indigenous and Local Communities.* University of California Press, Berkeley.

Ballbè, E. Gassiot

2007 The Archaeology of the Spanish Civil War: Recovering Memory and Historical Justice. In *Archaeology and Capitalism. From Ethics to Politics,* edited by Yannis Hamilakis and Philip Duke, pp. 84–102. Left Coast Press, Walnut Creek, California.

Barber, Gertrude A.

1950 *Marriages of Suffolk County, N.Y.: Taken from the "Republican Watchman," a Newspaper Published at Greenport, N.Y.* Accessible at Ancestry.com.

Barnes, Jodi

2011 Land Rich and Cash Poor: The Materiality of Poverty in Appalachia. *Historical Archaeology* 45(3): 26–40.

Barnes, Jodi (editor)

2011 *The Materiality of Freedom: Archaeologies of Postemancipation Life.* University of South Carolina Press, Columbia.

Barsh, Russel Lawrence

2002 "Colored" Seamen in the New England Whaling Industry: An Afro-Indian Consortium. In *Confounding the Color Line: The Indian-Black Experience in North America,* edited by James F. Brooks, pp. 76–107. University of Nebraska Press, Lincoln.

Battle-Baptiste, Whitney

2011 *Black Feminist Archaeology.* Left Coast Press, Walnut Creek, California.

Baxter, Jane E.

2005 *The Archaeology of Childhood: Children, Gender, and Material Culture.* AltaMira Press, Walnut Creek, California.

Beaudry, Mary C., Lauren J. Cook, and Stephen A. Mrozowski

1991 Artifacts and Active Voices: Material Culture as Social Discourse. In *The Archaeology of Inequality,* edited by Randall H. McGuire and Robert Paynter, pp. 150–191. Basil Blackwell, Oxford.

Bergen, Teunis G.

1867 *Genealogy of the Van Brunt Family.* Joel Munsell, Albany. https://archive.org/stream/genealogyofvanbr1867berg/genealogyofvanbr1867berg_djvu.txt, accessed March 26, 2019.

Bernbeck, Reinhard, and Susan Pollack

2007 "Grabe, wo du stehst!" An Archaeology of Perpetrators. In *Archaeology and Capitalism: From Ethics to Politics,* edited by Yannis Hamilakis and Philip Duke, eds., 217–233. Left Coast Press, Walnut Creek, California.

Bernstein, David J.

1990 Prehistoric Seasonality Studies in Coastal Southern New England. *American Anthropologist* 92:96–15.

1993 *Prehistoric Subsistence on the Southern New England Coast: The Record from Narragansett Bay.* Academic Press, New York.

2002 Late Woodland Use of Coastal Resources at Mount Sinai Harbor, Long Island, New York. In *A Lasting Impression: Coastal, Lithic and Ceramic Research in New England Archaeology,* edited by Jordan Kerber, pp. 27–40. Praeger, West Port, Connecticut.

Bernstein, David J., and Michael J. Lenardi

2008 The Use of Lithic Resources in a Coastal Environment: Quartz Technology on Long Island, New York. In *Current Approaches to the Analysis and Interpretation of Small Lithic Sites in the Northeast,* edited by Christina B. Rieth, pp. 101–110. New York State Museum Bulletin Series 508, Albany.

Bernstein, David J., Michael J. Lenardi, and Daria E. Merwin

1993 Archaeological Investigations at Eagle's Nest, Mount Sinai, Town of Brookhaven, Suffolk County, New York. Submitted to the Town of Brookhaven, New York. Copies available at the Institute for Long Island Archaeology, State University of New York at Stony Brook, Stony Brook, New York.

Bernstein, Iver

2005 Securing Freedom: The Challenges of Black Life in The Civil War. In *Slavery in New York,* edited by Ira Berlin and Leslie M. Harris, pp. 289–324. The New Press, New York.

Blakey, Michael L.

2001 Bioarchaeology of the African Diaspora in the Americas: Its Origins and Scope. *Annual Review of Anthropology* 30:387–422.

Bolster, W. Jeffrey

1997 *Black Jacks: African American Seamen in the Age of Sail.* Harvard University Press, Cambridge.

Brandon, Jamie C., and James M. Davidson

2005 The Landscape of Van Winkle's Mill: Identity, Myth, and Modernity in the Ozark Upland South. *Historical Archaeology* 39(3):113–131.

Brighton, Stephen

2001 Prices That Suit the Times: Shopping for Ceramics at the Five Points. *Historical Archaeology* 35(3):16–30.

Brody, Hugh

1981 *Maps and Dreams.* Pantheon, New York.

Brookhaven, New York

1880 *Records of the Town of Brookhaven up to 1800 as Compiled by the Town Clerk.* Compiled by the Town Clerk, Brookhaven, New York.

Brown, Kenneth L.

2004 Ethnographic Analogy, Archaeology, and the African Diaspora: Perspectives from a Tenant Community. *Historical Archaeology* 38(1):79–89.

Burkholder, Zoë A.

2011 *Color in the Classroom: How American Schools Taught Race, 1900–1954.* Oxford University Press, New York.

Cabak, Melanie A., Mark D. Groover, and Scott J. Wagers

1995 Health Care and the Wayman A.M.E. Church. *Historical Archaeology* 29(2): 55–76.

Caraher, William, and Brett Weber

2017 *The Bakken: An Archaeology of an Industrial Landscape.* North Dakota State University Press, Fargo.

Carter G. Woodson Center

2019 The Power of Sankofa: Know History. Carter G. Woodson Center, Berea College. https://www.berea.edu/cgwc/the-power-of-sankofa/, accessed May 22, 2019.

Castañeda, Quetzil E., and Christopher N. Matthews (editors)

2008 *Ethnographic Archaeologies: Reflections on Stakeholders and Archaeological Practices.* AltaMira Press, Walnut Creek, California.

Ceci, Lynn

1984 Shell Midden Deposits as Coastal Resources. *World Archaeology* 16(1):62–74.

Cerrato, Robert M., Kent G. Lightfoot, and Heather V. E. Wallace

1993 Prehistoric Shellfish-Harvesting Strategies: Implications from the Growth Patterns of Soft Shell Clams (*Mya arenaria*). *Antiquity* 67:358–369.

Colwell-Chanthaphonh, Chip, and T. J. Ferguson (editors)

2008 *Collaboration in Archaeological Practice: Engaging Descendant Communities.* AltaMira Press, Walnut Creek, California.

Crabtree, Pam

2018 Report on the Animal Bone Remains from the Hart House and the Tobias House, Setauket, New York. On file, Department of Anthropology, Montclair State University.

Davidson, James M.

2014 Deconstructing the Myth of the "Hand Charm": Mundane Clothing Fasteners and Their Curious Transformations into Supernatural Objects. *Historical Archaeology* 48(2):18–60.

2015 "A Cluster of Sacred Symbols": Interpreting an Act of Animal Sacrifice at Kingsley Plantation, Fort George Island, Florida (1814–1839). *International Journal of Historical Archaeology* 19(1):76–121.

Deagan, Kathleen A.

1983 *Spanish St. Augustine: The Archaeology of a Colonial Creole Community.* Academic Press, New York.

Deetz, James F.

1996 *In Small Things Forgotten: Archaeology and Early American Life.* Revised ed. Anchor, New York.

De León, Jason

2015 *The Land of Open Graves: Living and Dying on the Migrant Trail.* University of California Press, Berkeley.

Delle, James A.

2019 *The Archaeology of Northern Slavery and Freedom.* University Press of Florida, Gainesville.

de Tocqueville, Alexis

1988 [1835] *Democracy in America.* Edited by J. P. Mayer. Harper Perennial, New York.

Devantier-Thomas, Tate

2017 A Sperm Sewing Machine Oil Bottle from Aarhus. *Queensland Museum Network Blog,* November 15, 2017. https://blog.qm.qld.gov.au/2017/11/15/a-sperm-sewing-machine-oil-bottle-from-aarhus/, accessed May 22, 2019.

De Voe, Thomas F.

1862 *The Market Book: Containing a Historical Account of the Public Markets of the Cities of New York, Boston, Philadelphia and Brooklyn, With a Brief Descrip-*

tion of Every Article of Human Food Sold Therein, the Introduction of Cattle in America, and Notices of Many Remarkable Specimens. Printed for the author, New York.

Dippie, Brian W.

1982 *The Vanishing American: White Attitudes and US Indian Policy.* University Press of Kansas, Lawrence.

Discover Long Island

2019 Thompson House, c. 1709. Washington Spy Ring Trail. https://washingtonspytrail.com/the-thompson-house-c-1709/, accessed March 24, 2019.

Dixon, Joseph K.

2013 *The Vanishing Race: The Last Great Indian Council.* Doubleday, Page, Garden City, New York.

Douglass, Frederick

2003 [1895] *My Bondage, My Freedom.* Penguin, New York.

Du Bois, W. E. B.

1935 *Black Reconstruction in America, 1860–1880.* Harcourt Brace, New York.

Epperson, Terrence W.

1999 The Contested Commons: Archaeologies of Race, Repression, and Resistance in New York City. In *Historical Archaeologies of Capitalism,* edited by Mark P. Leone and Parker B. Potter Jr., pp. 81–110. Springer, Boston.

Fairbanks, Charles H.

1972 The Kingsley Slave Cabins in Duval County, Florida, 1968. *Conference on Historic Site Archaeology Papers 1972* 7:62–93.

Fennell, Christopher C.

2007 *Crossroads and Cosmologies: Diasporas and Ethnogenesis in the New World.* University Press of Florida, Gainesville.

Ferguson, Leland

1992 *Uncommon Ground: Archaeology and Early African America, 1650–1800.* Smithsonian University Press, Washington, DC.

Fitts, Robert K.

1996 The Landscapes of Northern Bondage. *Historical Archaeology* 30(2):54–73.

Frankenstein, Alfred

1968 *Painter of Rural America: William Sidney Mount, 1807–1868.* Suffolk Museum at Stony Brook, Stony Brook, New York.

1975 *William Sidney Mount.* Henry N. Abrams, New York.

Franklin, Maria

1997 "Power to the People": Sociopolitics and the Archaeology of Black Americans. *Historical Archaeology* 31(3):36–50.

2001 A Black Feminist-Inspired Archaeology? *Journal of Social Archaeology* 1(1):108–125.

Franklin, Maria, and Larry McKee

2004 African Diaspora Archaeologies: Present Insights and Expanding Discourses. *Historical Archaeology* 38(1):1–9.

Frederickson, George M.

2002 *Racism: A Short History.* Princeton University Press, Princeton.

Fullilove, Mindy T., and Roderick Wallace

2011 Serial Forced Displacement in American Cities, 1916–2010. *Journal of Urban Health* 88(3): 381–389.

Furman, Gabriel

1874 *Antiquities of Long Island, to Which Is Added a Bibliography by Henry Onderdonk, Jr.* Edited by Fran Moore. J. W. Bouton, New York.

Gabriel, Ralph Henry

1921 *The Evolution of Long Island: A Story of Land and Sea.* Yale University Press, New Haven.

Gellman, David N., and David Quigley (editors)

2003 *Jim Crow New York: A Documentary History of Race and Citizenship, 1777–1877.* New York University Press, New York.

Gigantino, James J.

2015 *The Ragged Road to Abolition: Slavery and Freedom in New Jersey, 1775–1865.* University of Pennsylvania Press, Philadelphia.

Glass, Barbara S.

2006 *African American Dance: An Illustrated History.* McFarland, New York.

Gonzalaz-Ruibal, Alfredo

2016 Archaeology and the Time of Modernity. *Historical Archaeology* 50(3):144–164.

Gorsline, Meg

2015 An Archaeology of Accountability: Recovering and Interrogating the "Invisible" Race. In *The Archaeology of Race in the Northeast,* edited by Christopher N. Matthews and Allison Manfra McGovern, pp. 291–310. University Press of Florida, Gainesville.

Gramly, Richard Michael, and Gretchen Gwynne

1979 Two Late Woodland Sites on Long Island Sound. *Bulletin of the Massachusetts Archaeological Society* 40(1):5–19.

Green, Theodore

1999 The Hart-Sells Connection. In *William Sidney Mount: Family, Friends, and Ideas,* edited by Elizabeth Kahn Kaplan, Robert W. Kenny, and Roger Wunderlich, pp. 63–67. Three Village Historical Society, Setauket.

Hall, Charles S.

1905 *Letters and Life of Samuel Holden Parsons.* Otseningo, Binghamton, New York.

Hall, Jacquelyn Dowd

2005 The Long Civil Rights Movement and the Political Uses of the Past. *Journal of American History* 91(4):1233–1263.

Hamilakis, Yannis

2007 From Ethics to Politics. In *Archaeology and Capitalism: From Ethics to Politics,* edited by Yannis Hamilakis and Philip Duke, pp. 15–40. Left Coast Press, Walnut Creek, California.

2017 Archaeologies of Forced and Undocumented Migration. *Journal of Contemporary Archaeology* 3(2):121–139.

Hamlet People Database

2011 Justice Nathaniel Brewster, Esq. Brookhaven/South Haven Hamlets and Their

People. http://www.brookhavensouthhaven.org/HamletPeople/tng/getperson.php?personID=I6218&tree=hamlet, accessed March 26, 2019.

Handsman, Russell G.

2011 Some Middle-Range Theory for Archaeological Studies of Wampanoag Indian Whaling. Paper prepared for the Annual Meeting of the Conference on New England Archaeology, Amherst, Massachusetts.

Hart-SellsFamily.com

2019 Hart-SellsFamily.com genealogy website. http://home.earthlink.net/~kds2/id2.html, accessed March 15, 2019.

Hayden, Delores

2003 *Building Suburbia: Green Fields and Urban Growth, 1820–2000.* Vintage, New York.

Henry, Meredith

2011 William Sidney Mount, *Eel Spearing at Setauket*, 1845. Art History of the Day. https://arthistoryoftheday.wordpress.com/2011/10/02/william-sidney-mount-eel-spearing-at-setauket-1845/, accessed March 15, 2019.

Holtorf, Cornelius

2018 Embracing Change: How Cultural Resilience Is Increased through Cultural Heritage. *World Archaeology* 50(1):1–12.

Hough, Franklin Benjamin

1857 *Census of the State of New York, for 1855; Taken in Pursuance of Article Third of the Constitution of the State, and of Chapter Sixty-Four of the Laws of 1855.* Printed by C. Van Benthuysen, Albany, New York. http://archive.org/details/cu31924078305582.

Hounshell, David A.

1984 *From the American System to Mass Production, 1800–1932.* Baltimore, Johns Hopkins University Press.

Independence Hall Association

2017 The Expansion of the Vote: A White Man's Democracy. *US History Online Textbook.* http://www.ushistory.org/us/23b.asp, accessed August 21, 2017.

Jackson, Kenneth T.

1987 *Crabgrass Frontier: The Suburbanization of the United States.* Oxford University Press, New York.

Johns, Elizabeth

1991 *American Genre Painting: The Politics of Everyday Life* Yale University Press, New Haven.

Kahrl, Andrew W.

2016 *The Land Was Ours: How Black Beaches Became White Wealth in the Coastal South.* University of North Carolina Press, Chapel Hill.

2018 *Free the Beaches: The Story of Ned Coll and the Battle for America's Most Exclusive Shoreline.* Yale University Press, New Haven.

Kaplan, Elizabeth Kahn, Robert W. Kenny, and Roger Wunderlich (editors)

1999 *William Sidney Mount: Family, Friends, and Ideas.* Three Village Historical Society, Setauket, New York.

Kelley, Robin D. G.
1996 *Race Rebels: Culture, Politics, and the Black Working Class.* The Free Press, New York.

Kendi, Ibram X.
2016 *Stamped from the Beginning: The Definitive History of Racist Ideas in America.* Nation Books, New York.

Kiddey, Rachel
2017 *Homeless Heritage: Collaborative Social Archaeology as Therapeutic Practice.* Oxford University Press, New York.

Klein, Howard
1986 *Three Village Guidebook: The Setaukets, Poquott, Old Field, and Stony Brook.* 2nd ed. Three Village Historical Society, East Setauket, New York.

Kourelis, Kostis
2017 If Place Remotely Matters: Camped in Greece's Contingent Countryside. *Journal of Contemporary Archaeology* 3(2):215–227.

Lamme, Rob
2015 A Brief History of Marbles (Including All That Marble Slang). *Mental Floss,* November 3, 2015. http://mentalfloss.com/article/29486/brief-history-marbles-including-all-marble-slang, accessed May 22, 2019.

Larkin, Karin, and Randall H. McGuire
2009 *The Archaeology of Class War: The Colorado Coalfield Strike of 1913–1914.* University of Colorado Press, Boulder.

LaRoche, Cheryl J., and Blakey, Michael L.
1997 Seizing Intellectual Power: The Dialogue at the New York African Burial Ground. *Historical Archaeology* 31:84–106.

Laws of the State of New York
1799 An Act For The Gradual Abolition of Slavery, passed March 29, 1799. In *Laws of the State of New York,* 22nd Session. http://www.rootsweb.ancestry.com/~nycayuga/land/towns/1799abolition.html, accessed August 21, 2017.

Lee, Virginia S.
2002 Unlearning: A Critical Element in the Learning Process. *Professional and Organizational Development Network in Higher Education, Essays on Teaching Excellence toward the Best in the Academy* 14(2).

Leone, Mark P.
1984 Interpreting Ideology in Historical Archaeology: The William Paca Garden in Annapolis, Maryland. In *Ideology, Power and Prehistory,* edited by Daniel Miller and Christopher Tilley, pp. 25–36. Cambridge University Press, Cambridge.
1988 The Georgian Order as the Order of Merchant Capitalism in Annapolis, Maryland. In *The Recovery of Meaning: Historical Archaeology in the Eastern United States,* edited by Mark P. Leone and Parker B. Potter Jr., pp. 235–261. Smithsonian Institution Press, Washington, DC.
2005 *The Archaeology of Liberty in an American Capital: Excavations in Annapolis.* University of California Press, Berkeley.

Leone, Mark P., Cheryl Janifer LaRoche, and Jennifer J. Barbiarz
2005 The Archaeology of Black Americans in Recent Times. *Annual Review of Anthropology* 34:575–598.
Leone, Mark P., and Paul A. Shackel
1987 Forks, Clocks, and Power. In *Mirror and Metaphor: Material and Social Constructions of Reality,* edited by Daniel Ingersoll, pp. 45–62. University Press of America, Lanham, Maryland.
Lhamon, W. T., Jr.
2000 *Raising Cain: Blackface Performance from Jim Crow to Hip Hop.* Harvard University Press, Cambridge, Massachusetts.
Liebmann, Matthew, and Uzma Z. Rizvi (editors)
2008 *Archaeology and the Postcolonial Critique.* AltaMira Press, Walnut Creek, California.
Lightfoot, Kent G., and Robert M. Cerrato
1988 Shellfish Exploitation in Coastal New York. *Journal of Field Archaeology* 15:141–144.
Linenebagh, Peter, and Marcus Rediker
2001 *The Many-Headed Hydra: Sailors, Slaves, Commoners, and the Hidden History of the Revolutionary Atlantic.* Verso, New York.
Little, Barbara J.
2007 *Historical Archaeology: Why the Past Matters.* Routledge, New York.
Little, Barbara J., and Paul A. Shackel (editors)
2007 *Archaeology as a Tool of Civic Engagement.* AltaMira Press, Walnut Creek, California.
Little, Barbara J., and Paul A. Shackel
2014 *Archaeology, Heritage, and Civic Engagement: Working toward the Public Good.* Left Coast Press, Walnut Creek, California.
Lockwood, Estelle D.
1999 Saga of the Strong Family. In *William Sidney Mount: Family, Friends, and Ideas,* edited by Elizabeth Kahn Kaplan, Robert W. Kenny, and Roger Wunderlich, pp. 44–53. Three Village Historical Society, Setauket.
Loften, Adam, and Emmanuel Vaughan-Lee
2019 Counter Mapping. *Emergence Magazine.* https://emergencemagazine.org/story/counter-mapping/.
Long Island Genealogy
2019 Research Tool for Use with Brookhaven Town Cemetery. Long Island Genealogy. http://longislandgenealogy.com/CemList.html, accessed March 22, 2019.
Longjohn, Tami, and Ariel Flajnik
2011 Internship research report on the Irving Hart Memorial Legion Hall. Prepared for Higher Ground Intercultural and Heritage Association and the Center for Public Archaeology, Hofstra University. On file, Higher Ground Intercultural and Heritage Association, Setauket, New York.
Longwood Central School District
2019 Censuses 1776–1900. http://longwood.k12.ny.us/community/longwood_journey/resources/censuses__1776-_1900_, accessed May 10, 2019.

Lott, Eric

1995 *Love and Theft: Blackface Minstrelsy and the American Working Class.* Oxford University Press, New York.

Lowenthal, David

1985 *The Past Is a Foreign Country.* Cambridge University Press, New York.

1998 *The Heritage Crusade and the Spoils of History.* Cambridge University Press, New York.

McDavid, Carol

1997 Descendants, Decisions, and Power: The Public Interpretation of the Archaeology of the Levi Jordan Plantation. *Historical Archaeology* 31(3):114–131.

McDavid, Carol, and Christopher N. Matthews (editors)

2016 *Perspectives from Historical Archaeology: Public and Community Archaeology.* Society for Historical Archaeology, Germantown, Maryland.

McGovern, Allison M.

2015a Disrupting the Narrative: Labor and Survivance for the Montaukett of Eastern Long Island. PhD dissertation, Department of Anthropology, City University of New York, New York.

2015b Facing "the End": Termination and Survivance among the Montaukett of Eastern Long Island, New York. In *The Archaeology of Race in the Northeast,* edited by Christopher N. Matthews and Allison Manfra McGovern, pp. 215–231. University Press of Florida, Gainesville.

McGuire, Randall H.

1992 *A Marxist Archaeology.* Academic Press, New York.

2008 *Archaeology as Political Action.* University of California Press, Berkeley.

McGuire, Randall H., Maria O'Donovan, and LouAnn Wurst

2005 Probing Praxis in Archaeology: The Last Eighty Years. *Rethinking Marxism* 17(3):355–372.

McGuire, Randall H., Dean Saitta, and Philip Duke

1998 Archaeology of the Colorado Coal Field War 1913–1914. *Radical History Review* 72:79–80.

McKenzie, Evan

1996 *Privatopia: Homeowner Associations and the Rise of Residential Private Government.* Yale University Press, New Haven.

McKnight, Justine

2017 Report on the Analysis of Flotation Samples Collected from the Silas Tobias Site (10353.000057), Setauket, Long Island, New York. On file, Department of Anthropology, Montclair State University, Montclair.

McManus, Edward J.

1966 *A History of Negro Slavery in New York.* Syracuse University Press, Syracuse, New York.

McNiven, Ian J., and Lynette Russell

2005 *Appropriated Pasts: Indigenous Peoples and the Colonial Culture of Archaeology.* AltaMira Press, Walnut Creek, California.

Mahar, William J.
1988 "Backside Albany" and Early Blackface Minstrelsy: A Contextual Study of America's First Blackface Song. *American Music* 6(1):1–27.
Marcus, Grania Bolton
1988 *Discovering the African American Experience in Suffolk County, 1620–1860*. Society for the Preservation of Long Island Antiquities/Amereon House, Mattituck, New York.
Matthews, Christopher N.
2010 *The Archaeology of American Capitalism.* University Press of Florida, Gainesville.
2011a Emancipation Landscapes: Archaeologies of Racial Modernity and the Public Sphere in Early New York. In *The Importance of Material Things, Vol. II,* edited by J. Shablitsky and M. Leone, pp. 69–91. Society for Historical Archaeology, Rockville, Maryland.
2011b Lonely Islands: Culture and Poverty in Archaeological Perspective. *Historical Archaeology* 45(3):41–54.
Matthews, Christopher N., and Allison Manfra McGovern (editors)
2015 *The Archaeology of Race in the Northeast.* University Press of Florida, Gainesville.
Maya People of Southern Belize
1997 *Maya Atlas: The Struggle to Preserve Maya Land in Southern Belize.* North Atlantic Books, Berkeley.
Melish, Joanne Pope
2000 *Disowning Slavery: Gradual Emancipation and "Race" in New England, 1780–1860*. Cornell University Press, Ithaca.
Meskell, Lynn
2002 Negative Heritage and Past Mastering. *Anthropological Quarterly* 75(3):557–574.
2018 *A Future in Ruins: UNESCO, World Heritage, and the Dream of Peace.* Oxford University Press, New York.
Morris, Annalies
2017 Materialities of Homeplace. *Historical Archaeology* 51(1):28–42.
Morrison, Toni
1992 *Playing in the Dark: Whiteness and the Literary Imagination.* Harvard University Press, Cambridge.
Muhammed, Khalil Gibran
2010 *The Condemnation of Blackness: Race, Crime, and the Making of Modern Urban America.* Harvard University Press, Cambridge, Massachusetts.
Mullins, Paul R.
1999a Race and the Genteel Consumer: Class and African-American Consumption, 1850–1930. *Historical Archaeology* 33(1):22–38.
1999b *Race and Affluence: An Archaeology of African America and Consumer Culture.* Kluwer Academic, New York.
2006 Racializing the Commonplace Landscape: An Archaeology of Urban Renewal along the Color Line. *World Archaeology* 38(1):60–71.

Mullins, Paul R., Kyle Huskins, and Susan B. Hyatt

2020 Race and the Water: Swimming, Sewers, and Structural Violence in African America. In *Archaeologies of Violence and Privilege,* edited by Christopher N. Matthews and Bradley D. Phillippi, University of New Mexico Press, Albuquerque.

Mullins, Paul R., and Lewis C. Jones

2011a Archaeologies of Race and Urban Poverty: The Politics of Slumming, Engagement, and the Color Line. *Historical Archaeology* 45(1):33–50.

2011b Race, Displacement, and Twentieth-Century University Landscapes: An Archaeology of Urban Renewal and Urban Universities. In *The Materiality of Freedom: Archaeologies of Postemancipation Life,* edited by Jodi A. Barnes, pp. 250–262. University of South Carolina Press.

National Archives and Records Administration

2010 US, Civil War Draft Registrations Records, 1863–1865. Records of the Provost Marshal General's Bureau (Civil War), Record Group 110. Washington, DC. Accessible at Ancestry.com.

National Register of Historic Places

2019 Frequently Asked Questions. National Register of Historic Places. https://nationalregisterofhistoricplaces.com/faq.html, accessed May 24, 2019.

Nelson, David Paul

2011 Culper Ring. In *Spies, Wiretaps, and Secret Operations: A-J.*, edited by Clenn P. Hastedt, p. 217. ABC-CLIO, Santa Barbara.

Nevins, Allan, and Milton Halsey Thomas (editors)

1952 *The Diary of George Templeton Strong.* Macmillan, New York.

New York Courts

2017 New York State Constitution of 1821. https://www.nycourts.gov/history/legal-history-new-york/documents/Publications_1821-NY-Constitution.pdf, accessed August 21, 2017.

New York State Archives

1865 New York State Census. 1865. Albany, New York. Accessible at Ancestry.com.

2018 Second Constitution of the State of New York, New York (State). Secretary of State, 1821. A1804. Digital Collections. http://digitalcollections.archives.nysed.gov/index.php/Detail/Collection/Show/collection_id/4903, accessed May 22, 2019.

New York State Historic Newspapers

2017 http://nyshistoricnewspapers.org/, accessed August 21, 2017.

Nida, Brandon

2013 Demystifying the Hidden Hand: Capital and the State at Blair Mountain. *Historical Archaeology* 47(3):52–68.

NYS Board for Historic Preservation

2015 162nd NYS Board for Historic Preservation Meeting Transcript. https://parks.ny.gov/newsroom/documents/162ndHPStateReviewBoardMeetingNotes.pdf, accessed March 15, 2019.

Orser, Charles E., Jr.

1988a The Archaeological Analysis of Plantation Society: Replacing Status and Caste with Economics and Power. *American Antiquity* 53:735–751.

1988b *The Material Basis of the Postbellum Tenant Plantation: Historical Archaeology in the South Carolina Piedmont.* University of Georgia Press, Athens.

1989 On Plantations and Patterns. *Historical Archaeology* 23(2): 28–40.

1991 The Continued Pattern of Dominance: Landlord and Tenant on the Postbellum Cotton Plantation. In *The Archaeology of Inequality,* edited by Robert Paynter and Randall H. McGuire, pp. 40–54. Basil Blackwell, Oxford.

1996 *Historical Archaeology of the Modern World.* Plenum Press, New York.

2007 *The Archaeology of Race and Racialization in Historic America.* University Press of Florida, Gainesville.

Otto, John

1980 Race and Class on Antebellum Plantations. In *Archaeological Perspectives on Ethnicity in America: Afro-American and Asian American Culture History,* edited by Robert L. Schuyler, pp. 3–13. Baywood, Farmingdale, New York.

Peluso, Nancy Lee

1995 Whose Woods are These? Counter-Mapping Forest Territories in Kalimantan, Indonesia. *Antipode* 27(4):383–406.

Perry, Warren, and Michael L. Blakey

1997 Archaeology as Community Service: The African Burial Ground Project in New York City. *North American Dialogue* 2(1): 45–51.

Perry, Warren R., Jean Howson, and Barbara A. Bianco (editors)

2009 *The Archaeology of the New York African Burial Ground, Part I.* Howard University Press, Washington.

Phillippi, Bradley D.

2016 *From Coercion to Compensation: Labor Systems and Spatial Practice on a Plural Farmstead, Long Island.* PhD dissertation, Department of Anthropology, Northwestern University, Evanston, Illinois.

Phillippi, Bradley D., and Christopher N. Matthews

2017 A Counter-Archaeology of Labor and Leisure in Setauket, New York. *World Archaeology* 49(3):357–371.

Prime, Nathaniel

1845 *A History of Long Island, from Its First Settlement by Europeans, to the Year 1845, with Special Reference to Its Ecclesiastical Concerns, in Two Parts: I, Its Physical Features and Civil Affairs; II, Annals of the Several Towns, Relating Chiefly to Ecclesiastical Matters.* Robert Carter, New York.

Rava, Ross T., and Christopher N. Matthews

2017 An Archaeological View of Slavery and Social Relations at Rock Hall, Lawrence, New York. *In Archaeologies of African American Life in the Upper Mid-Atlantic,* edited by Michael J. Gall and Richard F. Veit, pp. 55–69. University of Alabama Press, Tuscaloosa.

Rees, Jonathan

2013 *Industrialization and the Transformation of American Life: A Brief Introduction.* M. E. Sharpe, Armonk, New York.

Rico, Trinidad

2014 The Limits of a "Heritage at Risk" Framework: The Construction of Post-disaster Cultural Heritage in Banda Aceh, Indonesia. *Journal of Social Archaeology* 14(2):157–176.

Ritchie, William A.

1959 *The Stony Brook Site and Its Relation to Archaic and Transitional Cultures of Long Island.* New York State Museum and Science Service, Bul. 372. University of the State of New York, Albany.

1965 *The Archaeology of New York State.* Natural History Press, American Museum of Natural History, New York.

Roberts, Brian

2017 *Blackface Nation: Race, Reform, and Identity in American Popular Music, 1812–1925.* University of Chicago Press, Chicago.

Robertson, Bruce

1998 Who's Sitting at the Table? William Sidney Mount's *After Dinner,* 1834. *The Yale Journal of Criticism* 11(1):103–109.

Robinson, Cedric J.

2000 *Black Marxism: The Making of the Black Radical Tradition.* 2nd ed. University of North Carolina, Press, Chapel Hill.

Roediger, David R.

1991 *The Wages of Whiteness: Race and the Making of the American Working Class.* Verso, New York.

1999 The Pursuit of Whiteness: Property, Terror, and Expansion, 1790–1860. *Journal of the Early Republic* 19(4):579–600.

Roller, Michael

2013 Rewriting Narratives of Labor Violence: A Transnational Perspective of the Lattimer Massacre. *Historical Archaeology* 47(3):109–123.

Ronayne, Maggie

2007 The Culture of Caring and Its Destruction in the Middle East: Women's Work, Water, War and Archaeology. In *Archaeology and Capitalism: From Ethics to Politics,* edited by Yannis Hamilakis and Philip Duke, pp. 247–266. Left Coast Press, Walnut Creek, California.

Rose, Alexander

2007 *Washington's Spies: The Story of America's First Spy Ring.* Bantam Dell, New York.

Ross, Peter

1902 *A History of Long Island: From Its Earliest Settlement to the Present Time.* Lewis, New York.

Ruppel, Timothy, Jessica Neuwirth, Mark P. Leone, and Gladys-Marie Fry

2003 Hidden in View: African Spiritual Spaces in North American Landscapes. *Antiquity* 77(296):321–335.

Salive

2019 Eel Spear. Antique Tool Company. http://www.antiquetools.co.uk/articles/ee11.htm, accessed May 22, 2019.

Salwen, Bert

1962 Sea Levels and Archaeology in the Long Island Sound Area. *American Antiquity* 28(1): 46–55.

Schmidt, Peter R., and Jonathan R. Walz
2007 Re-representing African Pasts through Historical Archaeology. *American Antiquity* 72(1):53–70.
Schuyler, Robert L. (editor)
1980 *Archaeological Perspectives on Ethnicity in America: Afro-American and Asian American Culture History.* Baywood Monographs in Archaeology, Farmingdale, New York.
Scott, Kevin M.
2004 Rituals of Race: Mount, Melville, and Antebellum America. Ph.D. Dissertation, Purdue University, West Lafayette, Indiana.
SenGupta, Gunja
2009 *From Slavery to Poverty: The Racial Origins of Welfare in New York, 1840–1918.* New York University Press, New York.
Shackel, Paul A.
1993 *Personal Discipline and Material Culture: An Archaeology of Annapolis, Maryland, 1695–1870.* Knoxville, University of Tennessee Press.
1996 *Culture Change and the New Technology: An Archaeology of the Early American Industrial Era.* Plenum, New York.
Shackel Paul A., and Erve J. Chambers (editors)
2004 *Places in Mind: Public Archaeology as Applied Anthropology.* Routledge, New York.
Shupe, Barbara, Marlene Butler, Mary McCallum, Donna Sammis, Janet Steins, and Carolyn Woods (editors)
1982 Historical Population of Long Island Communities, 1790–1980. Long Island Regional Planning Board, Hauppauge, New York. https://www.suffolkcountyny.gov/Portals/0/formsdocs/planning/Research/Historical_pop.pdf.
Smedley, Audrey
2011 *Race in North America: Origin and Evolution of a Worldview.* Taylor and Francis, New York.
Smith, Christopher J.
2013 *The Creolization of American Culture: William Sidney Mount and the Roots of Blackface Minstrelsy.* University of Illinois Press, Urbana.
Smith, Laurajane
2004 *Archaeological Theory and the Politics of Cultural Heritage.* Routledge, New York.
2006 *Uses of Heritage.* Routledge, New York.
Smith, Laurajane, and Emma Waterton
2009 *Heritage, Communities and Archaeology.* Duckworth, London.
Smith, Linda Tuhiwai
1999 *Decolonizing Methodologies: Research and Indigenous People.* Zed Books, New York.
Stern, Marc J.
1991 The Social Utility of Failure: Long Island's Rubber Industry and the Setauket *Stetle,* 1876–1911. *Long Island Historical Journal* 4(1):15–35.
Stevens, William Oliver
1939 *Discovering Long Island.* Dodd, Mead, New York.

Stewart, James Brewer

1998 The Emergence of Racial Modernity and the Rise of the White North, 1790–1840. *Journal of the Early Republic* 18(2):181–217.

1999 Modernizing "Difference": The Political Meanings of Color in the Free United States, 1776–1840. *Journal of the Early Republic* 19(4):691–712.

Stottman, M. Jay (editor)

2010 *Archaeologists as Activists: Can Archaeologists Change the World?* University of Alabama Press, Tuscaloosa.

Straughsbaugh, John

2006 *Black Like You: Blackface, Whiteface, Insult and Imitation in American Popular Culture.* Tarcher/Penguin, New York.

Strong, John A.

1992 The Thirteen Tribes of Long Island: The History of a Myth. *Hudson Valley Regional Review* 9(2):39–73.

1998 *We Are Still Here: The Algonquian Peoples of Long Island Today.* Heart of the Lakes, Ovid, New York.

2006 *The Montaukett Indians of Eastern Long Island.* Syracuse University Press, Syracuse.

2011 *The Unkechaug Indians of Eastern Long Island: A History.* University of Oklahoma Press, Norman.

Strong, Kate

2013 *True Tales from the Early Days of Long Island.* Literary Licensing.

Sugrue, Thomas J.

2008 *Sweet Land of Liberty: The Forgotten Struggle for Civil Rights in the North.* Random House, New York.

Tallbear, Kim

2013 *Native American DNA: Tribal Belonging and the False Promise of Genetic Science.* University of Minnesota Press, Minneapolis.

Three Village Historical Society

2005 *The Setaukets, Old Field, and Poquott.* Images of America/Arcadia, Charleston, South Carolina.

2019 Chicken Hill: A Community Lost to Time. Three Village Historical Society. https://www.tvhs.org/current-exhibits?page_id=2021, accessed May 24, 2019.

Tobias, Simira

n.d. *A Knowing So Deep: A Tobias Genealogy.* Unpublished manuscript, in possession of the author.

Tri-Spy Tours

2019 About. Tri-Spy Tours. http://www.culper.com/about/, accessed March 14, 2019.

Tweedie, Mark

2014 *Exploratory Steatite Source Characterization in the Long Island Sound Watershed.* MA thesis, Department of Anthropology, Stony Brook University, Stony Brook.

2017 Stone Tools at Historic, Mixed-Heritage Settlements in North-Central Long Island, New York: Technology, Tradition, or Lithic Taphonomy at the Silas Tobias and Jacob Hart Households. On file, Department of Anthropology, Montclair State University, Montclair.

United States Department of Agriculture

1915 Service and Regulatory Announcements, Supplement, Notices of Judgements under the Food and Drugs Act. USDA, Washington, DC. https://books.google.com/books?id=6KkwAQAAMAAJ&pg=PA355&lpg=PA355&dq=Green+Mountain+Oil+(or+Magic+Pain+Destroyer)&source=bl&ots=BRB-HLhm31&sig=FQ3_miOa5D3mAHlvhnPBIoPzOEk&hl=en&sa=X&ved=0ahUKEwi_hP7PuIjcAhUHMt8KHUoABzkQ6AEIKTAA#v=onepage&q=Green%20Mountain%20oil%20(or%20Magic%20Pain%20Destroyer)&f=false, accessed May 14, 2019.

US Bureau of the Census

1902a *Twelfth Census of the Unite States Taken in the Year 1900, Volume VI. Agriculture, Part 2, Crops and Irrigation.* https://www.census.gov/library/publications/1902/dec/vol-06-agriculture.html, accessed May 23, 2019.

1902b *Twelfth Census of the Unite States Taken in the Year 1900, Volume V. Agriculture, Part 1, Farms, Livestock, and Animal Products.* https://www2.census.gov/library/publications/decennial/1900/volume-5/volume-5-p4.pdf, accessed 23 May 2019.

Ward, Christopher

1952 *War of the Revolution.* Macmillan, New York.

Waterton, Emma, and Steve Watson

2014 *The Semiotics of Heritage Tourism.* Channel View, Bristol.

Weik, Terry

1997 The Archaeology of Maroon Societies in the Americas: Resistance, Cultural Continuity, and Transformation in the African Diaspora. *Historical Archaeology* 31(2):81–92.

Weinberg, H. Barbara, and Carrie Rebora Barratt

2009 American Scenes of Everyday Life, 1840–1910. In *Heilbrunn Timeline of Art History.* Metropolitan Museum of Art, New York. http://www.metmuseum.org/toah/hd/scen/hd_scen.htm, accessed August 21, 2017.

Welch, Richard F.

1991 The World the Shipbuilders Made: An Entrepreneurial Elite on Nineteenth-Century Long Island. *Long Island Historical Journal* 4(1):35–44.

2015 Old Field South. In *Gardens of Eden: Long Island's Early Twentieth-Century Planned Communities*, edited by Robert B. MacKay, pp. 240–245. W. W. Norton, New York.

Wellman, Judith (editor)

2016 Cultural Resources Survey of Sites Relating to People of Color, Three Village Area (the Setaukets, Stony Brook, and Old Field) with a focus on the Bethel-Christian Avenue-Laurel Hill Town of Brookhaven Historic District. Prepared by Historical New York Research Associates, with contributions by Robert Lewis, Judith Burgess, Christopher Matthews, and Karen Martin. Submitted to Preserve New York. On file, Historical New York Associates.

Werner, Bell

1982 The Strong's Neck Site. In *The Second Coastal Archaeology Reader: 1900 to the Present,* edited by James Truex, pp. 202–213. Suffolk County Archaeological Association, Stony Brook.

White, William A., III

2017 Writ on the Landscape: Racialization, Whiteness, and River Street. *Historical Archaeology* 51(1):131–148.

Wilcox, Michael V.

2009a *The Pueblo Revolt and the Mythology of Conquest: An Indigenous Archaeology of Contact.* University of California Press, Berkeley.

2009b Marketing Conquest and the Vanishing Indian: An Indigenous Response to Jared Diamond's *Guns, Germs, and Steel* and *Collapse.* In *Questioning Collapse: Human Resilience, Ecological Vulnerability, and the Aftermath of Empire,* edited by Norman Yoffee and Patricia McAnany, pp. 113–142. Cambridge University Press, Cambridge.

2010 Marketing Conquest and the Vanishing Indian: An Indigenous Response to Jared Diamond's *Guns, Germs and Steel* and *Collapse. Journal of Social Archaeology* 10(1):93–117.

Wilkie, Laurie

1997 Secret and Sacred: Contextualizing the Artifacts of African-American Magic and Religion. *Historical Archaeology* 31(4):81–106.

Wines, Richard

1981 The Nineteenth-Century Agricultural Transition in an Eastern Long Island Community. *Agricultural History* 55(1):50–63.

Wood, Denis

2010 *Rethinking the Power of Maps.* Guilford Press, New York.

Woodson, Carter G.

1990 [1935] *The Mis-education of the Negro.* Africa World Press, Trenton, New Jersey.

Yamin, Rebecca

2001 From Tanning to Tea: The Evolution of a Neighborhood. *Historical Archaeology* 35(3):6–15.

Zimmerman, Larry J., Courtney Singleton, and Jessica Welch

2010 Activism and Creating a Translational Archaeology of Homelessness. *World Archaeology* 42(3):443–454.

INDEX

CHRISTOPHER N. MATTHEWS is professor of anthropology at Montclair State University. He is the author of *The Archaeology of American Capitalism* and the coeditor of *The Archaeology of Race in the Northeast.*

Cultural Heritage Studies
Edited by Paul A. Shackel, University of Maryland

Heritage of Value, Archaeology of Renown: Reshaping Archaeological Assessment and Significance, edited by Clay Mathers, Timothy Darvill, and Barbara J. Little (2005)
Archaeology, Cultural Heritage, and the Antiquities Trade, edited by Neil Brodie, Morag M. Kersel, Christina Luke, and Kathryn Walker Tubb (2006)
Archaeological Site Museums in Latin America, edited by Helaine Silverman (2006)
Crossroads and Cosmologies: Diasporas and Ethnogenesis in the New World, by Christopher C. Fennell (2007)
Ethnographies and Archaeologies: Iterations of the Past, edited by Lena Mortensen and Julie Hollowell (2009)
Cultural Heritage Management: A Global Perspective, edited by Phyllis Mauch Messenger and George S. Smith (2010; first paperback edition, 2014)
God's Fields: Landscape, Religion, and Race in Moravian Wachovia, by Leland Ferguson (2011; first paperback edition, 2013)
Ancestors of Worthy Life: Plantation Slavery and Black Heritage at Mount Clare, by Teresa S. Moyer (2015)
Slavery behind the Wall: An Archaeology of a Cuban Coffee Plantation, by Theresa A. Singleton (2015; first paperback edition, 2016)
Excavating Memory: Sites of Remembering and Forgetting, edited by Maria Theresia Starzmann and John R. Roby (2016)
Mythic Frontiers: Remembering, Forgetting, and Profiting with Cultural Heritage Tourism, by Daniel R. Maher (2016; first paperback edition, 2019)
Critical Theory and the Anthropology of Heritage Landscapes, by Melissa F. Baird (2017)
Heritage at the Interface: Interpretation and Identity, edited by Glenn Hooper (2018)
Cuban Cultural Heritage: A Rebel Past for a Revolutionary Nation, by Pablo Alonso González (2018)
The Rosewood Massacre: An Archaeology and History of Intersectional Violence, by Edward González-Tennant (2018; first paperback edition, 2019)
Race, Place, and Memory: Deep Currents in Wilmington, North Carolina, by Margaret M. Mulrooney (2018)
An Archaeology of Structural Violence: Life in a Twentieth-Century Coal Town, by Michael P. Roller (2018)
Colonialism, Community, and Heritage in Native New England, by Siobhan M. Hart (2019)
Pedagogy and Practice in Heritage Studies, edited by Susan J. Bender and Phyllis Mauch Messenger (2019)
History and Approaches to Heritage Studies, edited by Phyllis Mauch Messenger and Susan J. Bender (2019)
A Struggle for Heritage: Archaeology and Civil Rights in a Long Island Community, by Christopher N. Matthews (2020)